# THE A-TEAM
## SHOTGUN WEDDING

Co-plotted by **Joe Carnahan and Tom Waltz**

Written by **Tom Waltz**

Art by **Stephen Mooney**

Colors by **Alfredo Rodriguez**

Lettering by **Neil Uyetake**

Original Series Edits by **Chris Ryall**

Collection Edits by **Justin Eisinger**

Collection Design by **Neil Uyetake**

Cover by **John K. Snyder III**

Cover colors by **Jason Wright**

Special thanks to Debbie Olshan and Nicole Spiegel for their invaluable assistance.
www.IDWpublishing.com • ISBN: 978-1-60010-726-9 • 13 12 11 10 • 1 2 3 4

Operations: Ted Adams, Chief Executive Officer • Greg Goldstein, Chief Operating Officer • Matthew Ruzicka, CPA, Chief Financial Officer • Alan Payne, VP of Sales • Lorelei Bunjes, Dir. of Digital Services • AnnaMaria White, Marketing & PR Manager • Marci Hubbard, Executive Assistant • Alonzo Simon, Shipping Manager • Angela Loggins, Staff Accountant • Editorial: Chris Ryall, Publisher/Editor-in-Chief • Scott Dunbier, Editor, Special Projects • Andy Schmidt, Senior Editor • Bob Schreck, Senior Editor • Justin Eisinger, Editor • Kris Oprisko, Editor/Foreign Lic. • Denton J. Tipton, Editor • Tom Waltz, Editor • Mariah Huehner, Associate Editor • Carlos Guzman, Editorial Assistant • Design: Robbie Robbins, EVP/Sr. Graphic Artist • Neil Uyetake, Art Director • Chris Mowry, Graphic Artist • Amauri Osorio, Graphic Artist • Gilberto Lazcano, Production Assistant • Shawn Lee, Production Assistant

# CHAPTER ONE

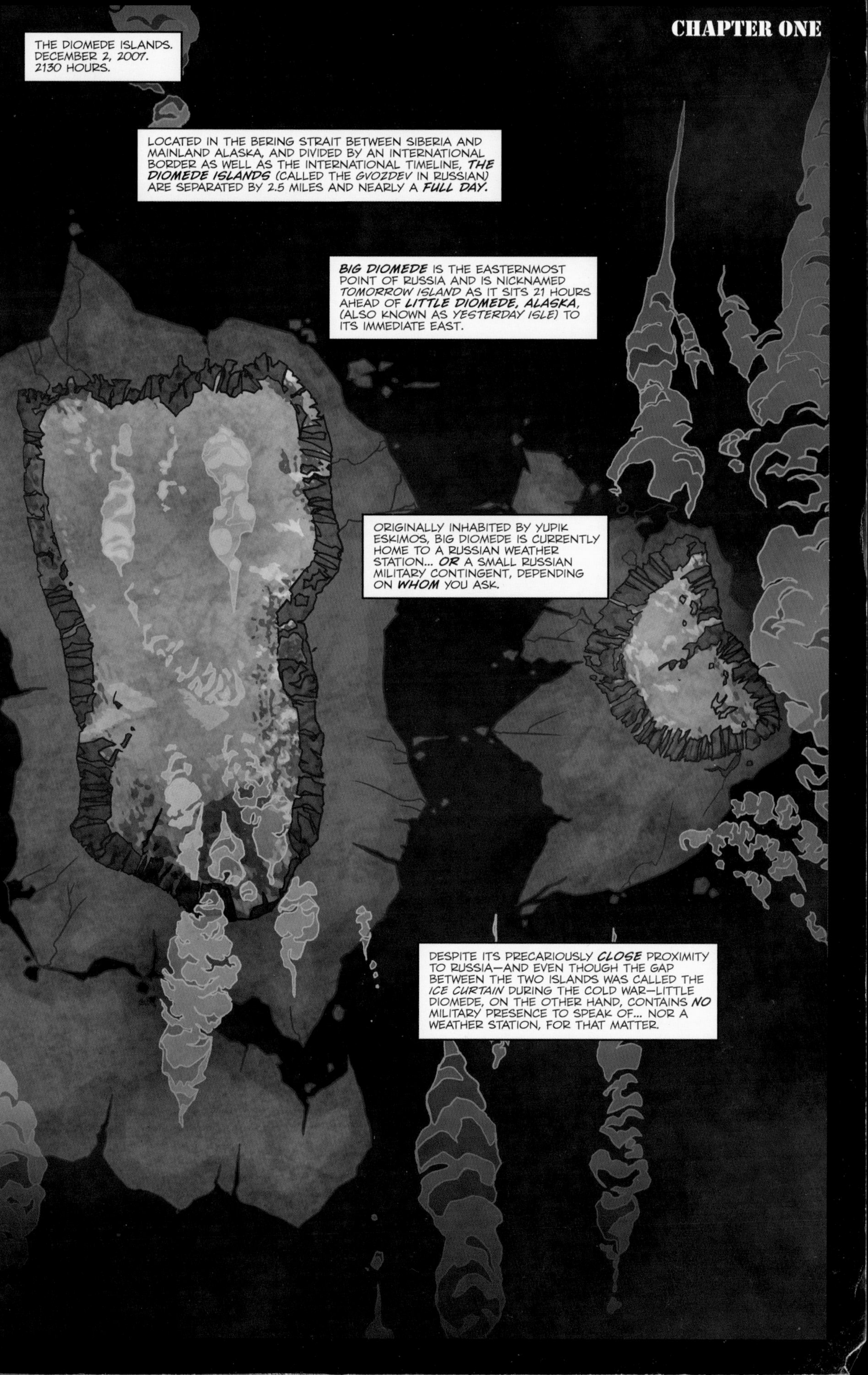
THE DIOMEDE ISLANDS. DECEMBER 2, 2007. 2130 HOURS.
LOCATED IN THE BERING STRAIT BETWEEN SIBERIA AND MAINLAND ALASKA, AND DIVIDED BY AN INTERNATIONAL BORDER AS WELL AS THE INTERNATIONAL TIMELINE, ***THE DIOMEDE ISLANDS*** (CALLED THE *GVOZDEV* IN RUSSIAN) ARE SEPARATED BY 2.5 MILES AND NEARLY A ***FULL DAY.***
***BIG DIOMEDE*** IS THE EASTERNMOST POINT OF RUSSIA AND IS NICKNAMED *TOMORROW ISLAND* AS IT SITS 21 HOURS AHEAD OF ***LITTLE DIOMEDE, ALASKA,*** (ALSO KNOWN AS *YESTERDAY ISLE*) TO ITS IMMEDIATE EAST.
ORIGINALLY INHABITED BY YUPIK ESKIMOS, BIG DIOMEDE IS CURRENTLY HOME TO A RUSSIAN WEATHER STATION... ***OR*** A SMALL RUSSIAN MILITARY CONTINGENT, DEPENDING ON ***WHOM*** YOU ASK.
DESPITE ITS PRECARIOUSLY ***CLOSE*** PROXIMITY TO RUSSIA—AND EVEN THOUGH THE GAP BETWEEN THE TWO ISLANDS WAS CALLED THE *ICE CURTAIN* DURING THE COLD WAR—LITTLE DIOMEDE, ON THE OTHER HAND, CONTAINS *NO* MILITARY PRESENCE TO SPEAK OF... NOR A WEATHER STATION, FOR THAT MATTER.

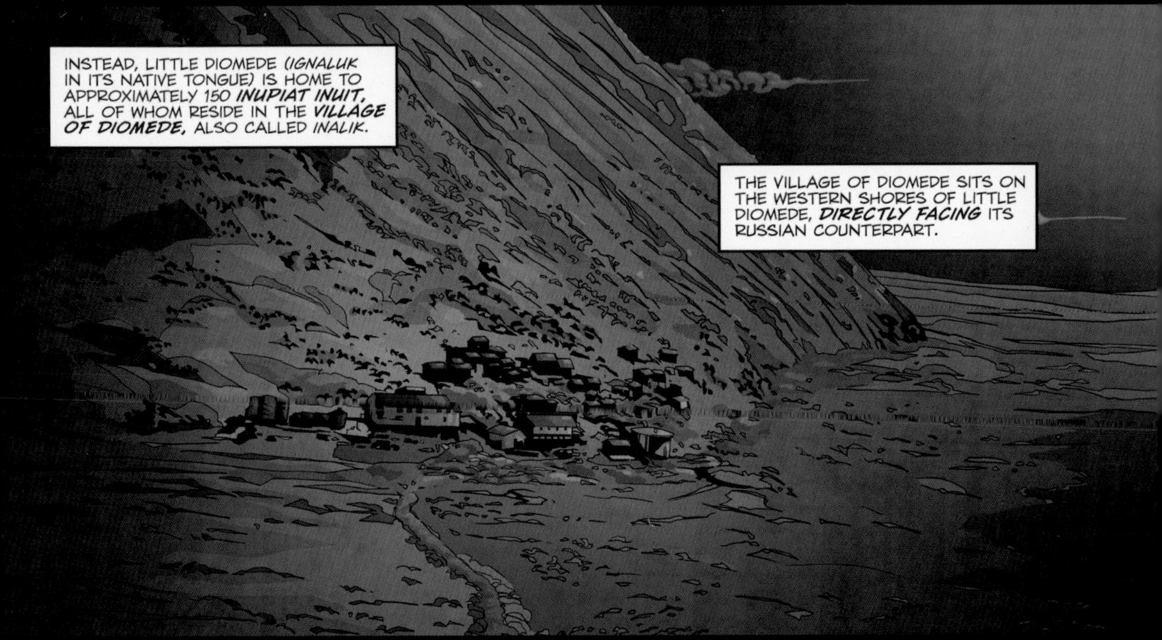
INSTEAD, LITTLE DIOMEDE (IGNALUK IN ITS NATIVE TONGUE) IS HOME TO APPROXIMATELY 150 INUPIAT INUIT, ALL OF WHOM RESIDE IN THE VILLAGE OF DIOMEDE, ALSO CALLED INALIK.
THE VILLAGE OF DIOMEDE SITS ON THE WESTERN SHORES OF LITTLE DIOMEDE, DIRECTLY FACING ITS RUSSIAN COUNTERPART.

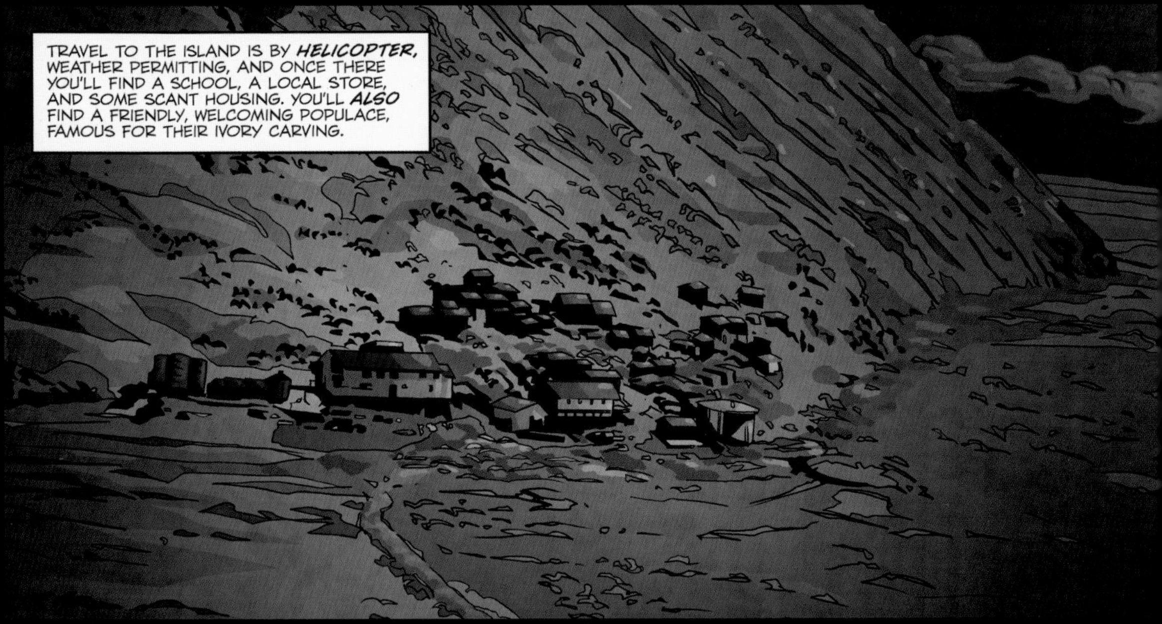
TRAVEL TO THE ISLAND IS BY HELICOPTER, WEATHER PERMITTING, AND ONCE THERE YOU'LL FIND A SCHOOL, A LOCAL STORE, AND SOME SCANT HOUSING. YOU'LL ALSO FIND A FRIENDLY, WELCOMING POPULACE, FAMOUS FOR THEIR IVORY CARVING.

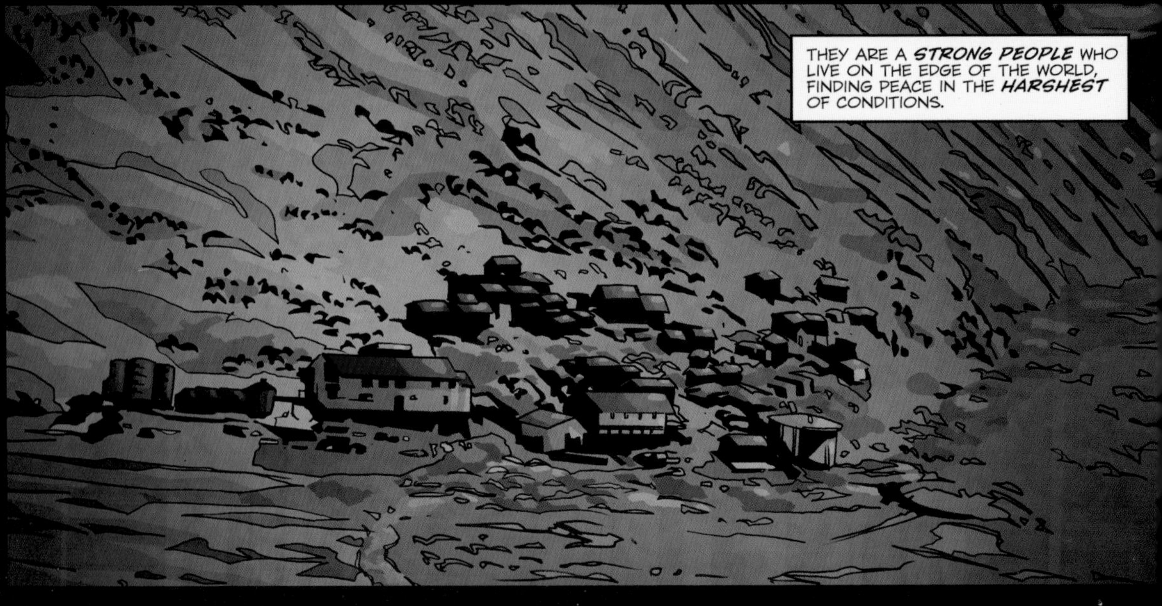
THEY ARE A STRONG PEOPLE WHO LIVE ON THE EDGE OF THE WORLD, FINDING PEACE IN THE HARSHEST OF CONDITIONS.

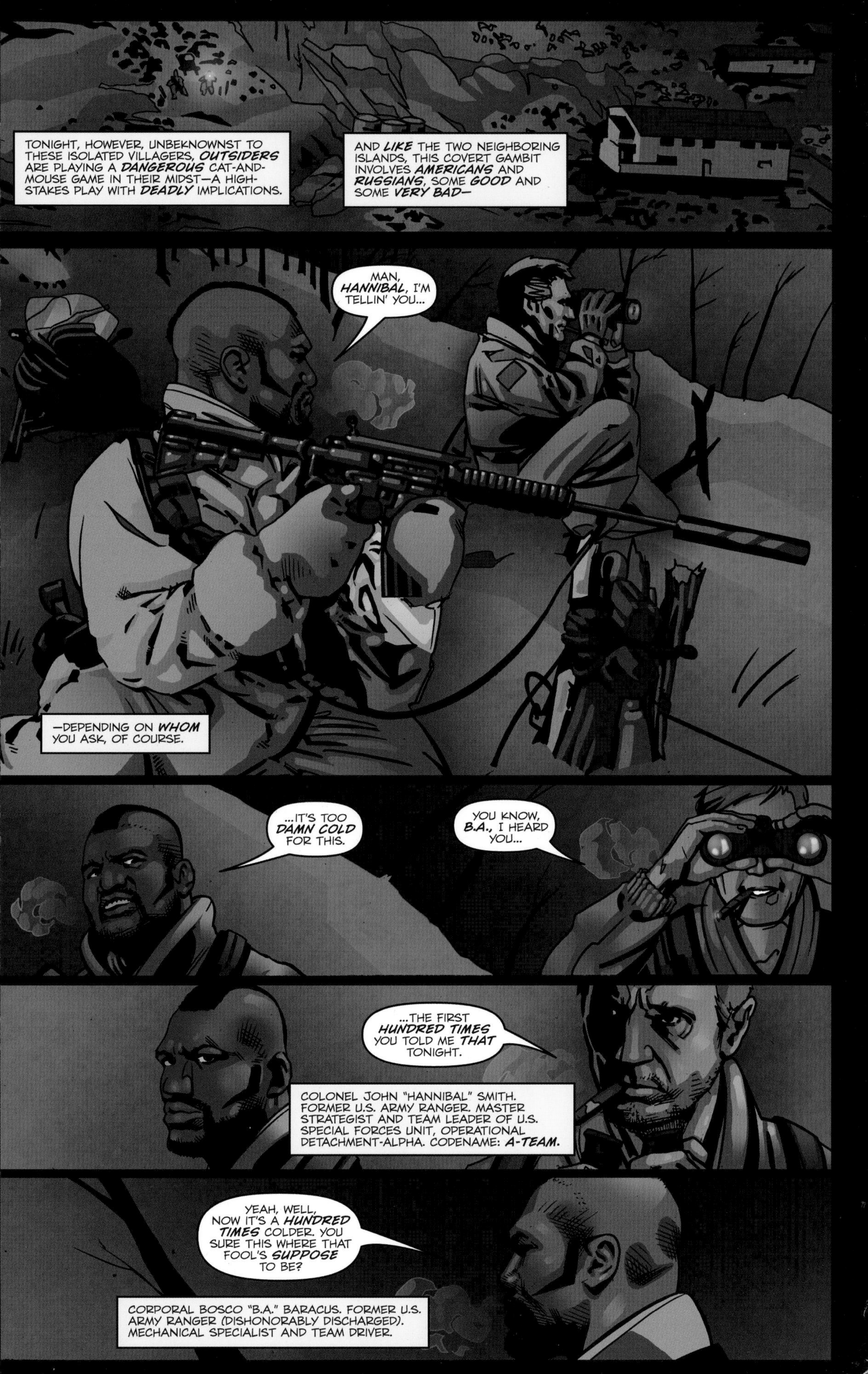
TONIGHT, HOWEVER, UNBEKNOWNST TO THESE ISOLATED VILLAGERS, OUTSIDERS ARE PLAYING A DANGEROUS CAT-AND-MOUSE GAME IN THEIR MIDST—A HIGH-STAKES PLAY WITH DEADLY IMPLICATIONS.
AND LIKE THE TWO NEIGHBORING ISLANDS, THIS COVERT GAMBIT INVOLVES AMERICANS AND RUSSIANS, SOME GOOD AND SOME VERY BAD—
MAN, HANNIBAL, I'M TELLIN' YOU...
—DEPENDING ON WHOM YOU ASK, OF COURSE.
...IT'S TOO DAMN COLD FOR THIS.
YOU KNOW, B.A., I HEARD YOU...
...THE FIRST HUNDRED TIMES YOU TOLD ME THAT TONIGHT.
COLONEL JOHN "HANNIBAL" SMITH. FORMER U.S. ARMY RANGER. MASTER STRATEGIST AND TEAM LEADER OF U.S. SPECIAL FORCES UNIT, OPERATIONAL DETACHMENT-ALPHA. CODENAME: A-TEAM.
YEAH, WELL, NOW IT'S A HUNDRED TIMES COLDER. YOU SURE THIS WHERE THAT FOOL'S SUPPOSE TO BE?
CORPORAL BOSCO "B.A." BARACUS. FORMER U.S. ARMY RANGER (DISHONORABLY DISCHARGED). MECHANICAL SPECIALIST AND TEAM DRIVER.

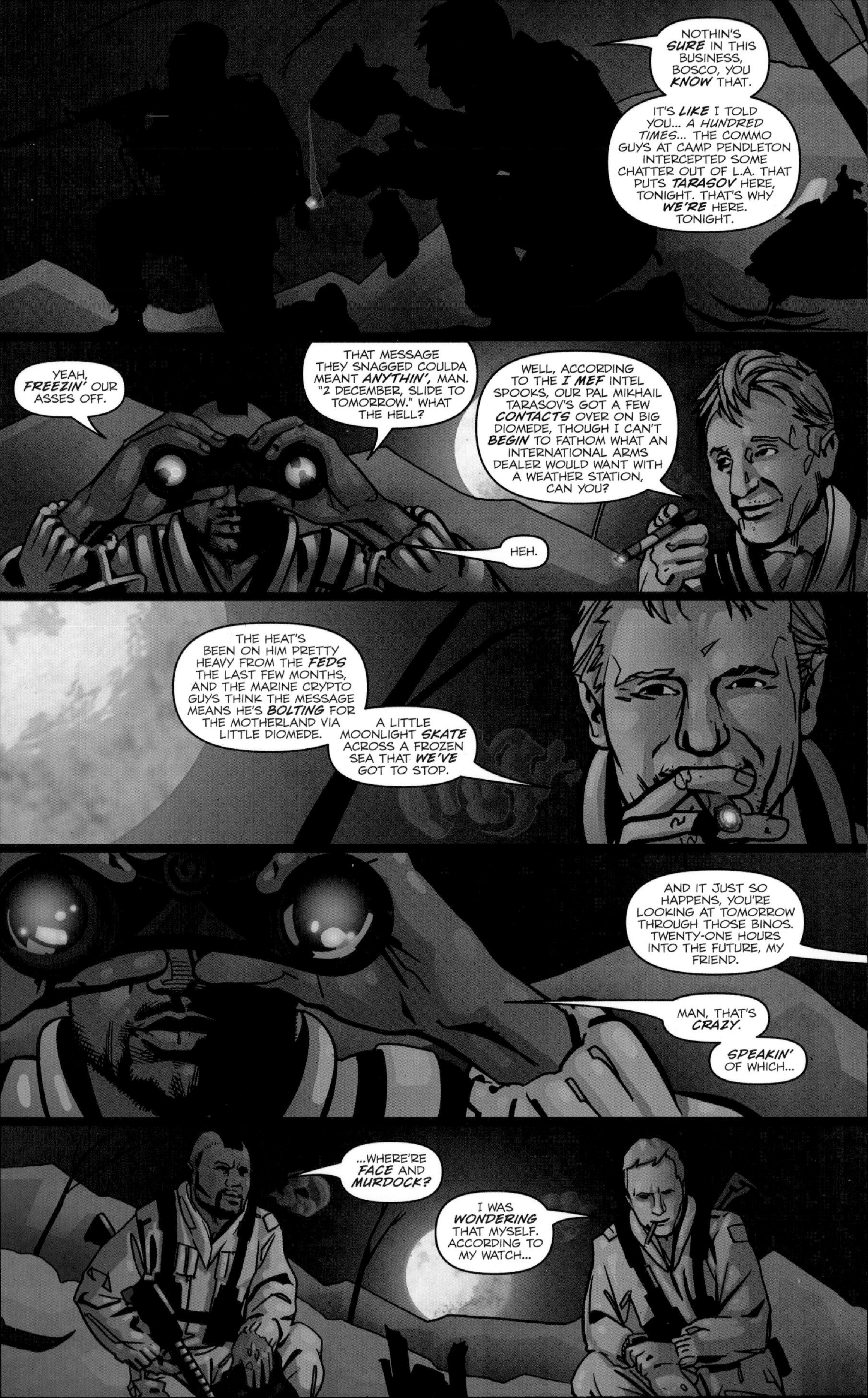
NOTHIN'S SURE IN THIS BUSINESS, BOSCO, YOU KNOW THAT.
IT'S LIKE I TOLD YOU... A HUNDRED TIMES... THE COMMO GUYS AT CAMP PENDLETON INTERCEPTED SOME CHATTER OUT OF L.A. THAT PUTS TARASOV HERE, TONIGHT. THAT'S WHY WE'RE HERE. TONIGHT.
YEAH, FREEZIN' OUR ASSES OFF.
THAT MESSAGE THEY SNAGGED COULDA MEANT ANYTHIN', MAN. "2 DECEMBER, SLIDE TO TOMORROW." WHAT THE HELL?
WELL, ACCORDING TO THE I MEF INTEL SPOOKS, OUR PAL MIKHAIL TARASOV'S GOT A FEW CONTACTS OVER ON BIG DIOMEDE, THOUGH I CAN'T BEGIN TO FATHOM WHAT AN INTERNATIONAL ARMS DEALER WOULD WANT WITH A WEATHER STATION, CAN YOU?
HEH.
THE HEAT'S BEEN ON HIM PRETTY HEAVY FROM THE FEDS THE LAST FEW MONTHS, AND THE MARINE CRYPTO GUYS THINK THE MESSAGE MEANS HE'S BOLTING FOR THE MOTHERLAND VIA LITTLE DIOMEDE.
A LITTLE MOONLIGHT SKATE ACROSS A FROZEN SEA THAT WE'VE GOT TO STOP.
AND IT JUST SO HAPPENS, YOU'RE LOOKING AT TOMORROW THROUGH THOSE BINOS. TWENTY-ONE HOURS INTO THE FUTURE, MY FRIEND.
MAN, THAT'S CRAZY.
SPEAKIN' OF WHICH...
...WHERE'RE FACE AND MURDOCK?
I WAS WONDERING THAT MYSELF. ACCORDING TO MY WATCH...

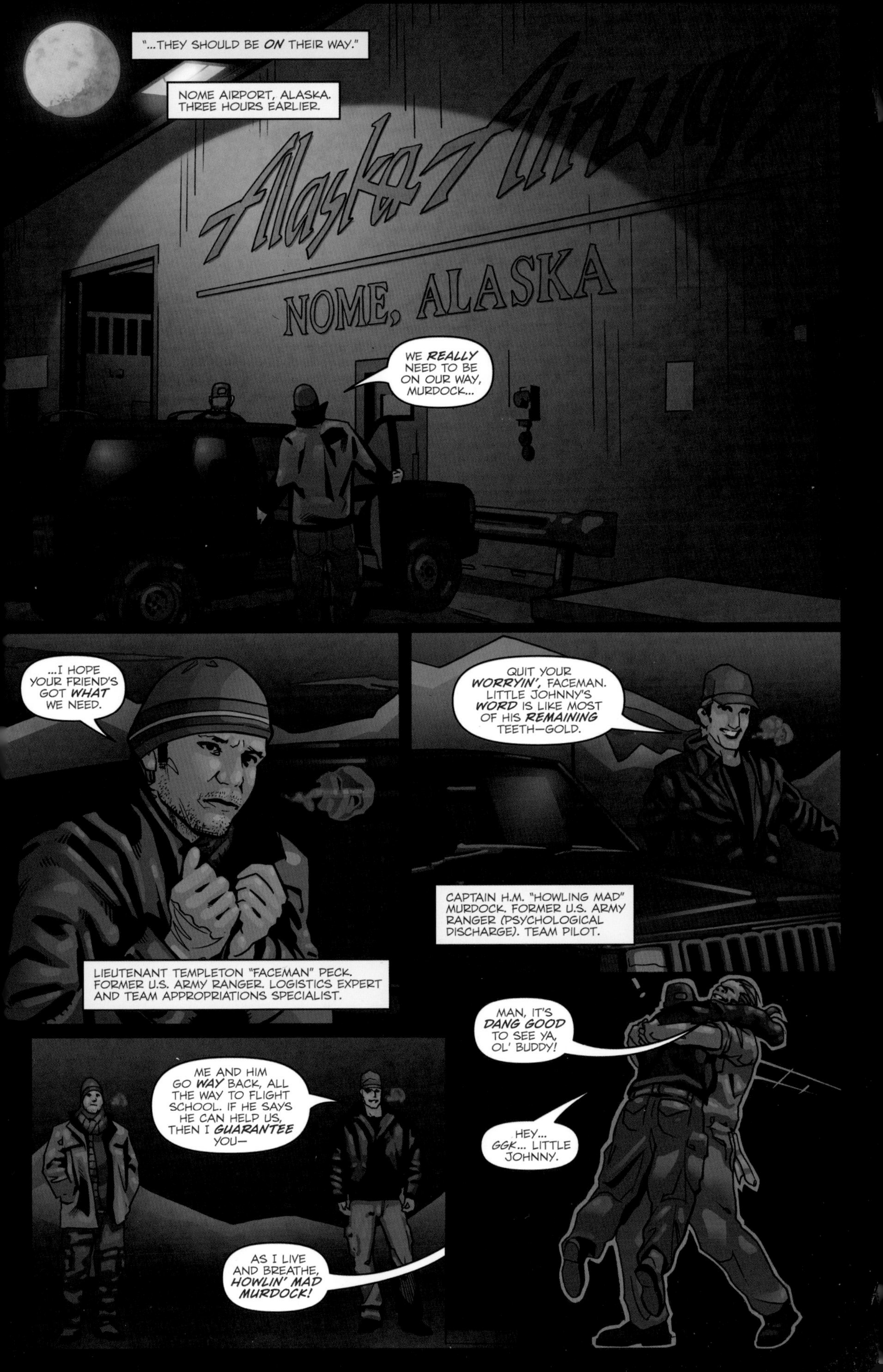
"...THEY SHOULD BE ON THEIR WAY."
NOME AIRPORT, ALASKA. THREE HOURS EARLIER.
Alaska Airways
NOME, ALASKA
WE REALLY NEED TO BE ON OUR WAY, MURDOCK...
...I HOPE YOUR FRIEND'S GOT WHAT WE NEED.
LIEUTENANT TEMPLETON "FACEMAN" PECK. FORMER U.S. ARMY RANGER. LOGISTICS EXPERT AND TEAM APPROPRIATIONS SPECIALIST.
QUIT YOUR WORRYIN', FACEMAN. LITTLE JOHNNY'S WORD IS LIKE MOST OF HIS REMAINING TEETH—GOLD.
CAPTAIN H.M. "HOWLING MAD" MURDOCK. FORMER U.S. ARMY RANGER (PSYCHOLOGICAL DISCHARGE). TEAM PILOT.
ME AND HIM GO WAY BACK, ALL THE WAY TO FLIGHT SCHOOL. IF HE SAYS HE CAN HELP US, THEN I GUARANTEE YOU—
AS I LIVE AND BREATHE, HOWLIN' MAD MURDOCK!
MAN, IT'S DANG GOOD TO SEE YA, OL' BUDDY!
HEY... GGK... LITTLE JOHNNY.

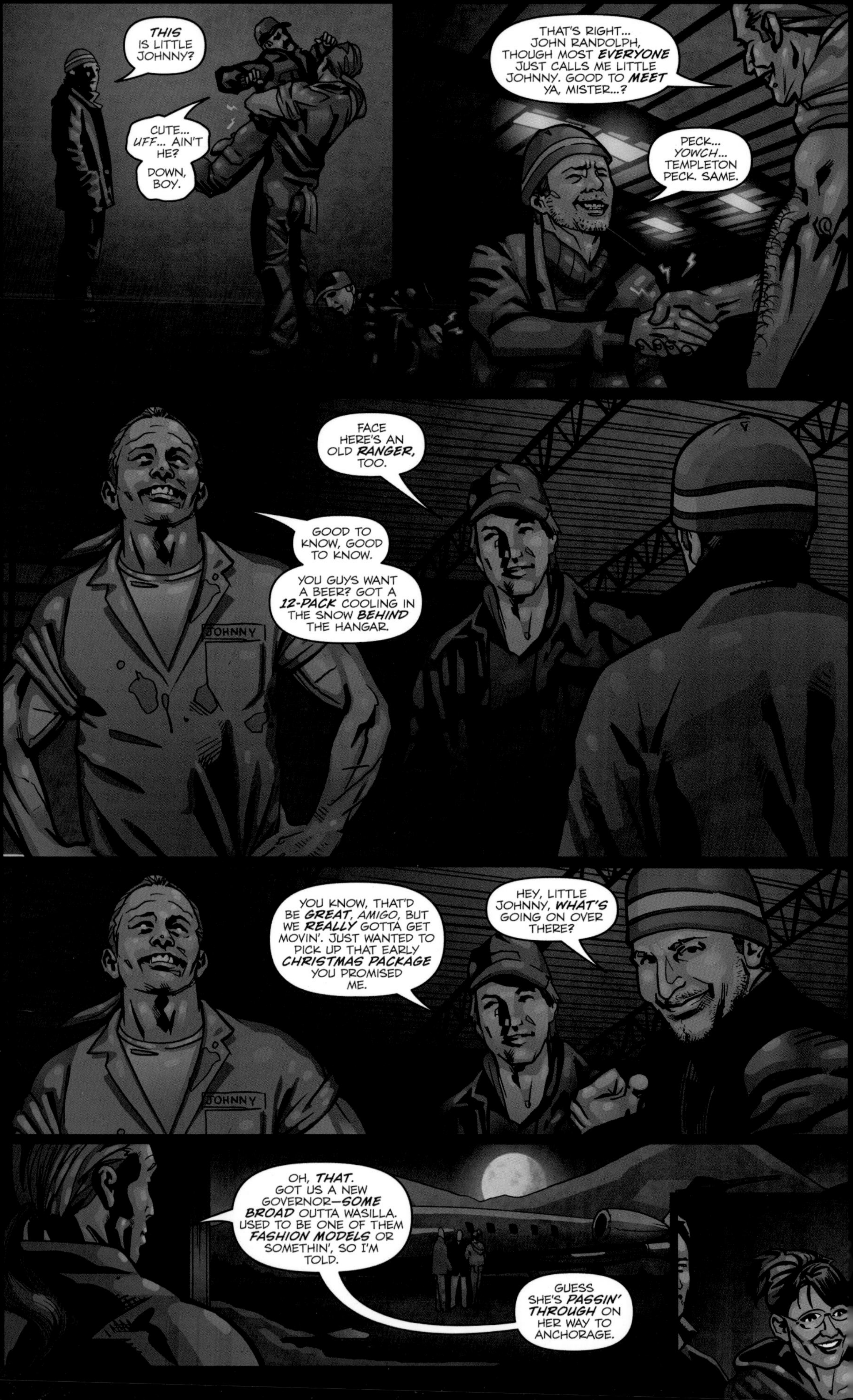
THIS IS LITTLE JOHNNY?
CUTE... UFF... AIN'T HE?
DOWN, BOY.
THAT'S RIGHT... JOHN RANDOLPH, THOUGH MOST EVERYONE JUST CALLS ME LITTLE JOHNNY. GOOD TO MEET YA, MISTER...?
PECK... YOWCH... TEMPLETON PECK. SAME.
FACE HERE'S AN OLD RANGER, TOO.
GOOD TO KNOW, GOOD TO KNOW.
YOU GUYS WANT A BEER? GOT A 12-PACK COOLING IN THE SNOW BEHIND THE HANGAR.
JOHNNY
YOU KNOW, THAT'D BE GREAT, AMIGO, BUT WE REALLY GOTTA GET MOVIN'. JUST WANTED TO PICK UP THAT EARLY CHRISTMAS PACKAGE YOU PROMISED ME.
HEY, LITTLE JOHNNY, WHAT'S GOING ON OVER THERE?
JOHNNY
OH, THAT. GOT US A NEW GOVERNOR—SOME BROAD OUTTA WASILLA. USED TO BE ONE OF THEM FASHION MODELS OR SOMETHIN', SO I'M TOLD.
GUESS SHE'S PASSIN' THROUGH ON HER WAY TO ANCHORAGE.

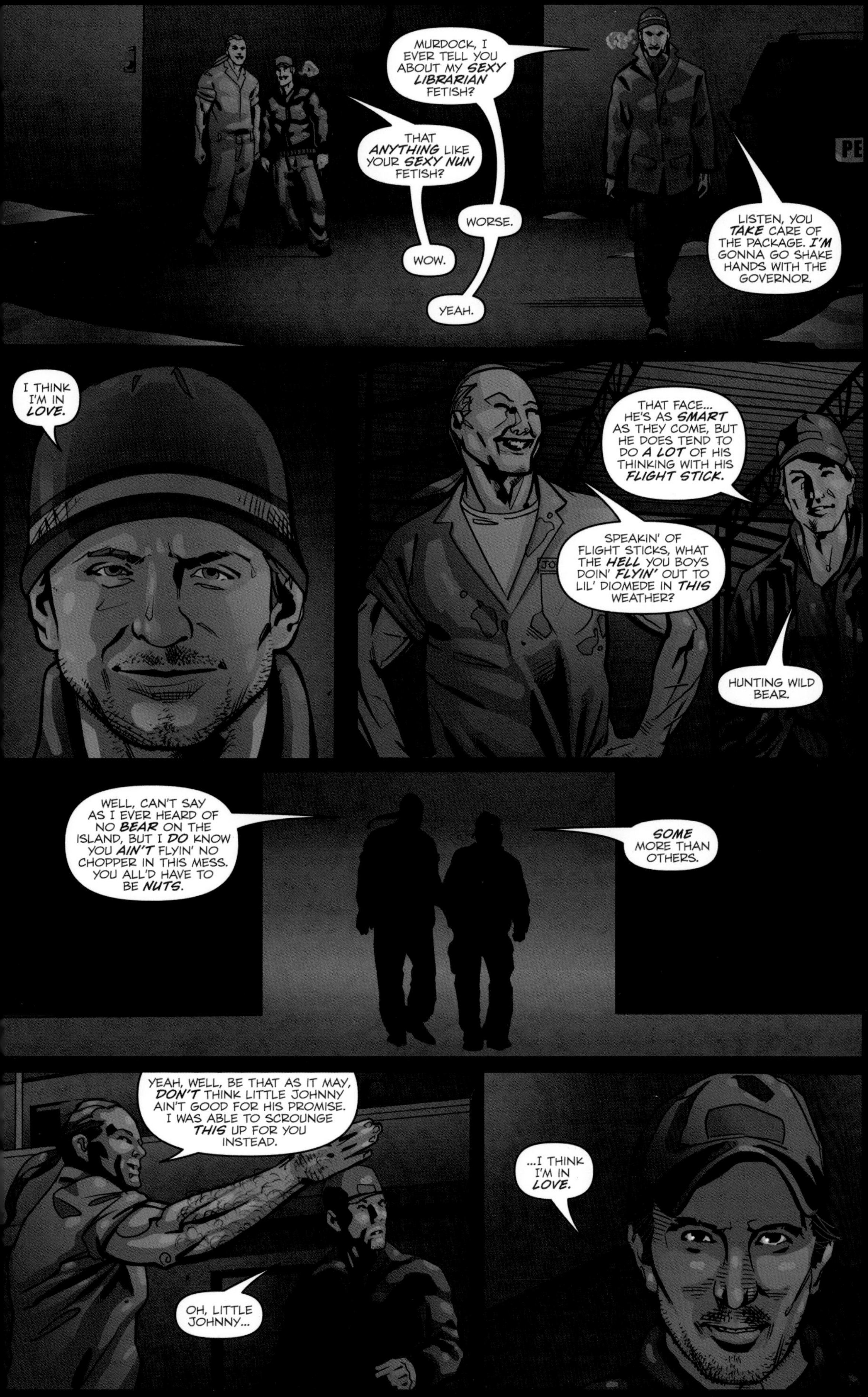
MURDOCK, I EVER TELL YOU ABOUT MY SEXY LIBRARIAN FETISH?
THAT ANYTHING LIKE YOUR SEXY NUN FETISH?
WORSE.
WOW.
YEAH.
LISTEN, YOU TAKE CARE OF THE PACKAGE. I'M GONNA GO SHAKE HANDS WITH THE GOVERNOR.
I THINK I'M IN LOVE.
THAT FACE... HE'S AS SMART AS THEY COME, BUT HE DOES TEND TO DO A LOT OF HIS THINKING WITH HIS FLIGHT STICK.
SPEAKIN' OF FLIGHT STICKS, WHAT THE HELL YOU BOYS DOIN' FLYIN' OUT TO LIL' DIOMEDE IN THIS WEATHER?
HUNTING WILD BEAR.
WELL, CAN'T SAY AS I EVER HEARD OF NO BEAR ON THE ISLAND, BUT I DO KNOW YOU AIN'T FLYIN' NO CHOPPER IN THIS MESS. YOU ALL'D HAVE TO BE NUTS.
SOME MORE THAN OTHERS.
YEAH, WELL, BE THAT AS IT MAY, DON'T THINK LITTLE JOHNNY AIN'T GOOD FOR HIS PROMISE. I WAS ABLE TO SCROUNGE THIS UP FOR YOU INSTEAD.
OH, LITTLE JOHNNY...
...I THINK I'M IN LOVE.

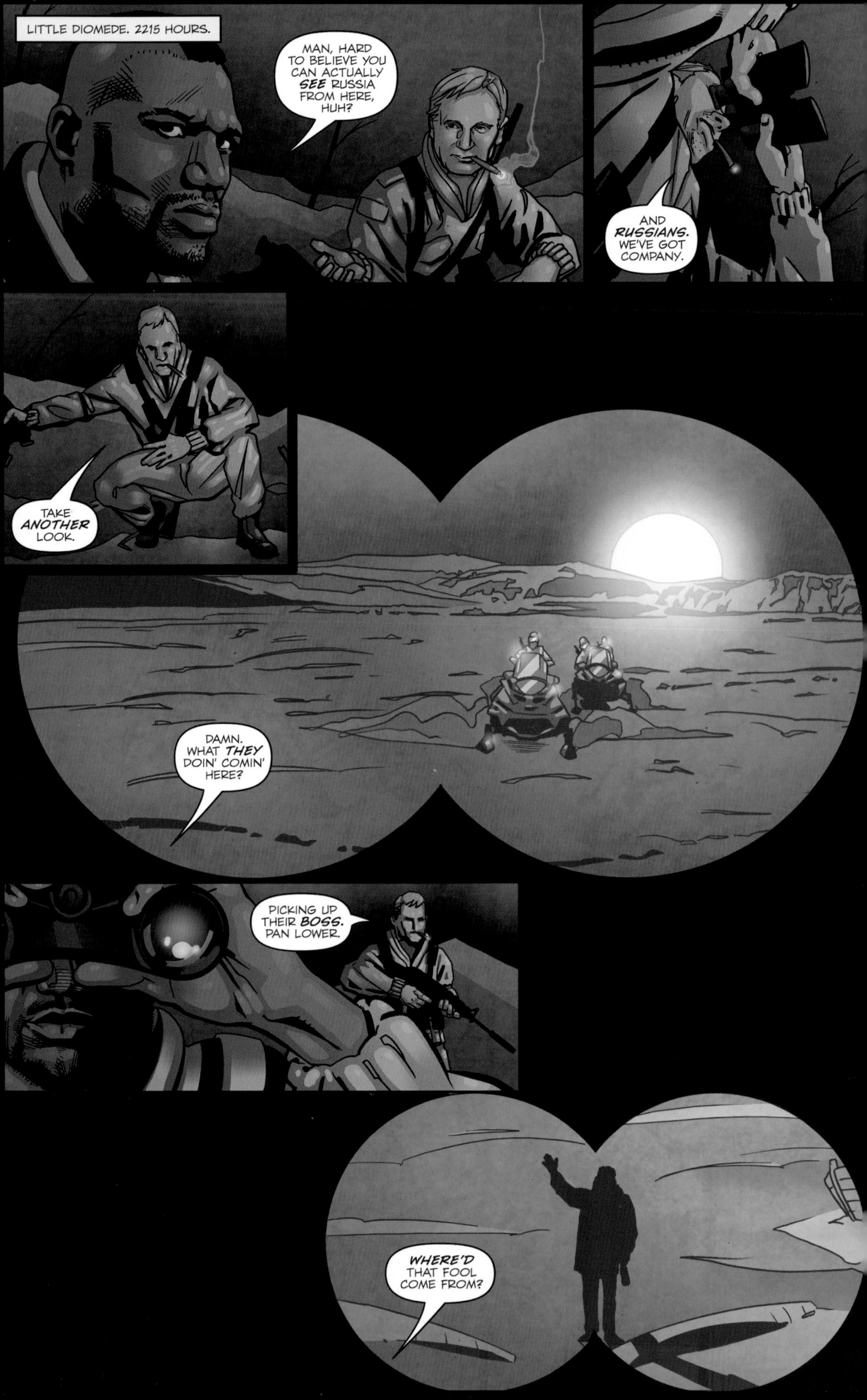
LITTLE DIOMEDE. 2215 HOURS.
MAN, HARD TO BELIEVE YOU CAN ACTUALLY SEE RUSSIA FROM HERE, HUH?
AND RUSSIANS. WE'VE GOT COMPANY.
TAKE ANOTHER LOOK.
DAMN. WHAT THEY DOIN' COMIN' HERE?
PICKING UP THEIR BOSS. PAN LOWER.
WHERE'D THAT FOOL COME FROM?

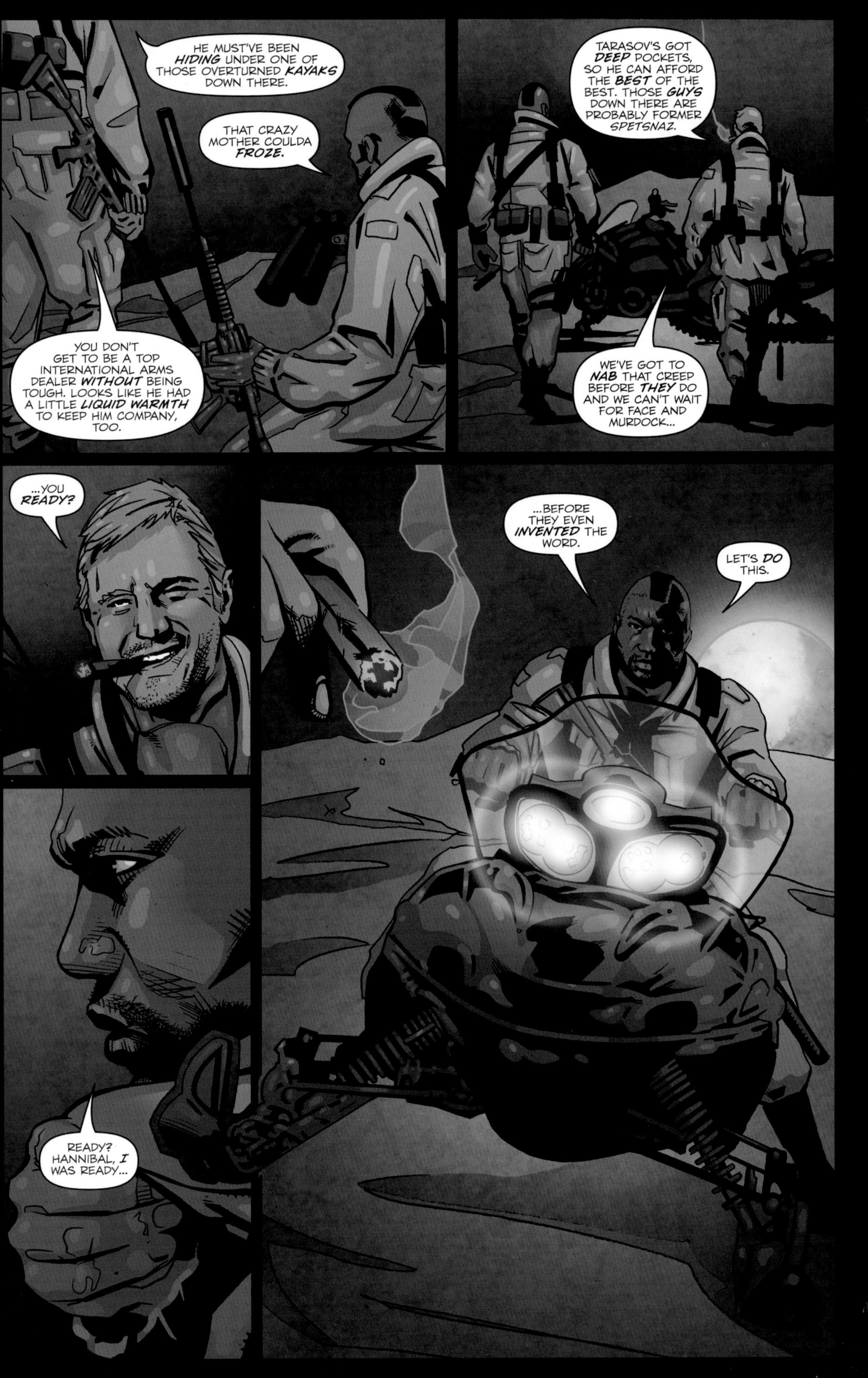
HE MUST'VE BEEN HIDING UNDER ONE OF THOSE OVERTURNED KAYAKS DOWN THERE.
THAT CRAZY MOTHER COULDA FROZE.
YOU DON'T GET TO BE A TOP INTERNATIONAL ARMS DEALER WITHOUT BEING TOUGH. LOOKS LIKE HE HAD A LITTLE LIQUID WARMTH TO KEEP HIM COMPANY, TOO.
TARASOV'S GOT DEEP POCKETS, SO HE CAN AFFORD THE BEST OF THE BEST. THOSE GUYS DOWN THERE ARE PROBABLY FORMER SPETSNAZ.
WE'VE GOT TO NAB THAT CREEP BEFORE THEY DO AND WE CAN'T WAIT FOR FACE AND MURDOCK...
...YOU READY?
READY? HANNIBAL, I WAS READY...
...BEFORE THEY EVEN INVENTED THE WORD.
LET'S DO THIS.

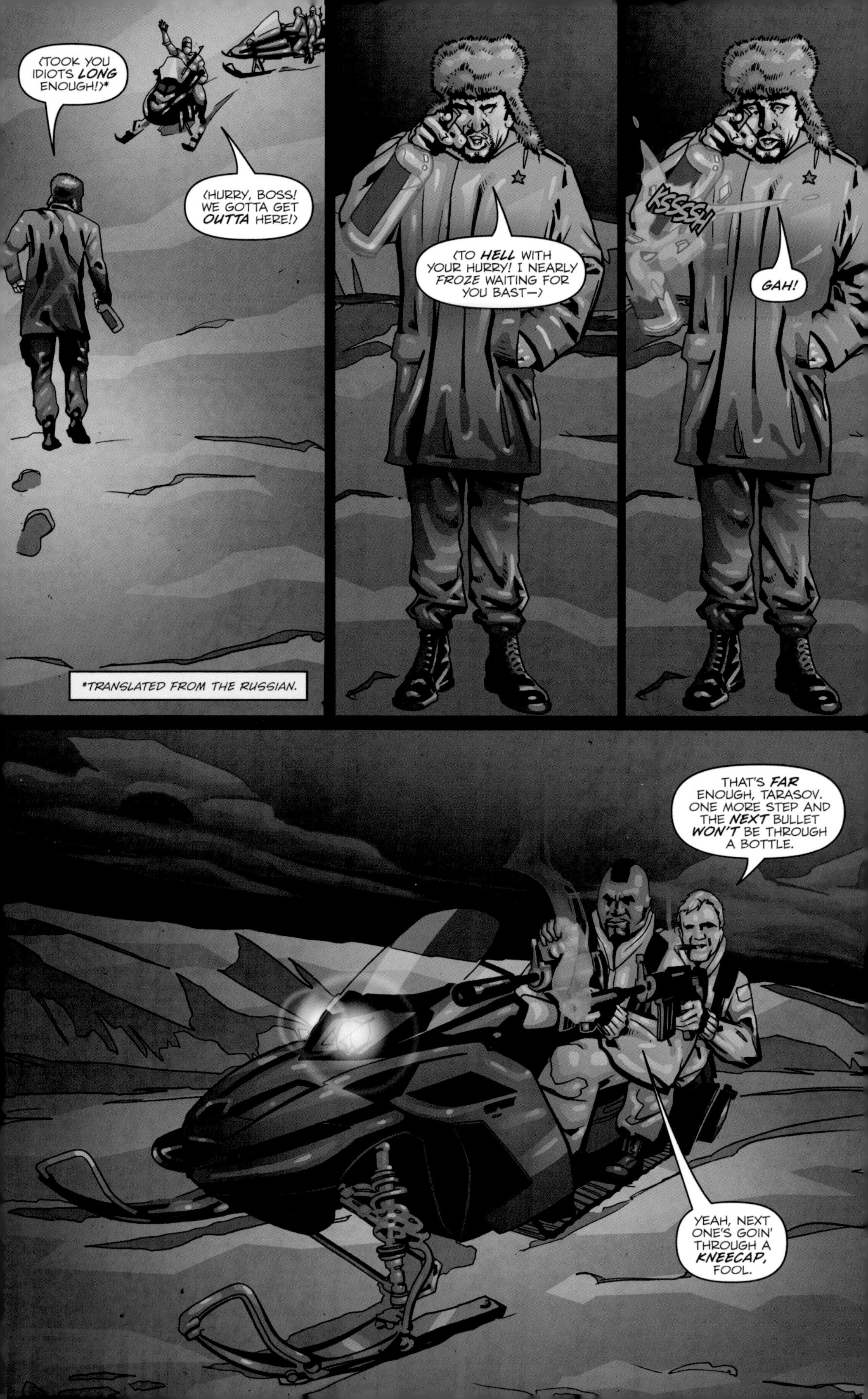
(TOOK YOU IDIOTS LONG ENOUGH!)*
(HURRY, BOSS! WE GOTTA GET OUTTA HERE!)
*TRANSLATED FROM THE RUSSIAN.
(TO HELL WITH YOUR HURRY! I NEARLY FROZE WAITING FOR YOU BAST—)
KSSSSH
GAH!
THAT'S FAR ENOUGH, TARASOV. ONE MORE STEP AND THE NEXT BULLET WON'T BE THROUGH A BOTTLE.
YEAH, NEXT ONE'S GOIN' THROUGH A KNEECAP, FOOL.

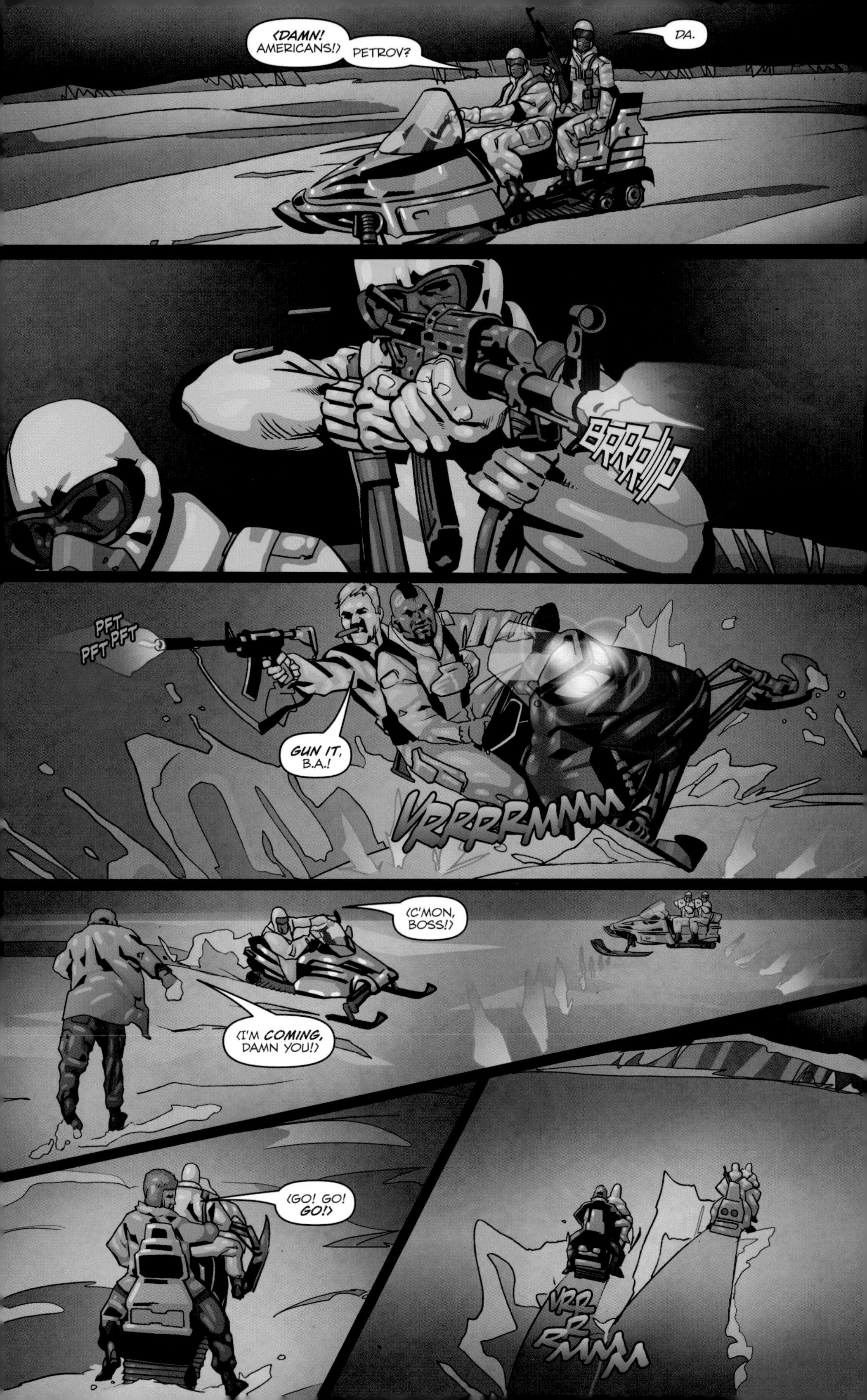
‹DAMN! AMERICANS!›
PETROV?
DA.
BRRRAP
PFT PFT PFT
GUN IT, B.A.!
VRRRRMMMM
‹C'MON, BOSS!›
‹I'M COMING, DAMN YOU!›
‹GO! GO! GO!›
VRRRRMMM

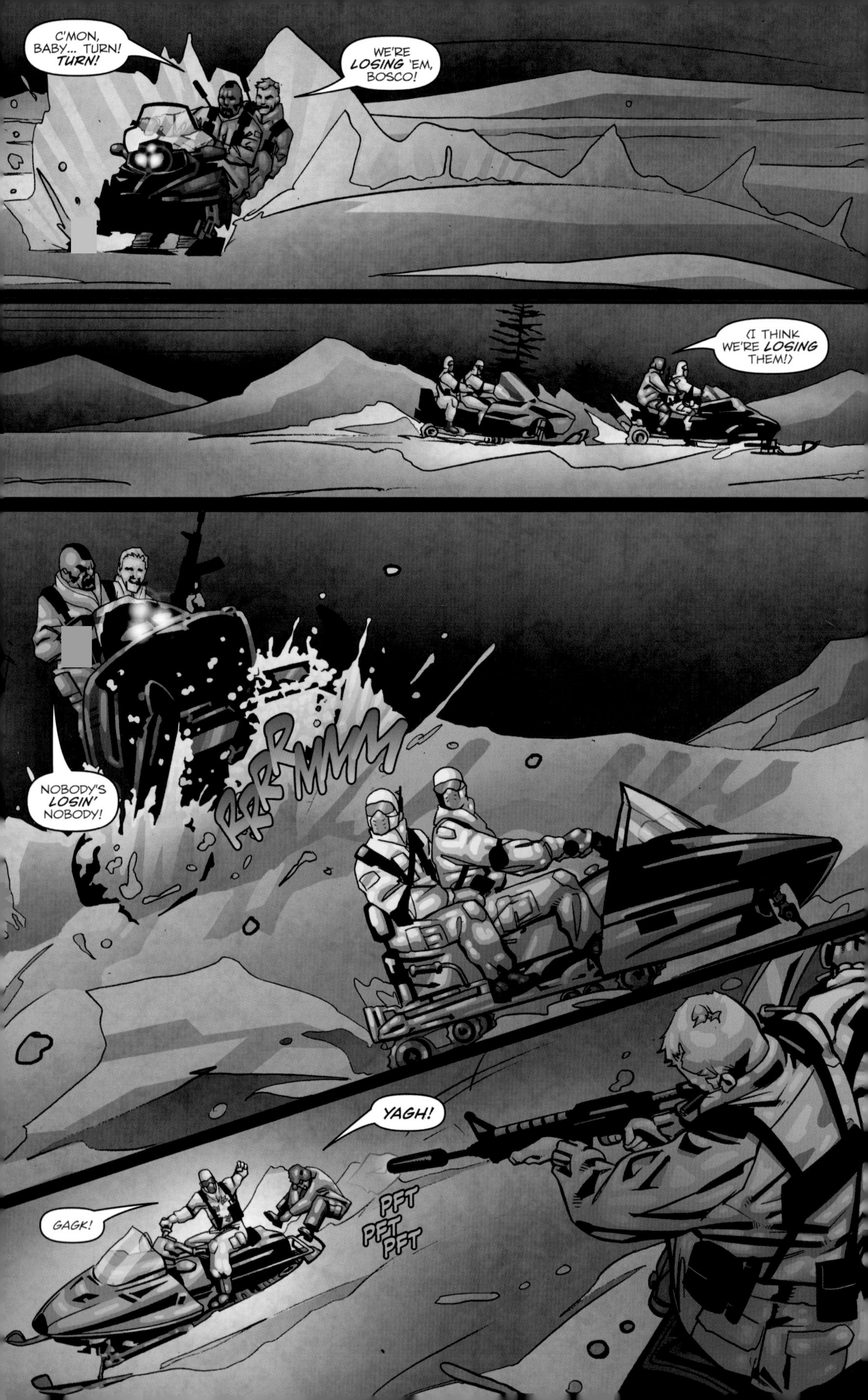
C'MON, BABY... TURN! TURN!
WE'RE LOSING 'EM, BOSCO!
(I THINK WE'RE LOSING THEM!)
NOBODY'S LOSIN' NOBODY!
RRRMMMM
YAGH!
GAGK!
PFT PFT PFT

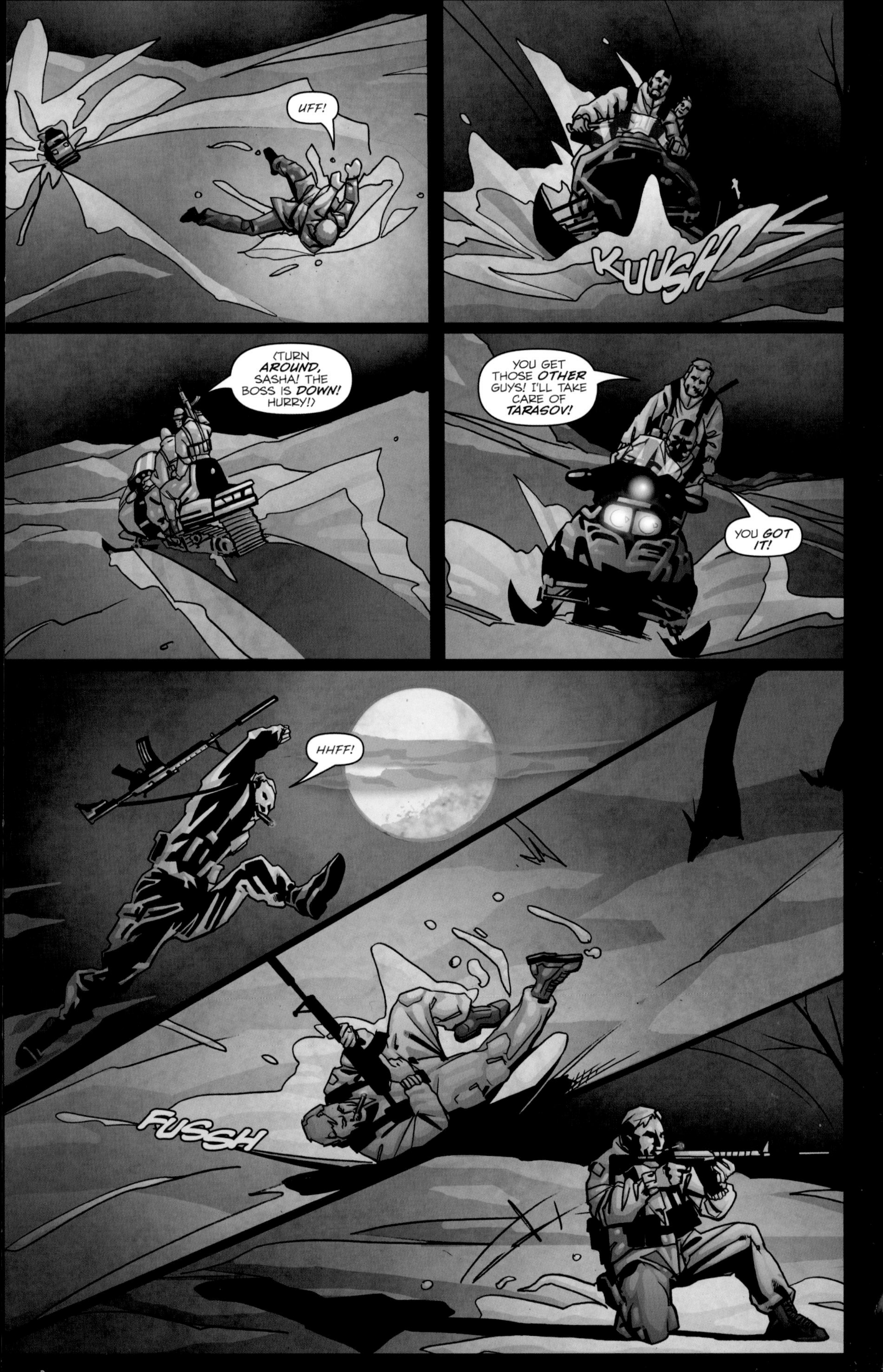
UFF!
KUUSH
(TURN AROUND, SASHA! THE BOSS IS DOWN! HURRY!)
YOU GET THOSE OTHER GUYS! I'LL TAKE CARE OF TARASOV!
YOU GOT IT!
HHFF!
FUSSH

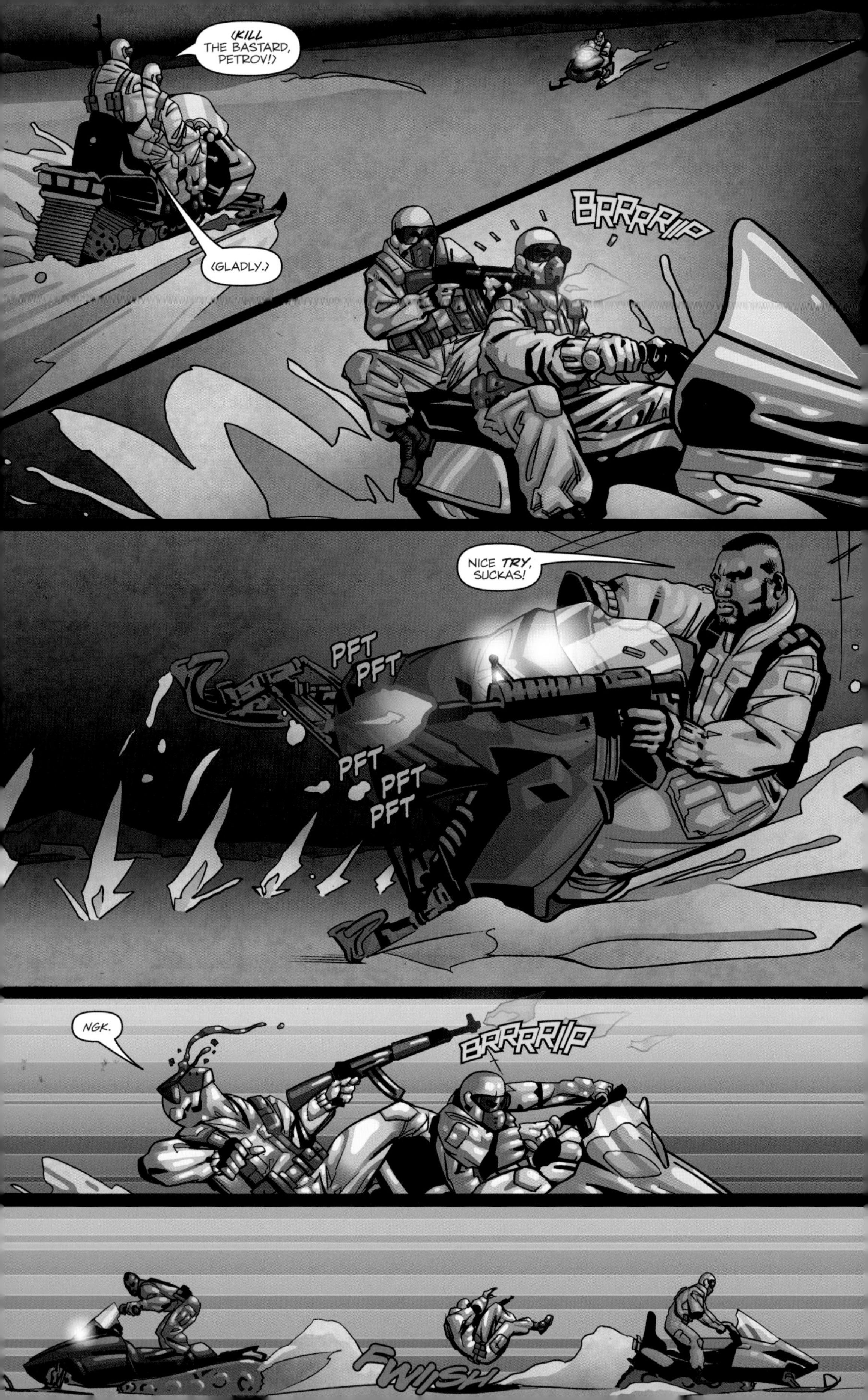

(KILL THE BASTARD, PETROV!)
(GLADLY.)
BRRRRIIP
NICE TRY, SUCKAS!
PFT
PFT
PFT
PFT
PFT
NGK.
BRRRRIIP
FWISH

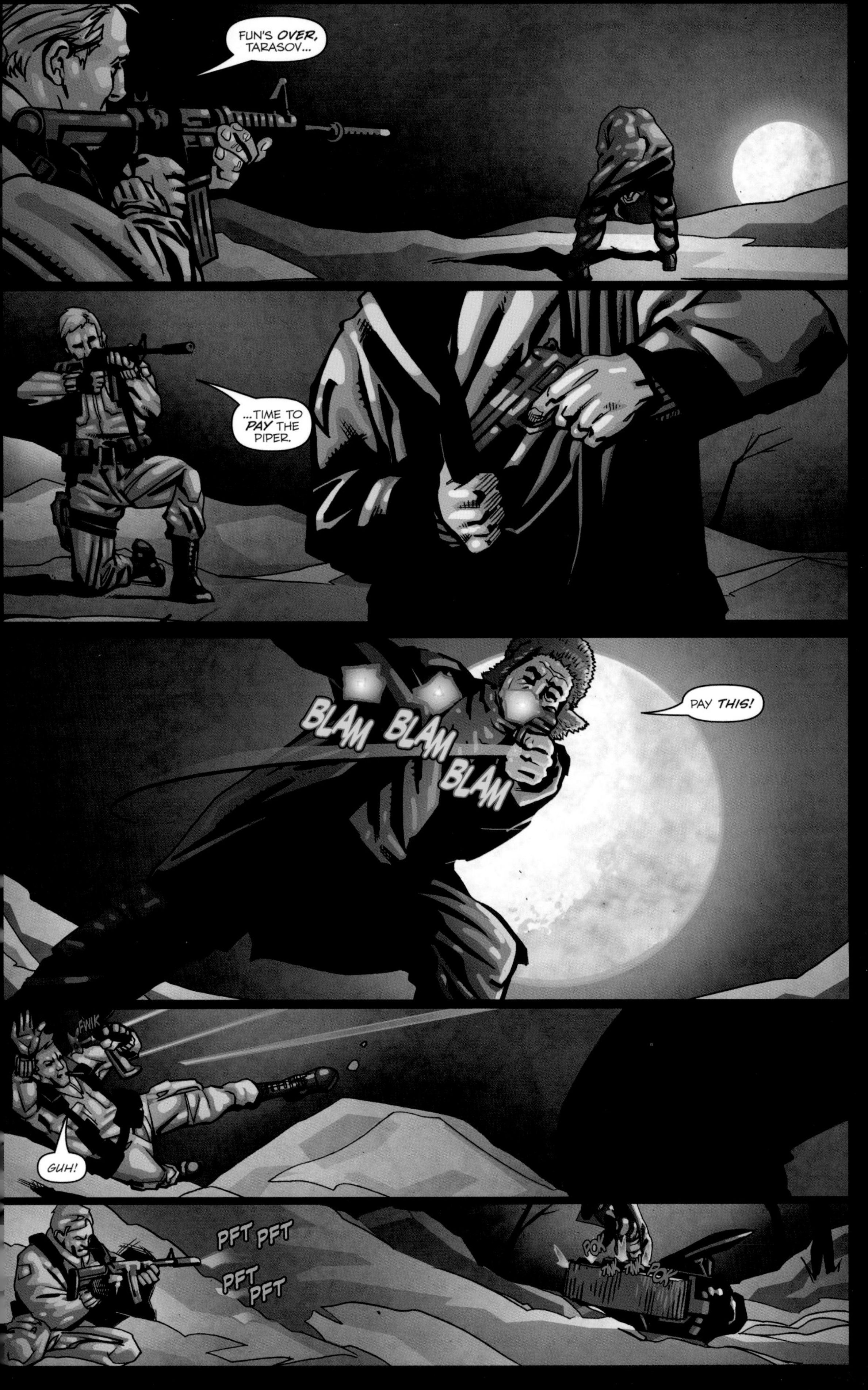
FUN'S *OVER,* TARASOV...
...TIME TO *PAY* THE PIPER.
BLAM BLAM BLAM
PAY *THIS!*
FWIK
*GUH!*
PFT PFT
PFT PFT
POK TINK TINK POK

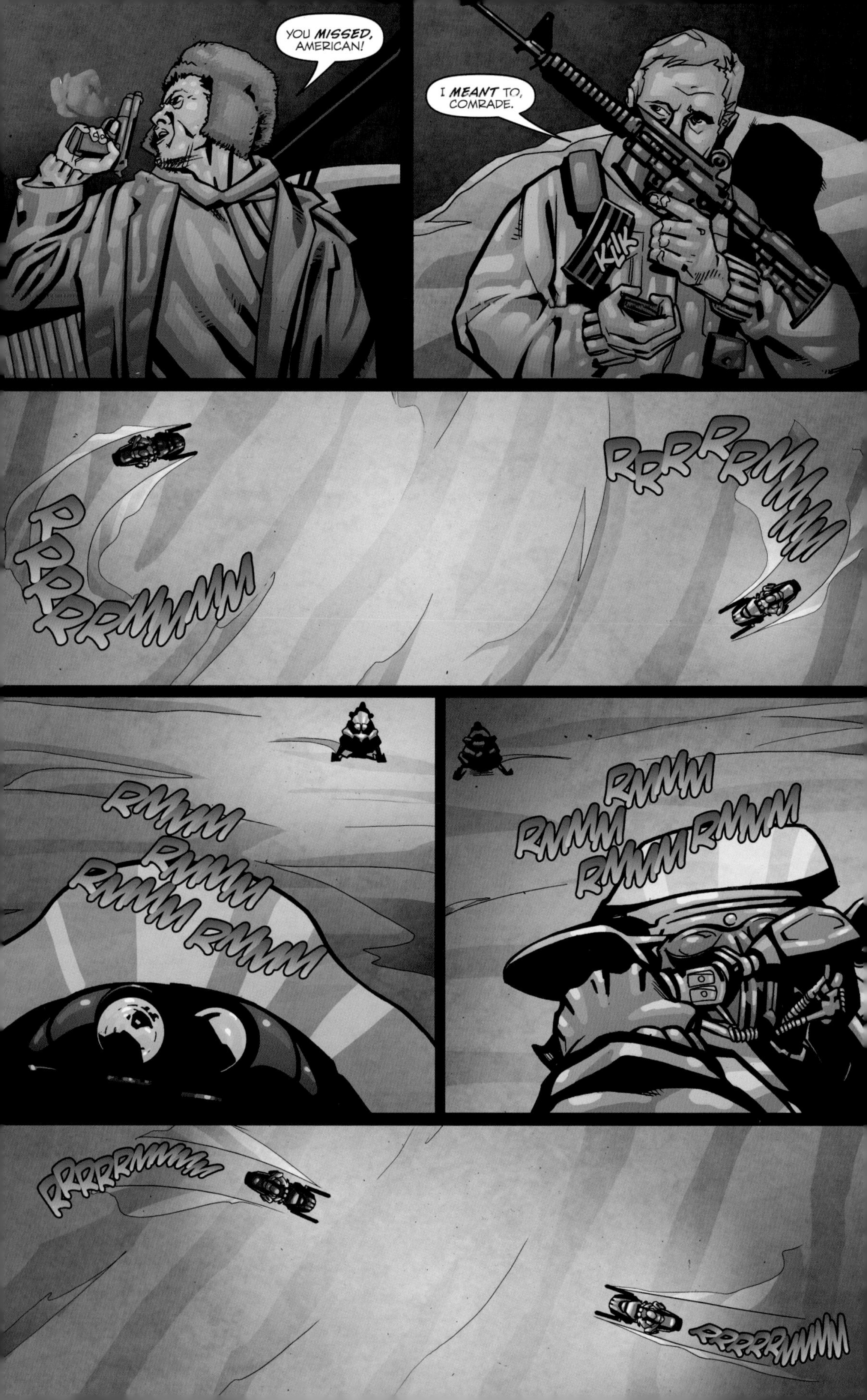
YOU **MISSED,** AMERICAN!
I **MEANT** TO, COMRADE.
KLIK
RRRRRMMMMM
RRRRRMMMMMM
RMMM
RMMM
RMMM RMMM
RMMM
RMMM
RMMM RMMM
RRRRRMMMMM
RRRRRMMMM

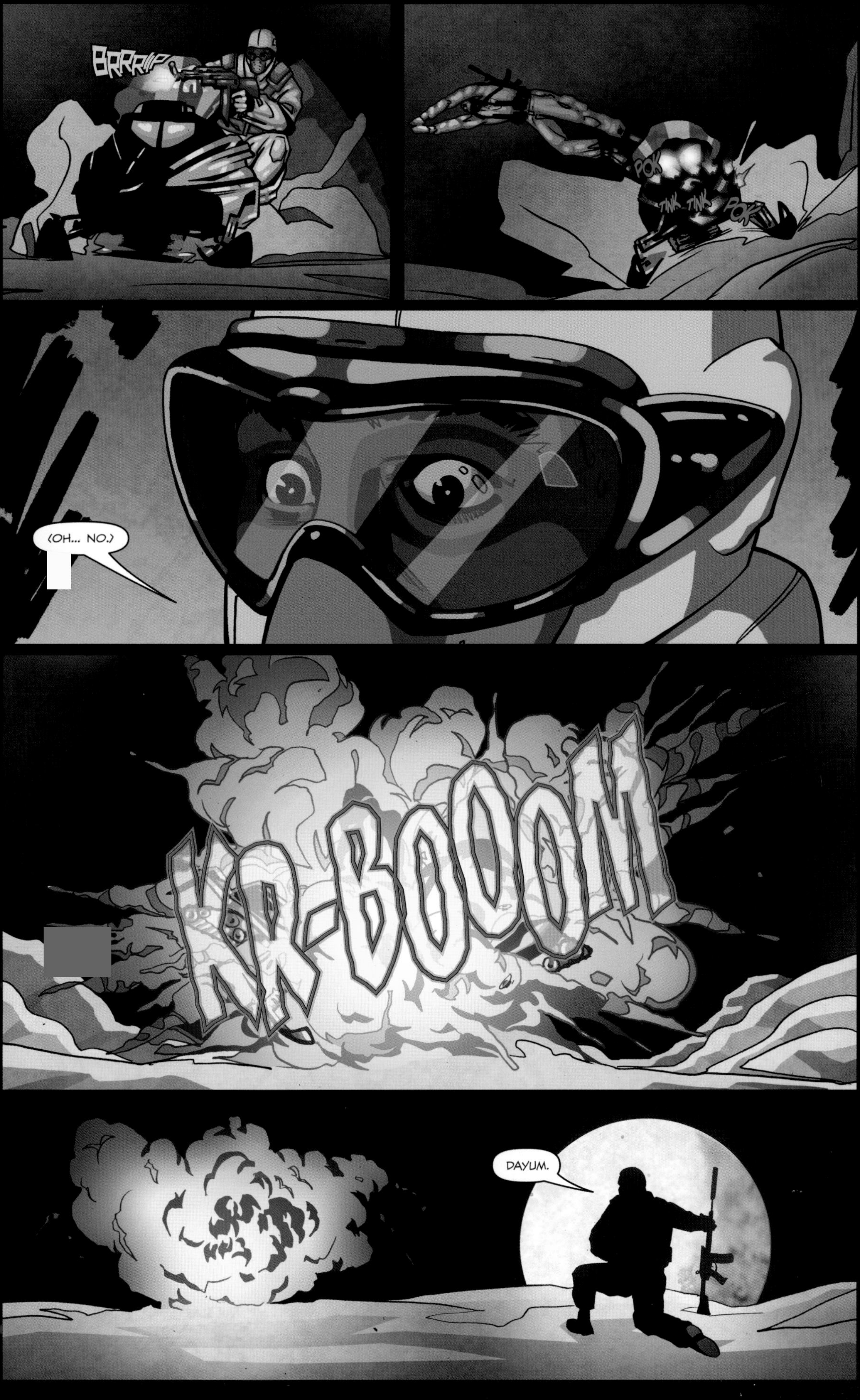
BRRRIIP
POK
TINK TINK
POK
(OH... NO.)
KR-BOOOM
DAYUM.

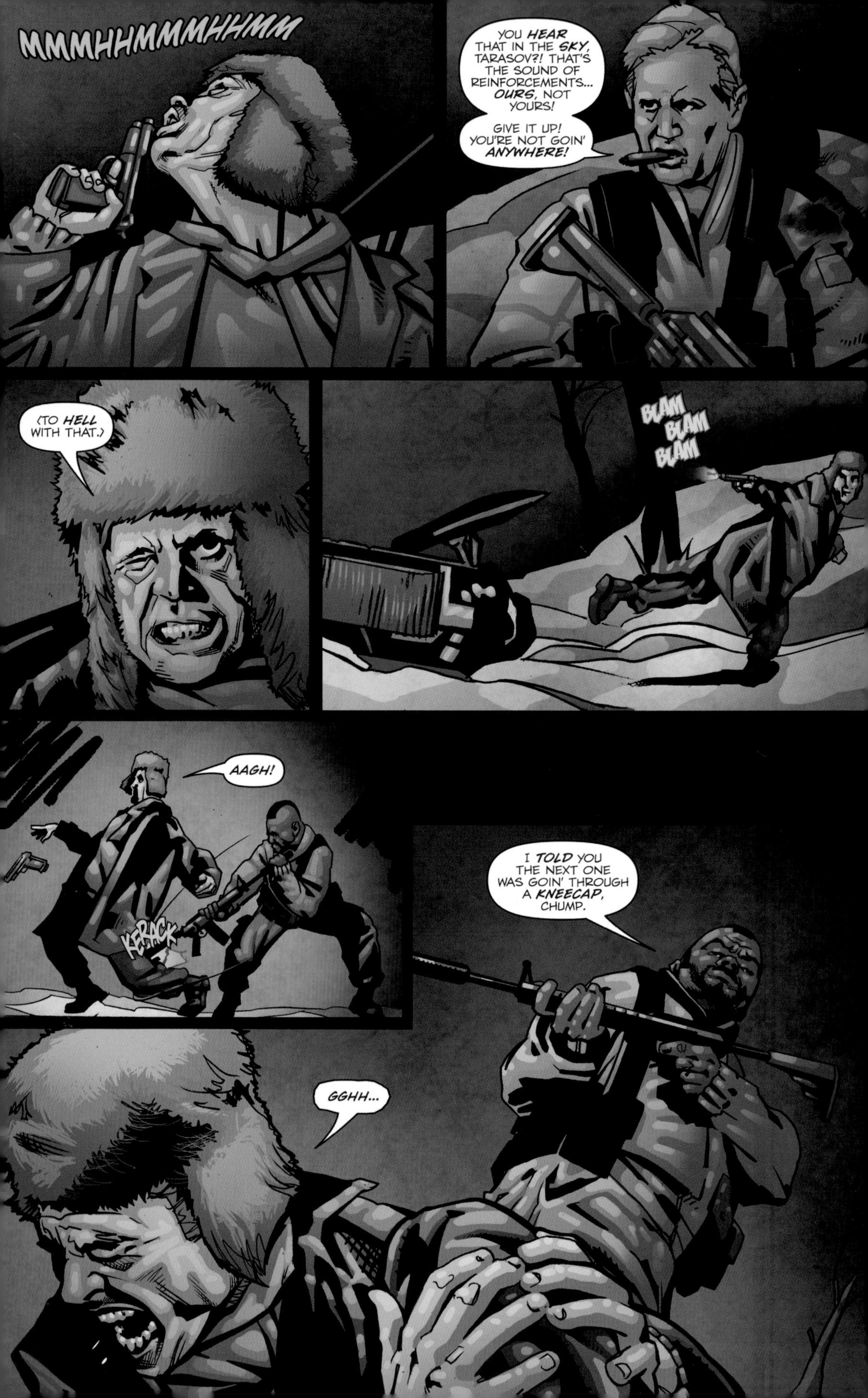
MMMHHMMMHHMM
YOU HEAR THAT IN THE SKY, TARASOV?! THAT'S THE SOUND OF REINFORCEMENTS... OURS, NOT YOURS!
GIVE IT UP! YOU'RE NOT GOIN' ANYWHERE!
‹TO HELL WITH THAT.›
BLAM
BLAM
BLAM
AAGH!
KERACK
I TOLD YOU THE NEXT ONE WAS GOIN' THROUGH A KNEECAP, CHUMP.
GGHH...

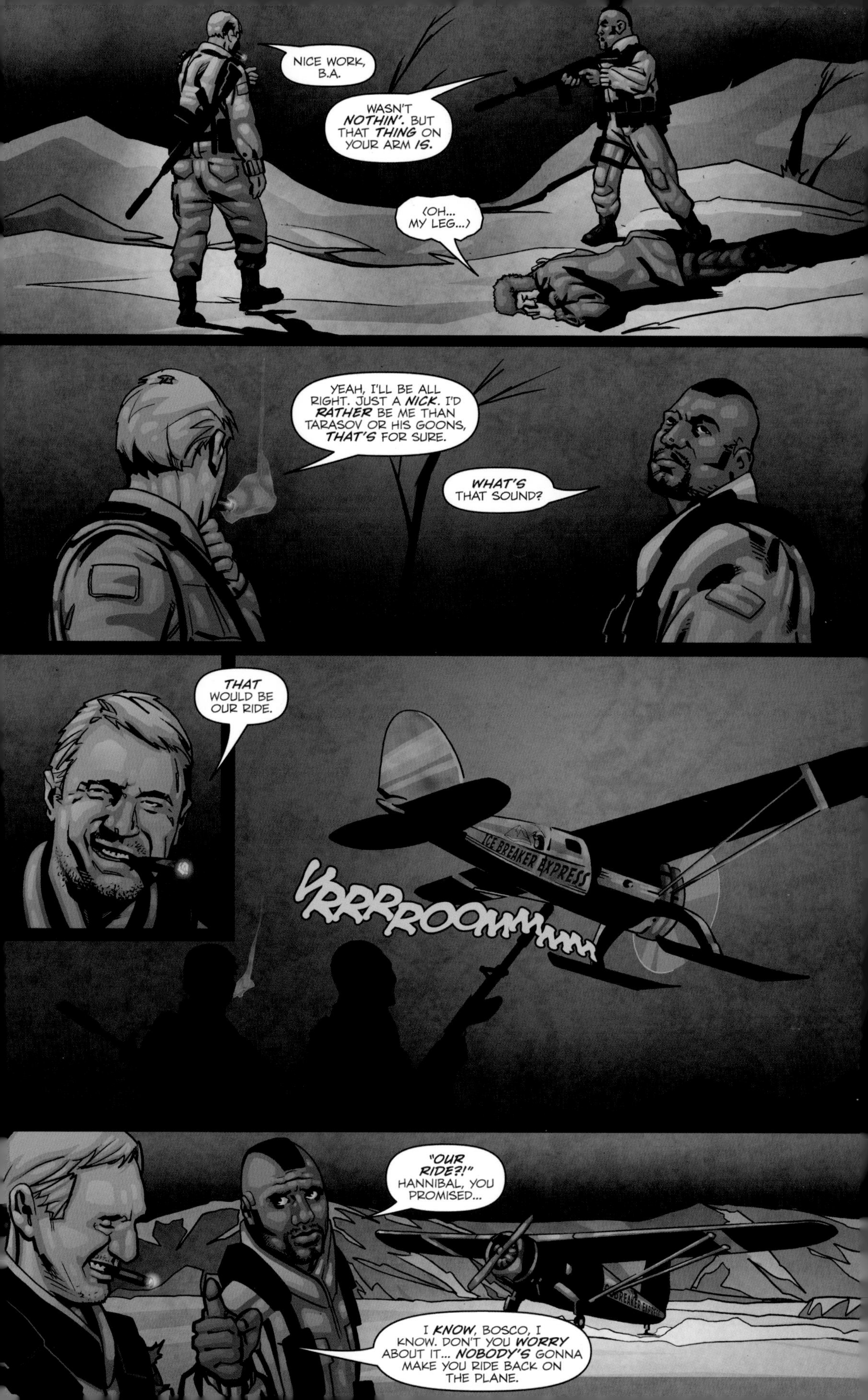
NICE WORK, B.A.
WASN'T NOTHIN'. BUT THAT THING ON YOUR ARM IS.
(OH... MY LEG...)
YEAH, I'LL BE ALL RIGHT. JUST A NICK. I'D RATHER BE ME THAN TARASOV OR HIS GOONS, THAT'S FOR SURE.
WHAT'S THAT SOUND?
THAT WOULD BE OUR RIDE.
ICE BREAKER EXPRESS
VRRRROOMMMM
"OUR RIDE?!" HANNIBAL, YOU PROMISED...
I KNOW, BOSCO, I KNOW. DON'T YOU WORRY ABOUT IT... NOBODY'S GONNA MAKE YOU RIDE BACK ON THE PLANE.

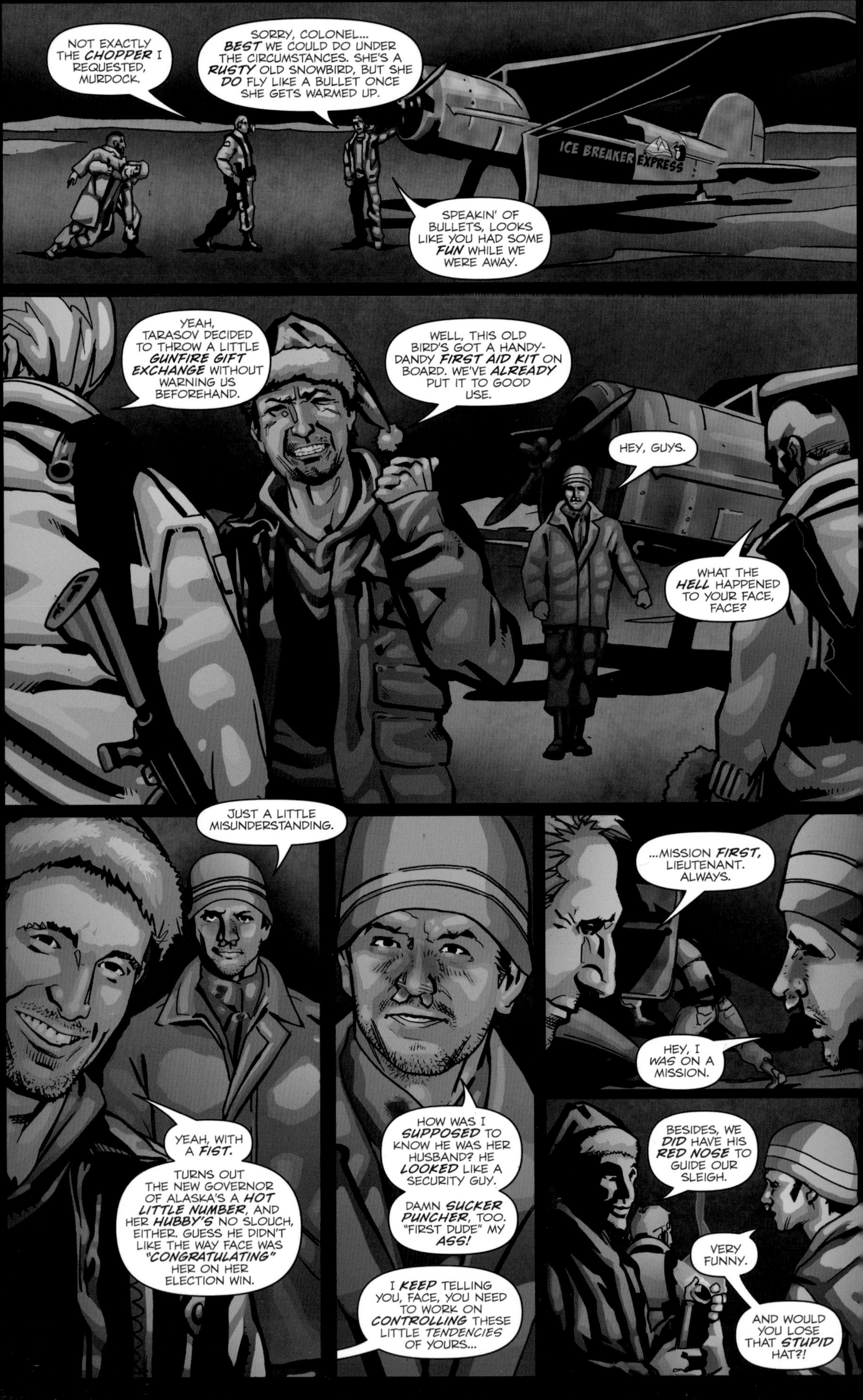
NOT EXACTLY THE CHOPPER I REQUESTED, MURDOCK.
SORRY, COLONEL... BEST WE COULD DO UNDER THE CIRCUMSTANCES. SHE'S A RUSTY OLD SNOWBIRD, BUT SHE DO FLY LIKE A BULLET ONCE SHE GETS WARMED UP.
ICE BREAKER EXPRESS
SPEAKIN' OF BULLETS, LOOKS LIKE YOU HAD SOME FUN WHILE WE WERE AWAY.
YEAH, TARASOV DECIDED TO THROW A LITTLE GUNFIRE GIFT EXCHANGE WITHOUT WARNING US BEFOREHAND.
WELL, THIS OLD BIRD'S GOT A HANDY-DANDY FIRST AID KIT ON BOARD. WE'VE ALREADY PUT IT TO GOOD USE.
HEY, GUYS.
WHAT THE HELL HAPPENED TO YOUR FACE, FACE?
JUST A LITTLE MISUNDERSTANDING.
YEAH, WITH A FIST.
TURNS OUT THE NEW GOVERNOR OF ALASKA'S A HOT LITTLE NUMBER, AND HER HUBBY'S NO SLOUCH, EITHER. GUESS HE DIDN'T LIKE THE WAY FACE WAS "CONGRATULATING" HER ON HER ELECTION WIN.
HOW WAS I SUPPOSED TO KNOW HE WAS HER HUSBAND? HE LOOKED LIKE A SECURITY GUY.
DAMN SUCKER PUNCHER, TOO. "FIRST DUDE" MY ASS!
I KEEP TELLING YOU, FACE, YOU NEED TO WORK ON CONTROLLING THESE LITTLE TENDENCIES OF YOURS...
...MISSION FIRST, LIEUTENANT. ALWAYS.
HEY, I WAS ON A MISSION.
BESIDES, WE DID HAVE HIS RED NOSE TO GUIDE OUR SLEIGH.
VERY FUNNY.
AND WOULD YOU LOSE THAT STUPID HAT?!

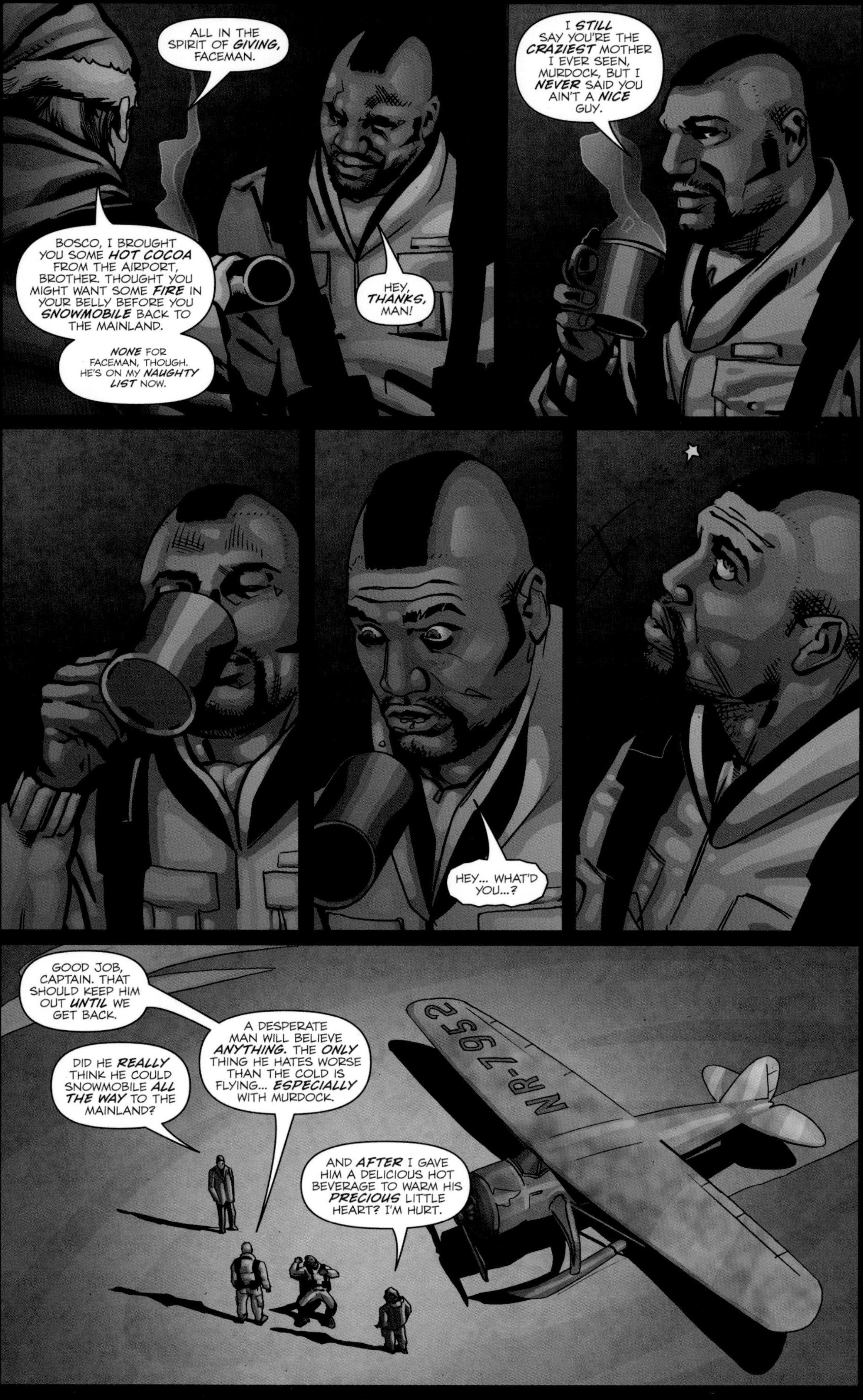
ALL IN THE SPIRIT OF GIVING, FACEMAN.
BOSCO, I BROUGHT YOU SOME HOT COCOA FROM THE AIRPORT, BROTHER. THOUGHT YOU MIGHT WANT SOME FIRE IN YOUR BELLY BEFORE YOU SNOWMOBILE BACK TO THE MAINLAND.
NONE FOR FACEMAN, THOUGH. HE'S ON MY NAUGHTY LIST NOW.
HEY, THANKS, MAN!
I STILL SAY YOU'RE THE CRAZIEST MOTHER I EVER SEEN, MURDOCK, BUT I NEVER SAID YOU AIN'T A NICE GUY.
HEY... WHAT'D YOU...?
GOOD JOB, CAPTAIN. THAT SHOULD KEEP HIM OUT UNTIL WE GET BACK.
DID HE REALLY THINK HE COULD SNOWMOBILE ALL THE WAY TO THE MAINLAND?
A DESPERATE MAN WILL BELIEVE ANYTHING. THE ONLY THING HE HATES WORSE THAN THE COLD IS FLYING... ESPECIALLY WITH MURDOCK.
AND AFTER I GAVE HIM A DELICIOUS HOT BEVERAGE TO WARM HIS PRECIOUS LITTLE HEART? I'M HURT.
NR-7952

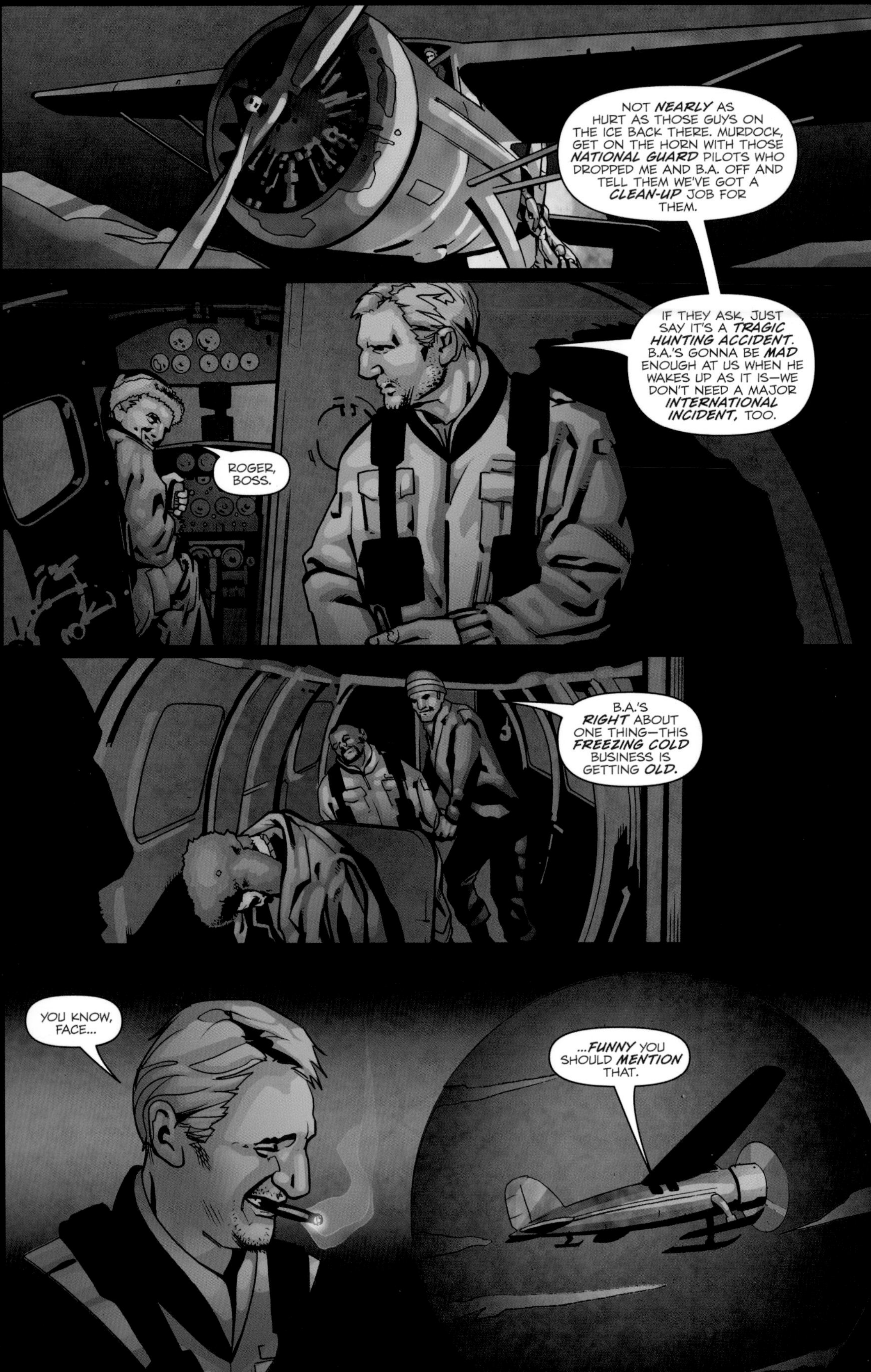
NOT NEARLY AS HURT AS THOSE GUYS ON THE ICE BACK THERE. MURDOCK, GET ON THE HORN WITH THOSE NATIONAL GUARD PILOTS WHO DROPPED ME AND B.A. OFF AND TELL THEM WE'VE GOT A CLEAN-UP JOB FOR THEM.
IF THEY ASK, JUST SAY IT'S A TRAGIC HUNTING ACCIDENT. B.A.'S GONNA BE MAD ENOUGH AT US WHEN HE WAKES UP AS IT IS—WE DON'T NEED A MAJOR INTERNATIONAL INCIDENT, TOO.
ROGER, BOSS.
B.A.'S RIGHT ABOUT ONE THING—THIS FREEZING COLD BUSINESS IS GETTING OLD.
YOU KNOW, FACE...
...FUNNY YOU SHOULD MENTION THAT.

# CHAPTER TWO

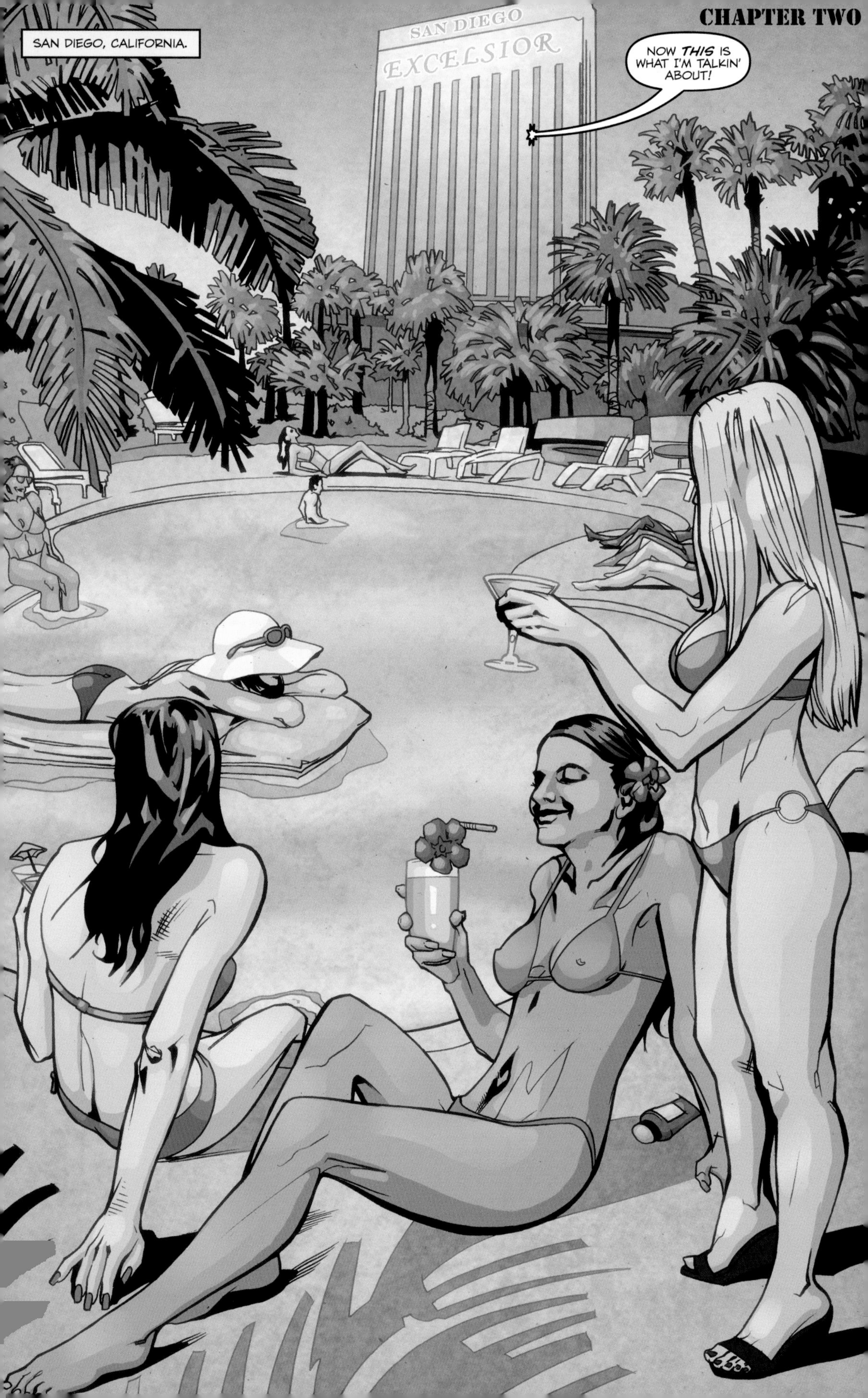
SAN DIEGO, CALIFORNIA.
SAN DIEGO
EXCELSIOR
NOW *THIS* IS WHAT I'M TALKIN' ABOUT!

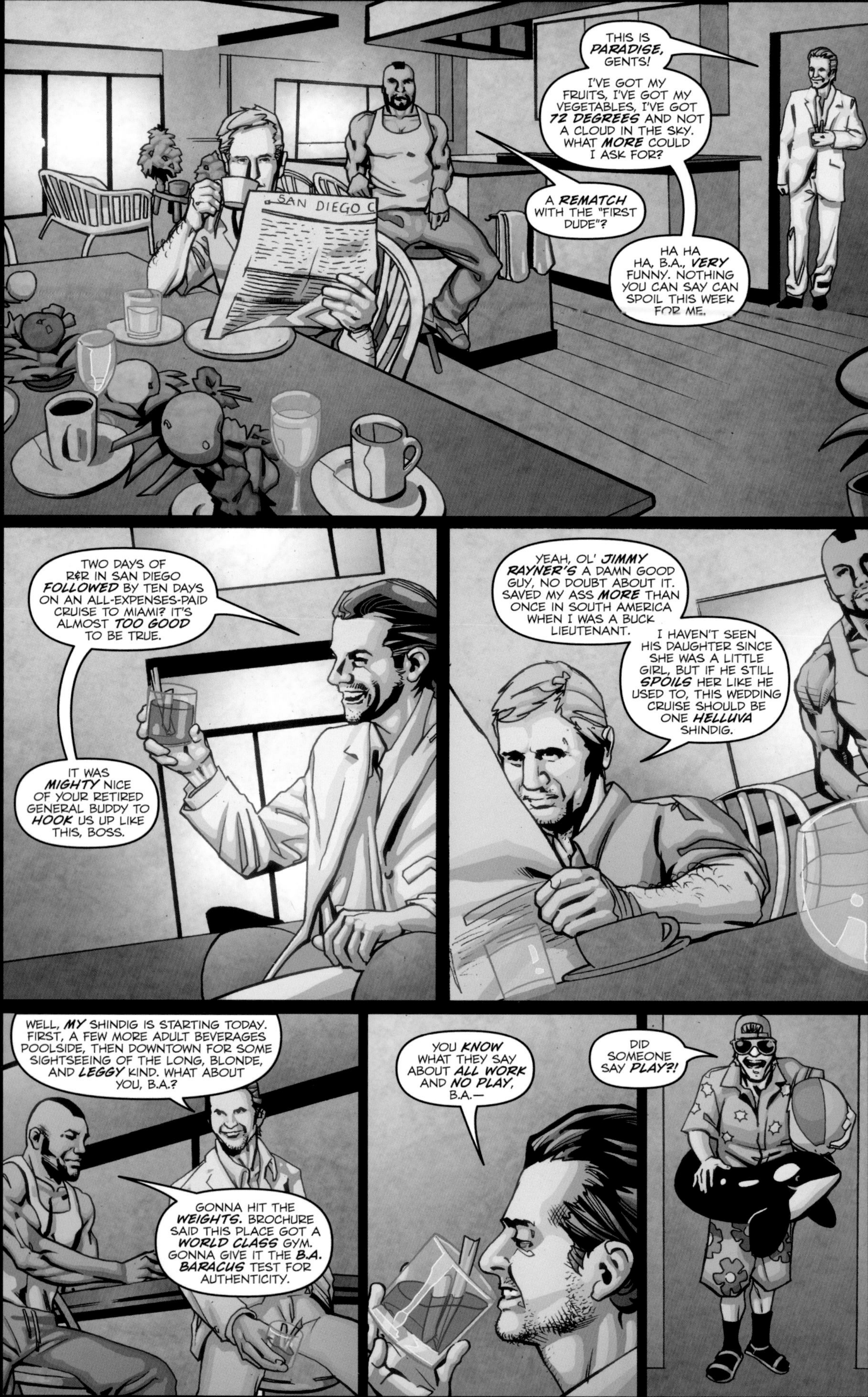
THIS IS PARADISE, GENTS!
I'VE GOT MY FRUITS, I'VE GOT MY VEGETABLES, I'VE GOT 72 DEGREES AND NOT A CLOUD IN THE SKY. WHAT MORE COULD I ASK FOR?
A REMATCH WITH THE "FIRST DUDE"?
HA HA HA, B.A., VERY FUNNY. NOTHING YOU CAN SAY CAN SPOIL THIS WEEK FOR ME.
SAN DIEGO C
TWO DAYS OF R&R IN SAN DIEGO FOLLOWED BY TEN DAYS ON AN ALL-EXPENSES-PAID CRUISE TO MIAMI? IT'S ALMOST TOO GOOD TO BE TRUE.
IT WAS MIGHTY NICE OF YOUR RETIRED GENERAL BUDDY TO HOOK US UP LIKE THIS, BOSS.
YEAH, OL' JIMMY RAYNER'S A DAMN GOOD GUY, NO DOUBT ABOUT IT. SAVED MY ASS MORE THAN ONCE IN SOUTH AMERICA WHEN I WAS A BUCK LIEUTENANT.
I HAVEN'T SEEN HIS DAUGHTER SINCE SHE WAS A LITTLE GIRL, BUT IF HE STILL SPOILS HER LIKE HE USED TO, THIS WEDDING CRUISE SHOULD BE ONE HELLUVA SHINDIG.
WELL, MY SHINDIG IS STARTING TODAY. FIRST, A FEW MORE ADULT BEVERAGES POOLSIDE, THEN DOWNTOWN FOR SOME SIGHTSEEING OF THE LONG, BLONDE, AND LEGGY KIND. WHAT ABOUT YOU, B.A.?
GONNA HIT THE WEIGHTS. BROCHURE SAID THIS PLACE GOT A WORLD CLASS GYM. GONNA GIVE IT THE B.A. BARACUS TEST FOR AUTHENTICITY.
YOU KNOW WHAT THEY SAY ABOUT ALL WORK AND NO PLAY, B.A.—
DID SOMEONE SAY PLAY?!

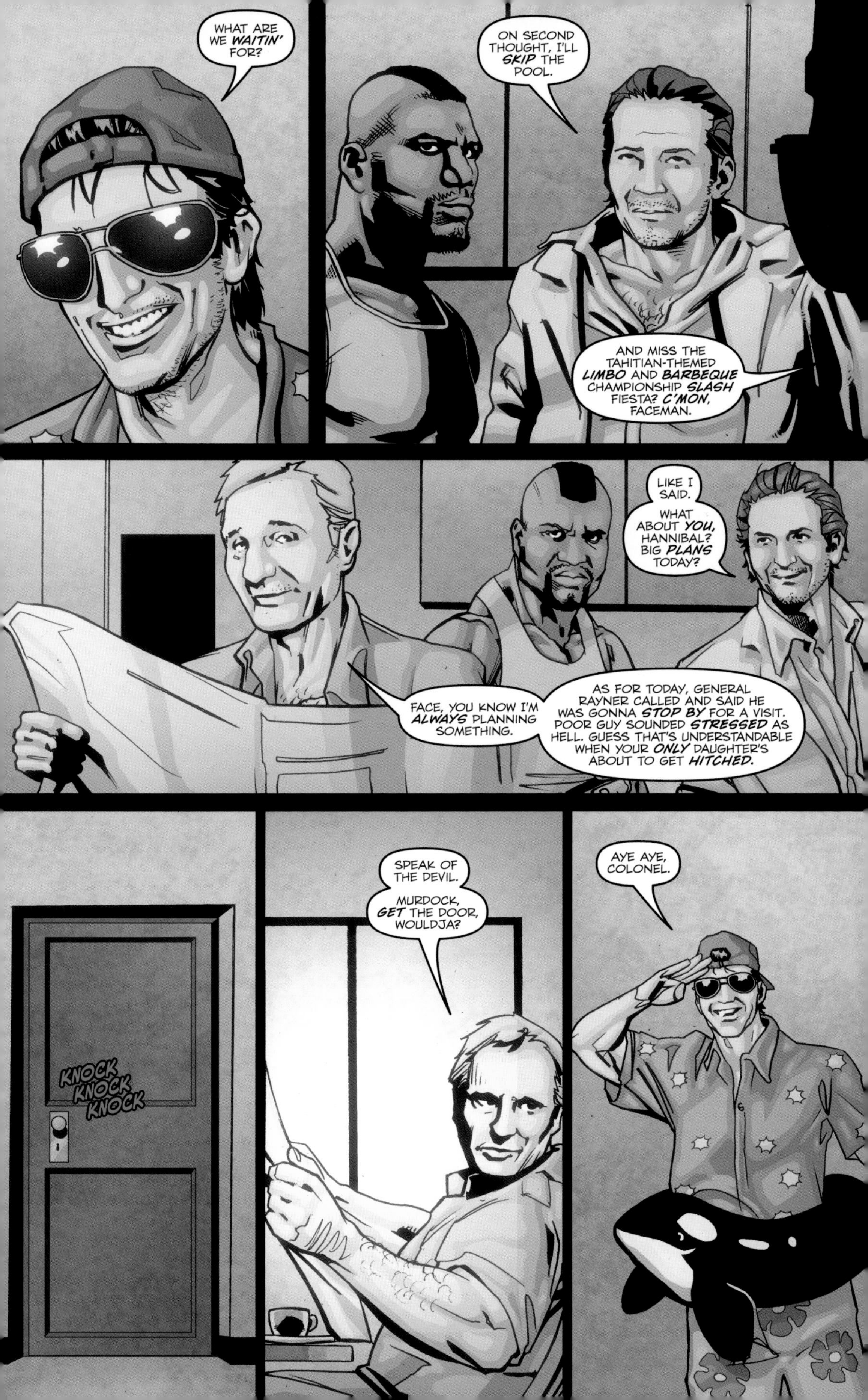
WHAT ARE WE WAITIN' FOR?
ON SECOND THOUGHT, I'LL SKIP THE POOL.
AND MISS THE TAHITIAN-THEMED LIMBO AND BARBEQUE CHAMPIONSHIP SLASH FIESTA? C'MON, FACEMAN.
LIKE I SAID.
WHAT ABOUT YOU, HANNIBAL? BIG PLANS TODAY?
FACE, YOU KNOW I'M ALWAYS PLANNING SOMETHING.
AS FOR TODAY, GENERAL RAYNER CALLED AND SAID HE WAS GONNA STOP BY FOR A VISIT. POOR GUY SOUNDED STRESSED AS HELL. GUESS THAT'S UNDERSTANDABLE WHEN YOUR ONLY DAUGHTER'S ABOUT TO GET HITCHED.
KNOCK KNOCK KNOCK
SPEAK OF THE DEVIL.
MURDOCK, GET THE DOOR, WOULDJA?
AYE AYE, COLONEL.

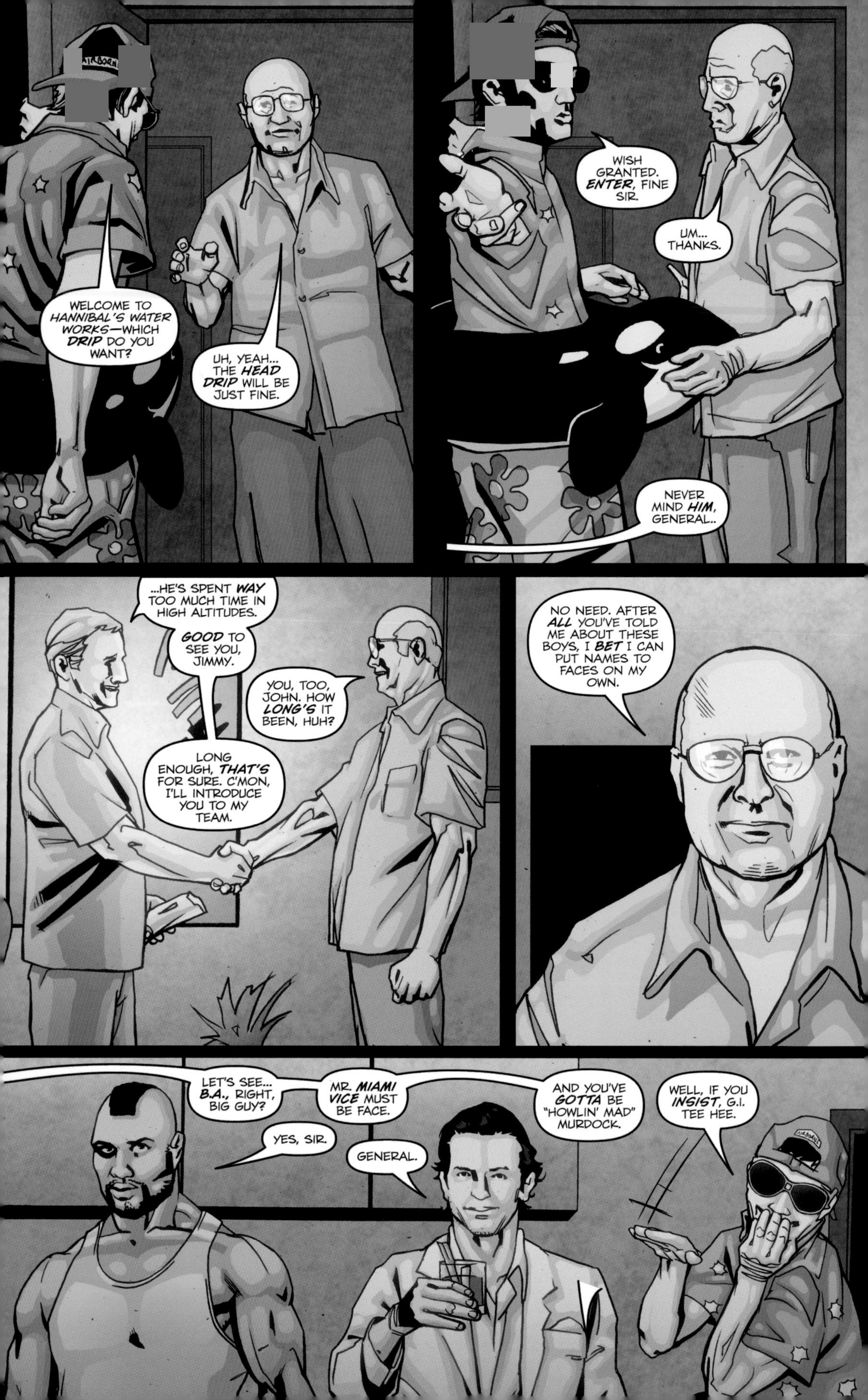
WELCOME TO HANNIBAL'S WATER WORKS—WHICH DRIP DO YOU WANT?
UH, YEAH... THE HEAD DRIP WILL BE JUST FINE.
WISH GRANTED. ENTER, FINE SIR.
UM... THANKS.
NEVER MIND HIM, GENERAL..
...HE'S SPENT WAY TOO MUCH TIME IN HIGH ALTITUDES.
GOOD TO SEE YOU, JIMMY.
YOU, TOO, JOHN. HOW LONG'S IT BEEN, HUH?
LONG ENOUGH, THAT'S FOR SURE. C'MON, I'LL INTRODUCE YOU TO MY TEAM.
NO NEED. AFTER ALL YOU'VE TOLD ME ABOUT THESE BOYS, I BET I CAN PUT NAMES TO FACES ON MY OWN.
LET'S SEE... B.A., RIGHT, BIG GUY?
YES, SIR.
MR. MIAMI VICE MUST BE FACE.
GENERAL.
AND YOU'VE GOTTA BE "HOWLIN' MAD" MURDOCK.
WELL, IF YOU INSIST, G.I. TEE HEE.

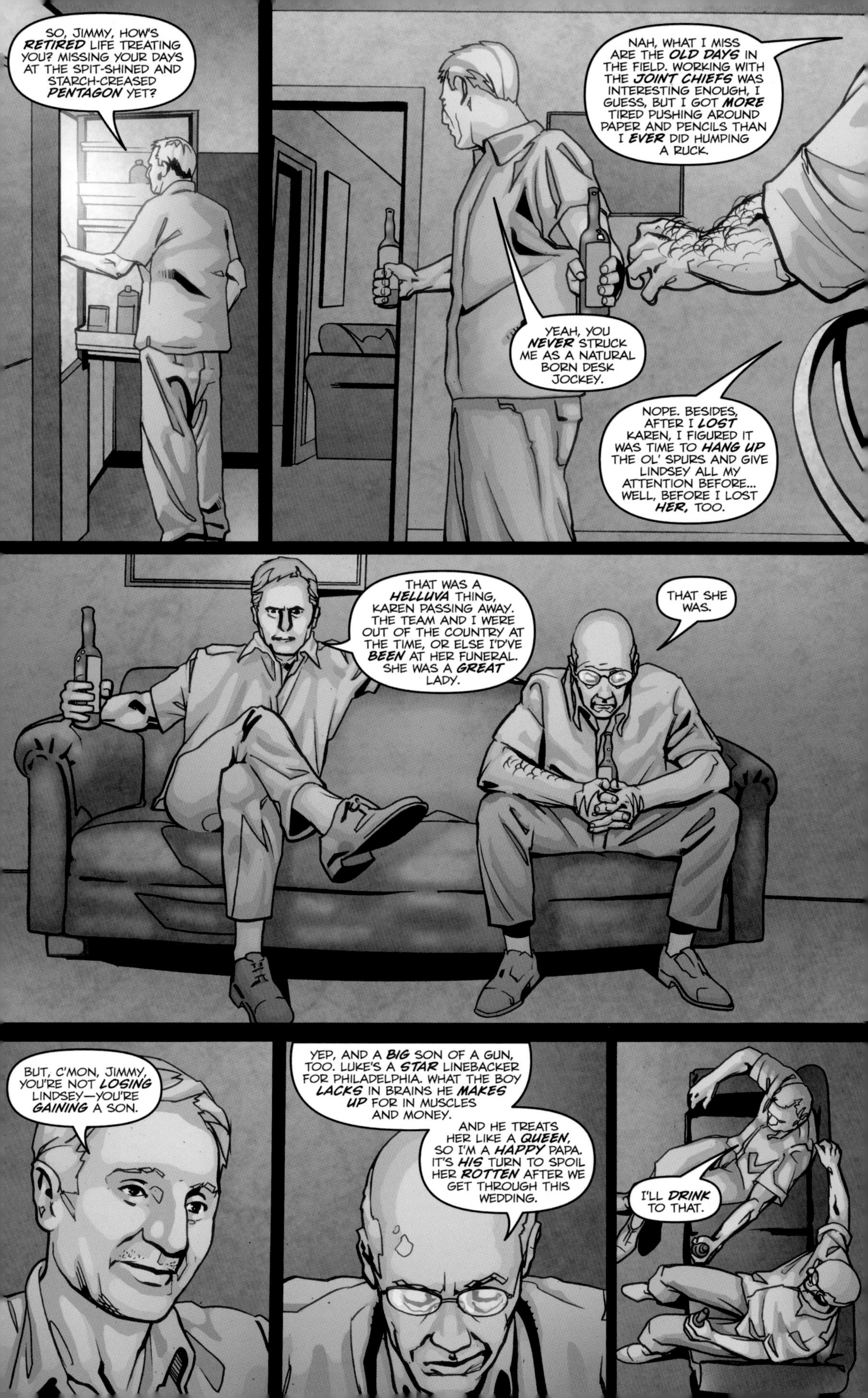
SO, JIMMY, HOW'S RETIRED LIFE TREATING YOU? MISSING YOUR DAYS AT THE SPIT-SHINED AND STARCH-CREASED PENTAGON YET?
NAH, WHAT I MISS ARE THE OLD DAYS IN THE FIELD. WORKING WITH THE JOINT CHIEFS WAS INTERESTING ENOUGH, I GUESS, BUT I GOT MORE TIRED PUSHING AROUND PAPER AND PENCILS THAN I EVER DID HUMPING A RUCK.
YEAH, YOU NEVER STRUCK ME AS A NATURAL BORN DESK JOCKEY.
NOPE. BESIDES, AFTER I LOST KAREN, I FIGURED IT WAS TIME TO HANG UP THE OL' SPURS AND GIVE LINDSEY ALL MY ATTENTION BEFORE... WELL, BEFORE I LOST HER, TOO.
THAT WAS A HELLUVA THING, KAREN PASSING AWAY. THE TEAM AND I WERE OUT OF THE COUNTRY AT THE TIME, OR ELSE I'D'VE BEEN AT HER FUNERAL. SHE WAS A GREAT LADY.
THAT SHE WAS.
BUT, C'MON, JIMMY, YOU'RE NOT LOSING LINDSEY—YOU'RE GAINING A SON.
YEP, AND A BIG SON OF A GUN, TOO. LUKE'S A STAR LINEBACKER FOR PHILADELPHIA. WHAT THE BOY LACKS IN BRAINS HE MAKES UP FOR IN MUSCLES AND MONEY.
AND HE TREATS HER LIKE A QUEEN, SO I'M A HAPPY PAPA. IT'S HIS TURN TO SPOIL HER ROTTEN AFTER WE GET THROUGH THIS WEDDING.
I'LL DRINK TO THAT.

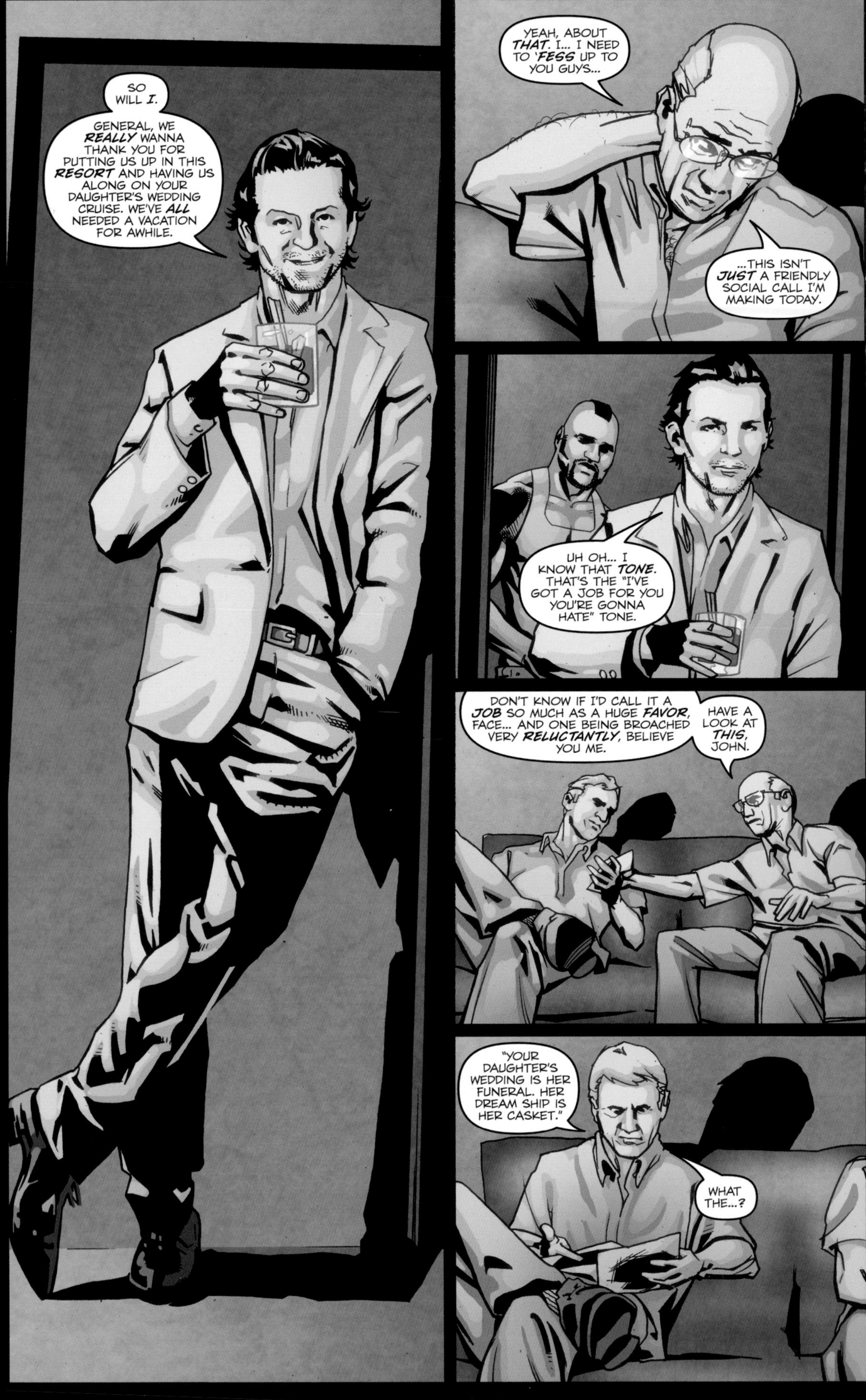
SO WILL I.
GENERAL, WE REALLY WANNA THANK YOU FOR PUTTING US UP IN THIS RESORT AND HAVING US ALONG ON YOUR DAUGHTER'S WEDDING CRUISE. WE'VE ALL NEEDED A VACATION FOR AWHILE.
YEAH, ABOUT THAT. I... I NEED TO 'FESS UP TO YOU GUYS...
...THIS ISN'T JUST A FRIENDLY SOCIAL CALL I'M MAKING TODAY.
UH OH... I KNOW THAT TONE. THAT'S THE "I'VE GOT A JOB FOR YOU YOU'RE GONNA HATE" TONE.
DON'T KNOW IF I'D CALL IT A JOB SO MUCH AS A HUGE FAVOR, FACE... AND ONE BEING BROACHED VERY RELUCTANTLY, BELIEVE YOU ME.
HAVE A LOOK AT THIS, JOHN.
"YOUR DAUGHTER'S WEDDING IS HER FUNERAL. HER DREAM SHIP IS HER CASKET."
WHAT THE...?

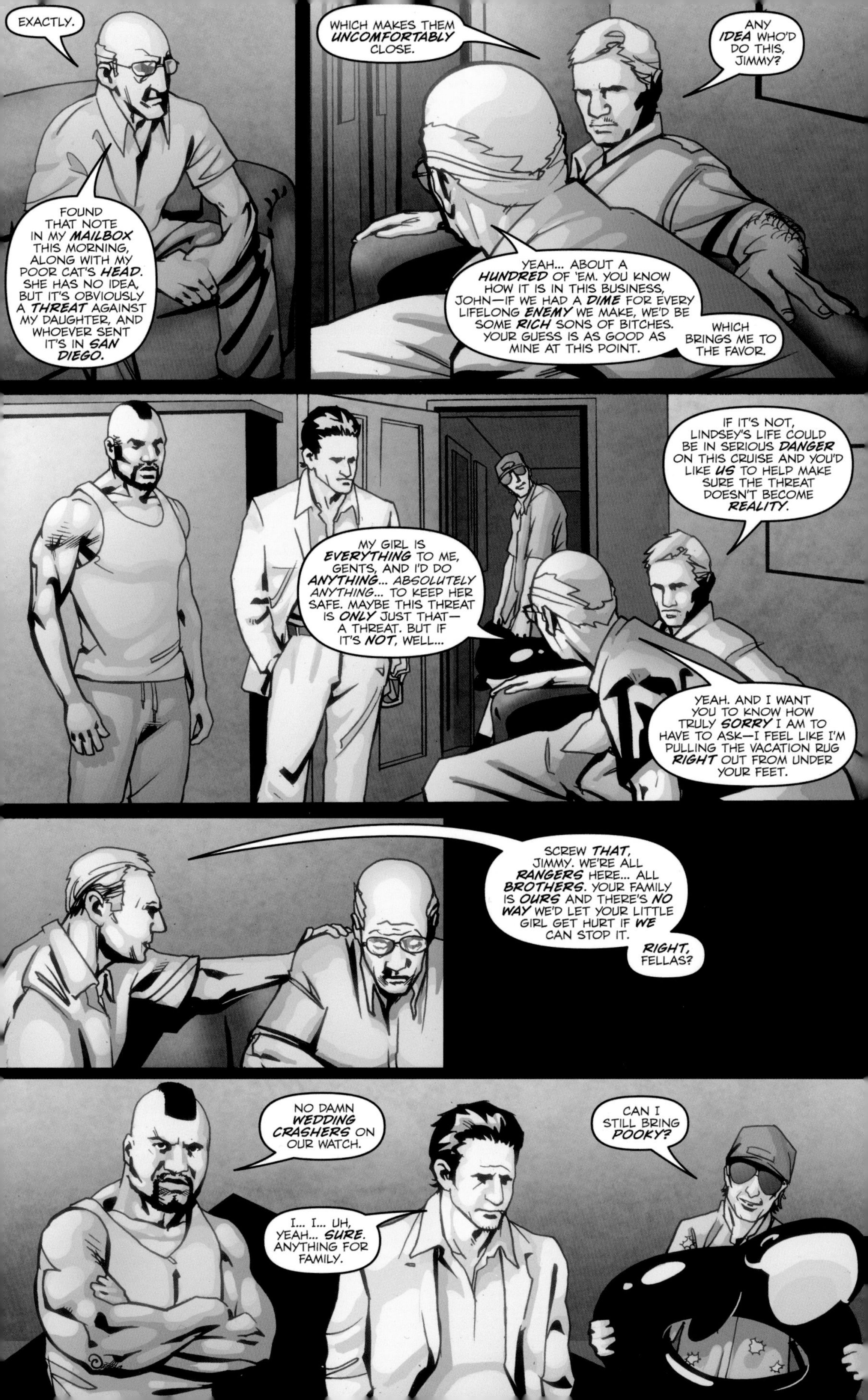
EXACTLY.
FOUND THAT NOTE IN MY MAILBOX THIS MORNING, ALONG WITH MY POOR CAT'S HEAD. SHE HAS NO IDEA, BUT IT'S OBVIOUSLY A THREAT AGAINST MY DAUGHTER, AND WHOEVER SENT IT'S IN SAN DIEGO.
WHICH MAKES THEM UNCOMFORTABLY CLOSE.
ANY IDEA WHO'D DO THIS, JIMMY?
YEAH... ABOUT A HUNDRED OF 'EM. YOU KNOW HOW IT IS IN THIS BUSINESS, JOHN—IF WE HAD A DIME FOR EVERY LIFELONG ENEMY WE MAKE, WE'D BE SOME RICH SONS OF BITCHES. YOUR GUESS IS AS GOOD AS MINE AT THIS POINT.
WHICH BRINGS ME TO THE FAVOR.
MY GIRL IS EVERYTHING TO ME, GENTS, AND I'D DO ANYTHING... ABSOLUTELY ANYTHING... TO KEEP HER SAFE. MAYBE THIS THREAT IS ONLY JUST THAT—A THREAT. BUT IF IT'S NOT, WELL...
IF IT'S NOT, LINDSEY'S LIFE COULD BE IN SERIOUS DANGER ON THIS CRUISE AND YOU'D LIKE US TO HELP MAKE SURE THE THREAT DOESN'T BECOME REALITY.
YEAH. AND I WANT YOU TO KNOW HOW TRULY SORRY I AM TO HAVE TO ASK—I FEEL LIKE I'M PULLING THE VACATION RUG RIGHT OUT FROM UNDER YOUR FEET.
SCREW THAT, JIMMY. WE'RE ALL RANGERS HERE... ALL BROTHERS. YOUR FAMILY IS OURS AND THERE'S NO WAY WE'D LET YOUR LITTLE GIRL GET HURT IF WE CAN STOP IT.
RIGHT, FELLAS?
NO DAMN WEDDING CRASHERS ON OUR WATCH.
I... I... UH, YEAH... SURE. ANYTHING FOR FAMILY.
CAN I STILL BRING POOKY?

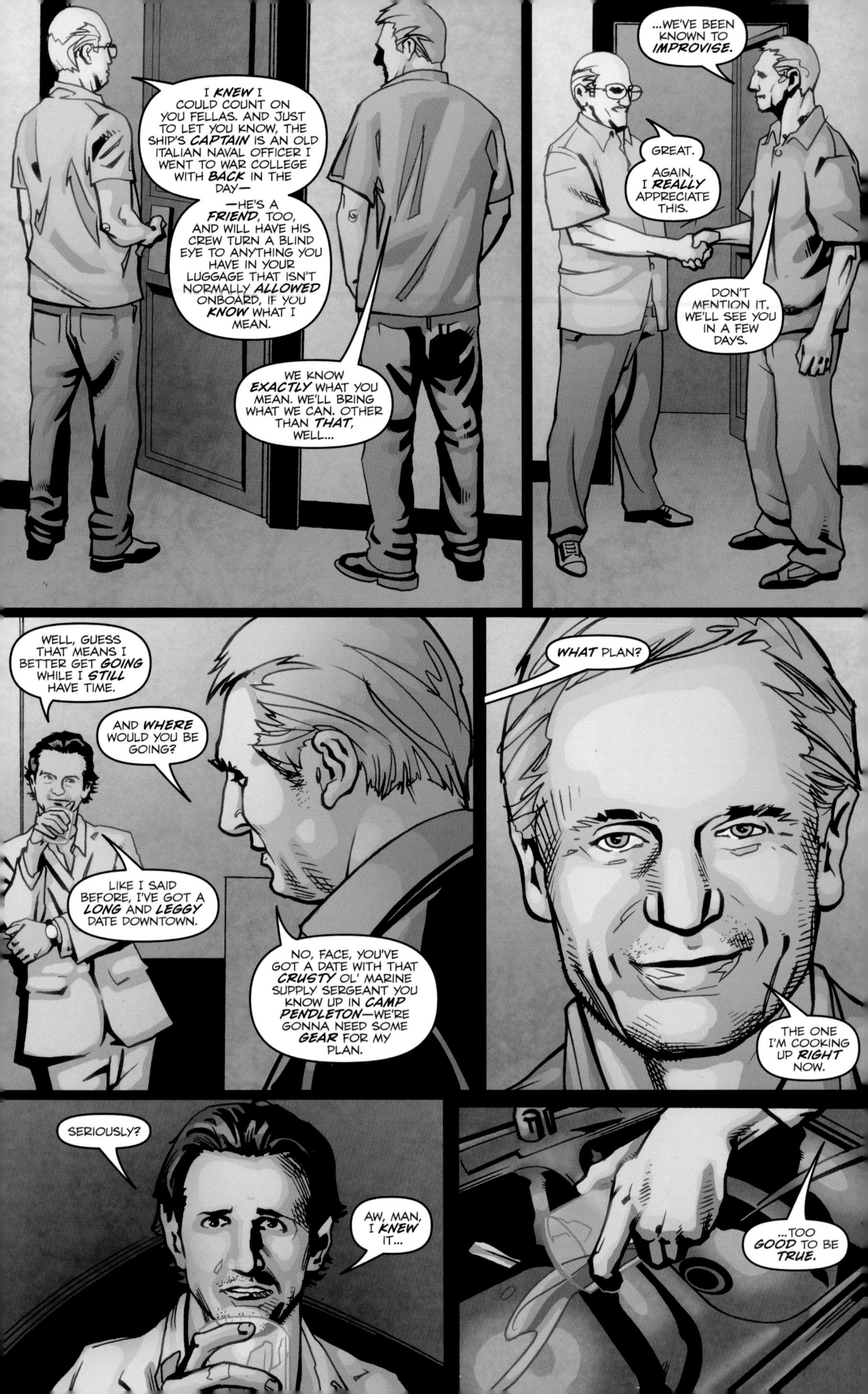
I KNEW I COULD COUNT ON YOU FELLAS. AND JUST TO LET YOU KNOW, THE SHIP'S CAPTAIN IS AN OLD ITALIAN NAVAL OFFICER I WENT TO WAR COLLEGE WITH BACK IN THE DAY—
—HE'S A FRIEND, TOO, AND WILL HAVE HIS CREW TURN A BLIND EYE TO ANYTHING YOU HAVE IN YOUR LUGGAGE THAT ISN'T NORMALLY ALLOWED ONBOARD, IF YOU KNOW WHAT I MEAN.
WE KNOW EXACTLY WHAT YOU MEAN. WE'LL BRING WHAT WE CAN. OTHER THAN THAT, WELL...
...WE'VE BEEN KNOWN TO IMPROVISE.
GREAT.
AGAIN, I REALLY APPRECIATE THIS.
DON'T MENTION IT. WE'LL SEE YOU IN A FEW DAYS.
WELL, GUESS THAT MEANS I BETTER GET GOING WHILE I STILL HAVE TIME.
AND WHERE WOULD YOU BE GOING?
LIKE I SAID BEFORE, I'VE GOT A LONG AND LEGGY DATE DOWNTOWN.
NO, FACE, YOU'VE GOT A DATE WITH THAT CRUSTY OL' MARINE SUPPLY SERGEANT YOU KNOW UP IN CAMP PENDLETON—WE'RE GONNA NEED SOME GEAR FOR MY PLAN.
WHAT PLAN?
THE ONE I'M COOKING UP RIGHT NOW.
SERIOUSLY?
AW, MAN, I KNEW IT...
...TOO GOOD TO BE TRUE.

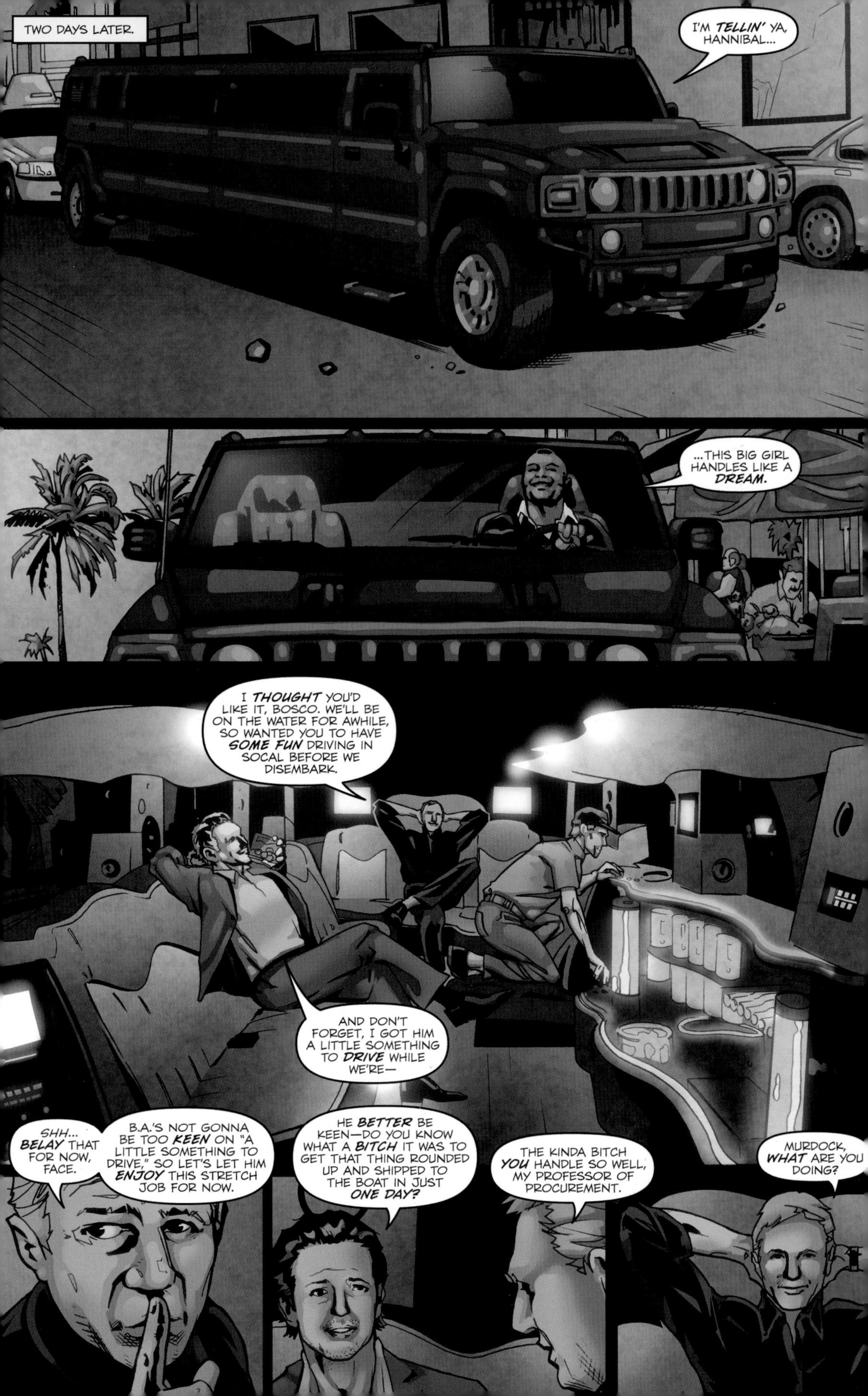
TWO DAYS LATER.
I'M TELLIN' YA, HANNIBAL...
...THIS BIG GIRL HANDLES LIKE A DREAM.
I THOUGHT YOU'D LIKE IT, BOSCO. WE'LL BE ON THE WATER FOR AWHILE, SO WANTED YOU TO HAVE SOME FUN DRIVING IN SOCAL BEFORE WE DISEMBARK.
AND DON'T FORGET, I GOT HIM A LITTLE SOMETHING TO DRIVE WHILE WE'RE—
SHH... BELAY THAT FOR NOW, FACE.
B.A.'S NOT GONNA BE TOO KEEN ON "A LITTLE SOMETHING TO DRIVE," SO LET'S LET HIM ENJOY THIS STRETCH JOB FOR NOW.
HE BETTER BE KEEN—DO YOU KNOW WHAT A BITCH IT WAS TO GET THAT THING ROUNDED UP AND SHIPPED TO THE BOAT IN JUST ONE DAY?
THE KINDA BITCH YOU HANDLE SO WELL, MY PROFESSOR OF PROCUREMENT.
MURDOCK, WHAT ARE YOU DOING?

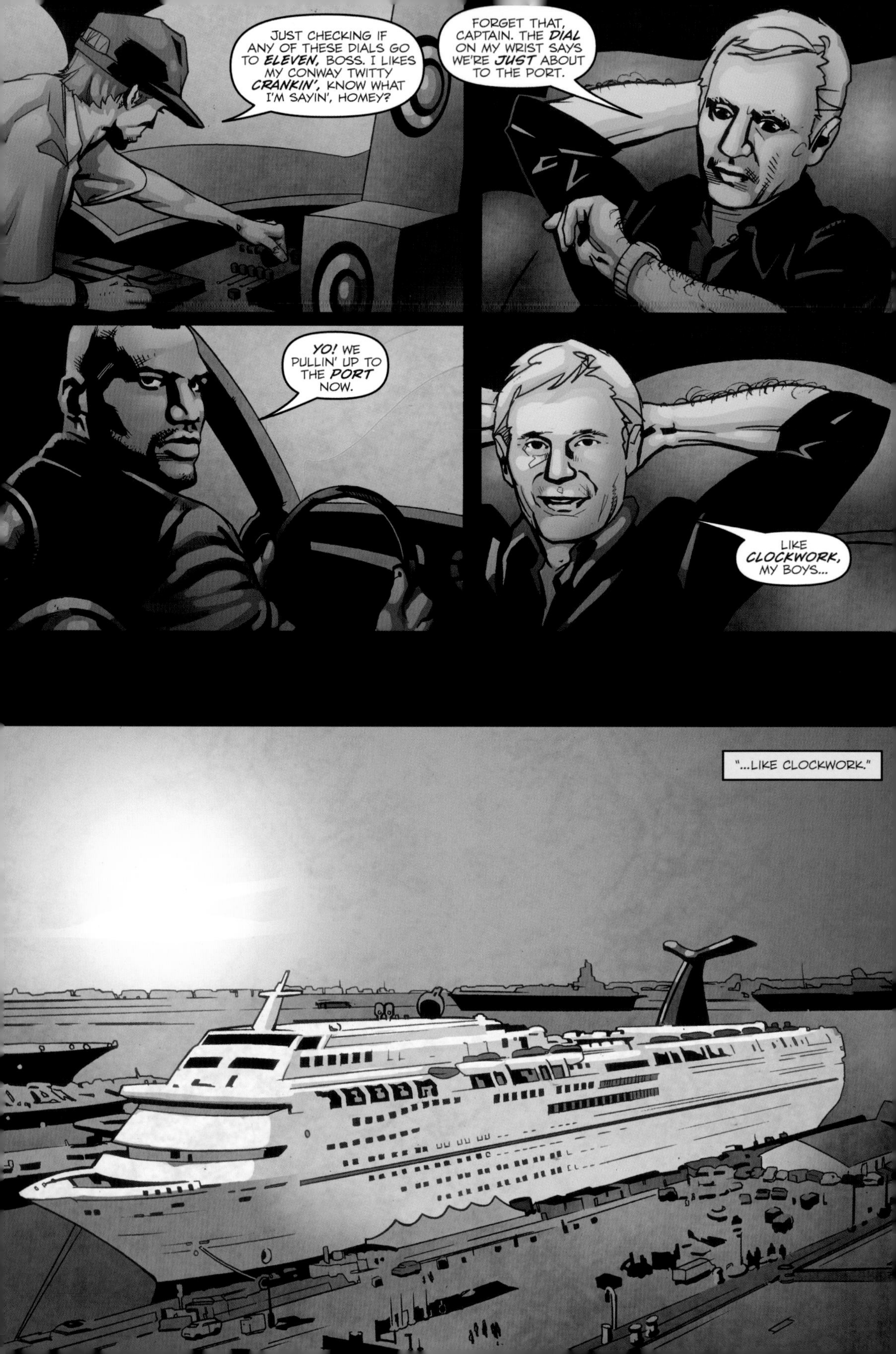
JUST CHECKING IF ANY OF THESE DIALS GO TO ELEVEN, BOSS. I LIKES MY CONWAY TWITTY CRANKIN', KNOW WHAT I'M SAYIN', HOMEY?
FORGET THAT, CAPTAIN. THE DIAL ON MY WRIST SAYS WE'RE JUST ABOUT TO THE PORT.
YO! WE PULLIN' UP TO THE PORT NOW.
LIKE CLOCKWORK, MY BOYS...
"...LIKE CLOCKWORK."

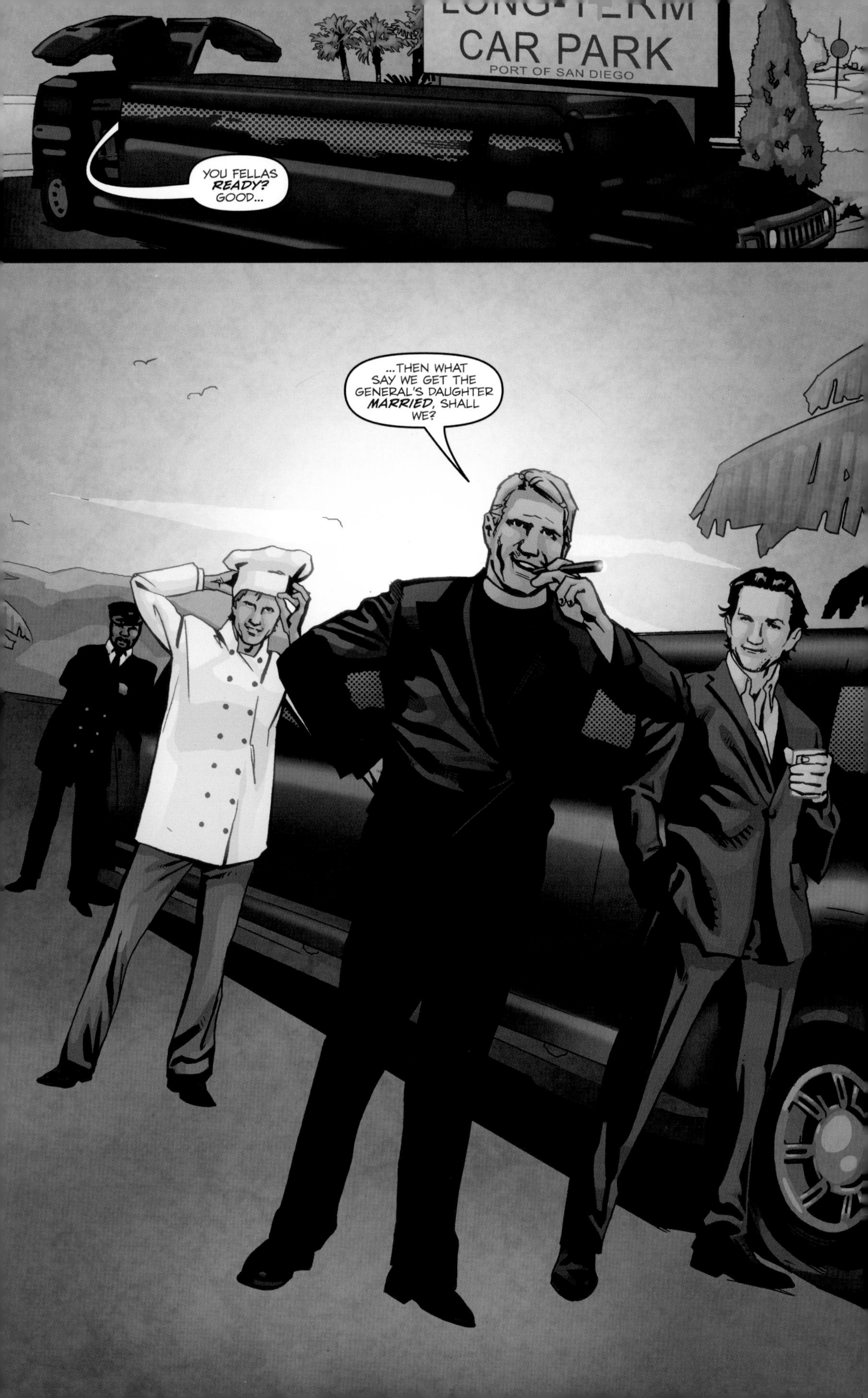
CAR PARK
PORT OF SAN DIEGO
YOU FELLAS *READY?* GOOD...
...THEN WHAT SAY WE GET THE GENERAL'S DAUGHTER *MARRIED*, SHALL WE?

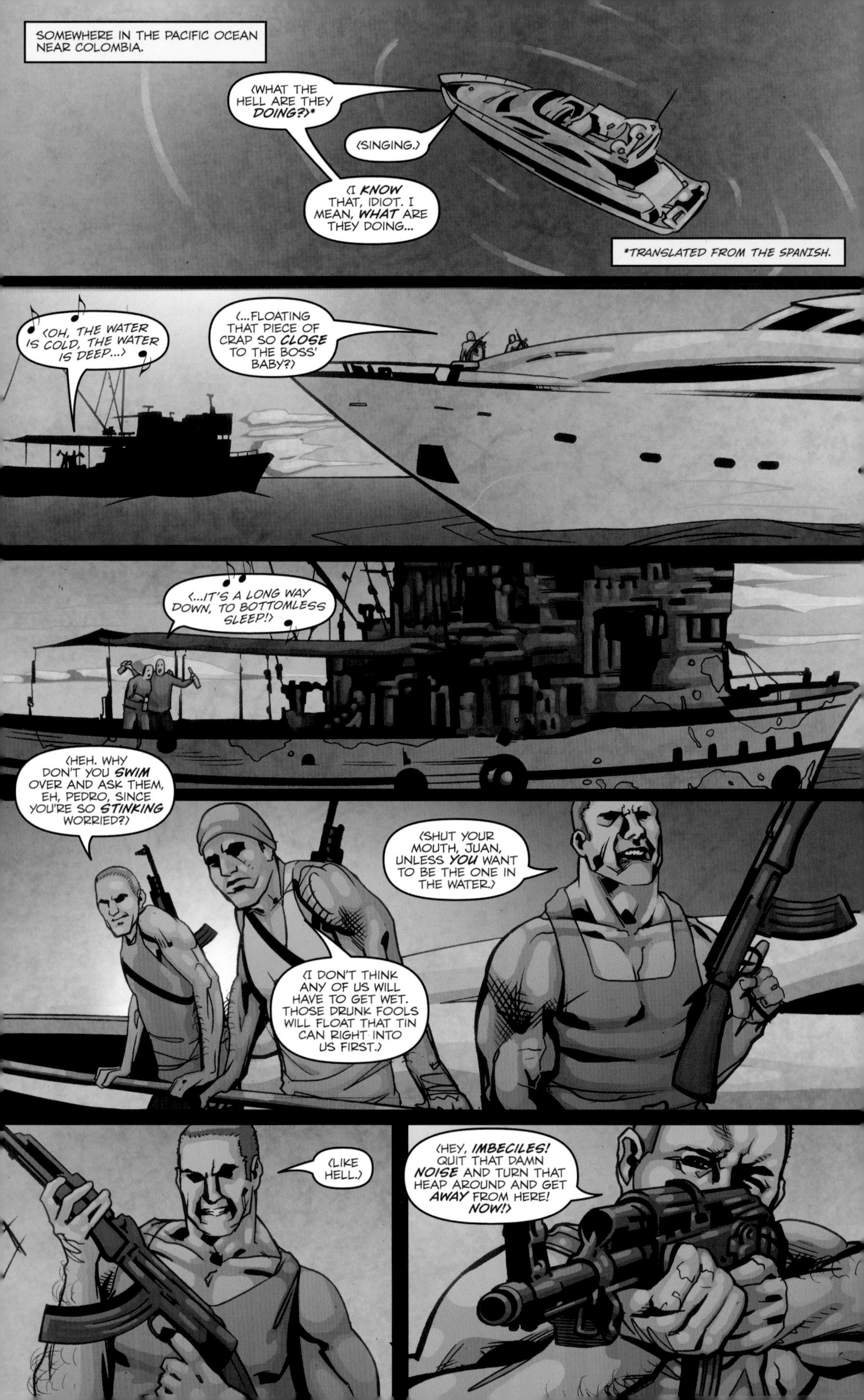

SOMEWHERE IN THE PACIFIC OCEAN NEAR COLOMBIA.
‹WHAT THE HELL ARE THEY DOING?›*
‹SINGING.›
‹I KNOW THAT, IDIOT. I MEAN, WHAT ARE THEY DOING...
*TRANSLATED FROM THE SPANISH.
‹OH, THE WATER IS COLD, THE WATER IS DEEP...›
‹...FLOATING THAT PIECE OF CRAP SO CLOSE TO THE BOSS' BABY?›
‹...IT'S A LONG WAY DOWN, TO BOTTOMLESS SLEEP!›
‹HEH. WHY DON'T YOU SWIM OVER AND ASK THEM, EH, PEDRO, SINCE YOU'RE SO STINKING WORRIED?›
‹SHUT YOUR MOUTH, JUAN, UNLESS YOU WANT TO BE THE ONE IN THE WATER.›
‹I DON'T THINK ANY OF US WILL HAVE TO GET WET. THOSE DRUNK FOOLS WILL FLOAT THAT TIN CAN RIGHT INTO US FIRST.›
‹LIKE HELL.›
‹HEY, IMBECILES! QUIT THAT DAMN NOISE AND TURN THAT HEAP AROUND AND GET AWAY FROM HERE! NOW!›

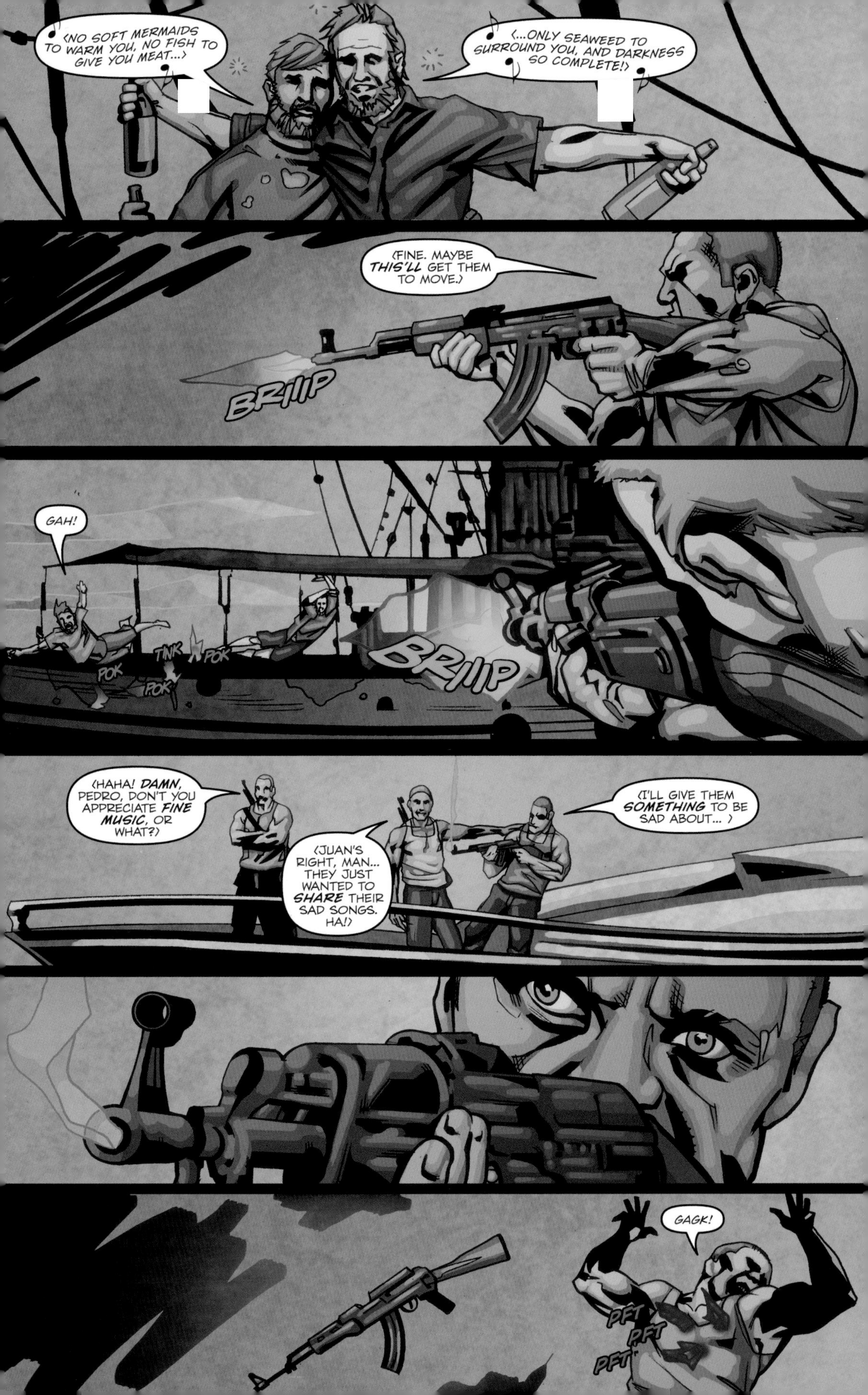
‹NO SOFT MERMAIDS TO WARM YOU, NO FISH TO GIVE YOU MEAT...›
‹...ONLY SEAWEED TO SURROUND YOU, AND DARKNESS SO COMPLETE!›
‹FINE. MAYBE **THIS'LL** GET THEM TO MOVE.›
BRIIIP
GAH!
TINK
POK
POK
POK
BRIIIP
‹HAHA! **DAMN,** PEDRO, DON'T YOU APPRECIATE **FINE MUSIC,** OR WHAT?›
‹JUAN'S RIGHT, MAN... THEY JUST WANTED TO **SHARE** THEIR SAD SONGS. HA!›
‹I'LL GIVE THEM **SOMETHING** TO BE SAD ABOUT... ›
GAGK!
PFT
PFT
PFT

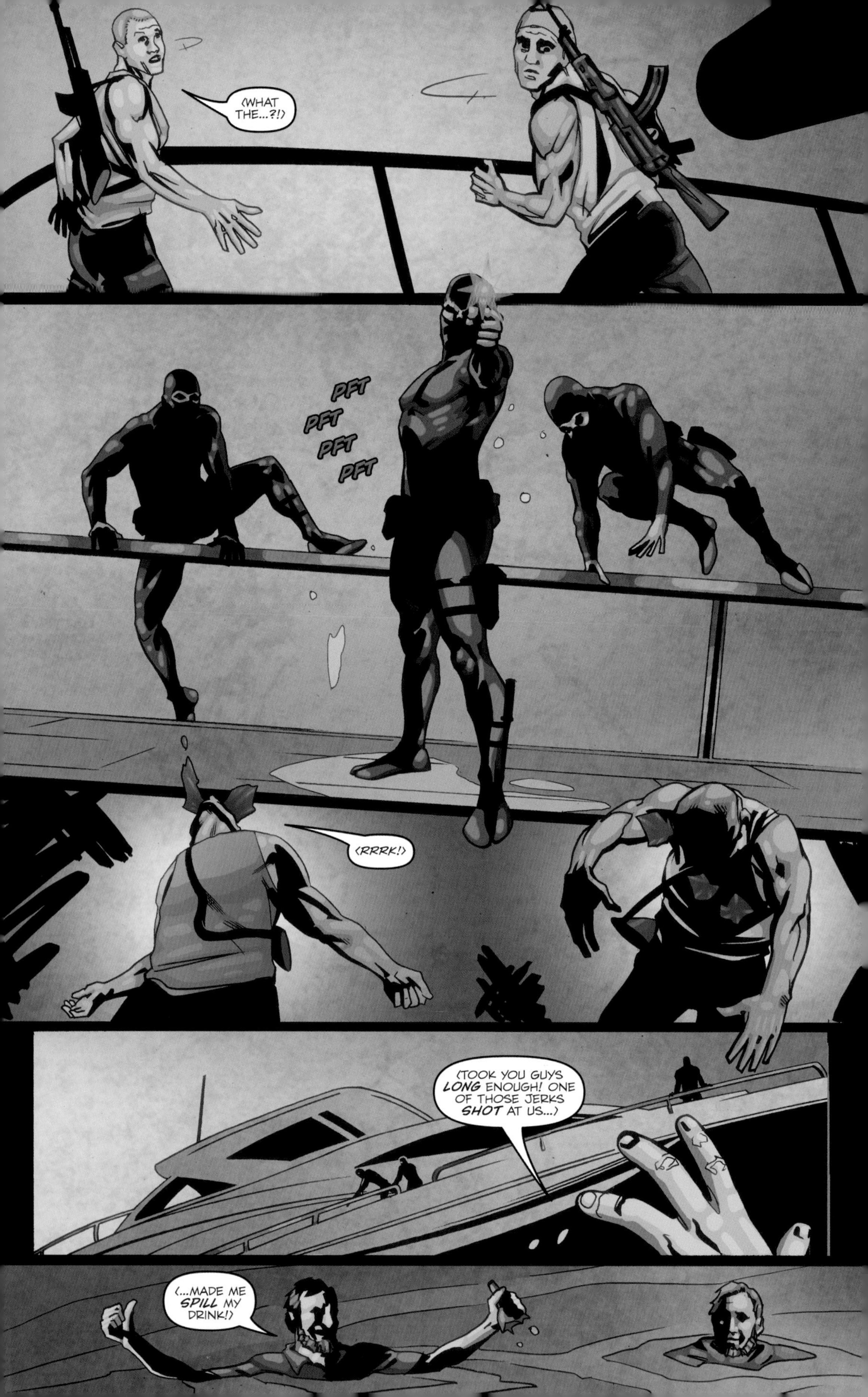

‹WHAT THE...?!›
PFT
PFT
PFT
PFT
‹RRRK!›
‹TOOK YOU GUYS LONG ENOUGH! ONE OF THOSE JERKS SHOT AT US...›
‹...MADE ME SPILL MY DRINK!›

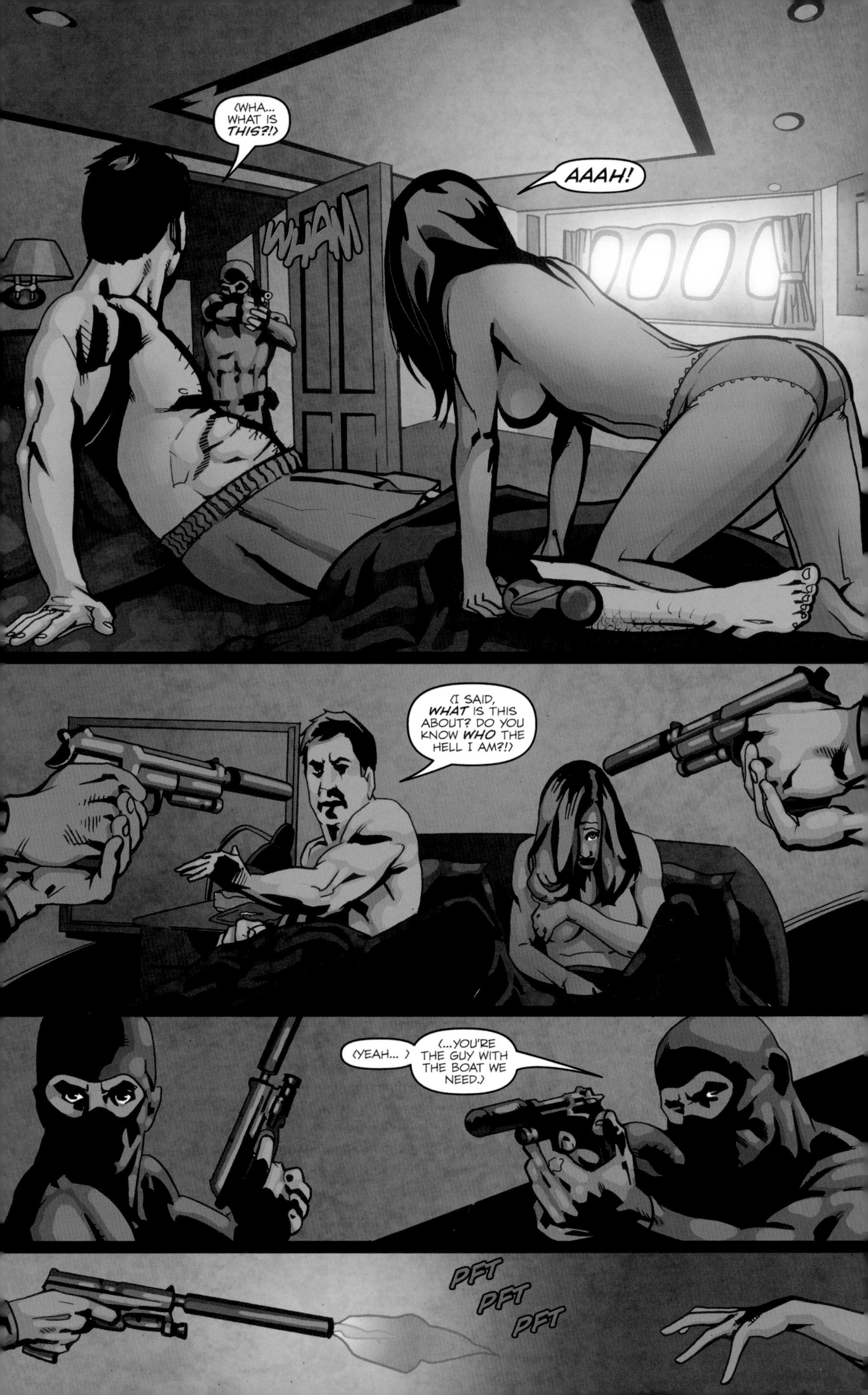
(WHA... WHAT IS THIS?!)
AAAH!
WHAM
(I SAID, WHAT IS THIS ABOUT? DO YOU KNOW WHO THE HELL I AM?!)
(YEAH... )
(...YOU'RE THE GUY WITH THE BOAT WE NEED.)
PFT
PFT
PFT

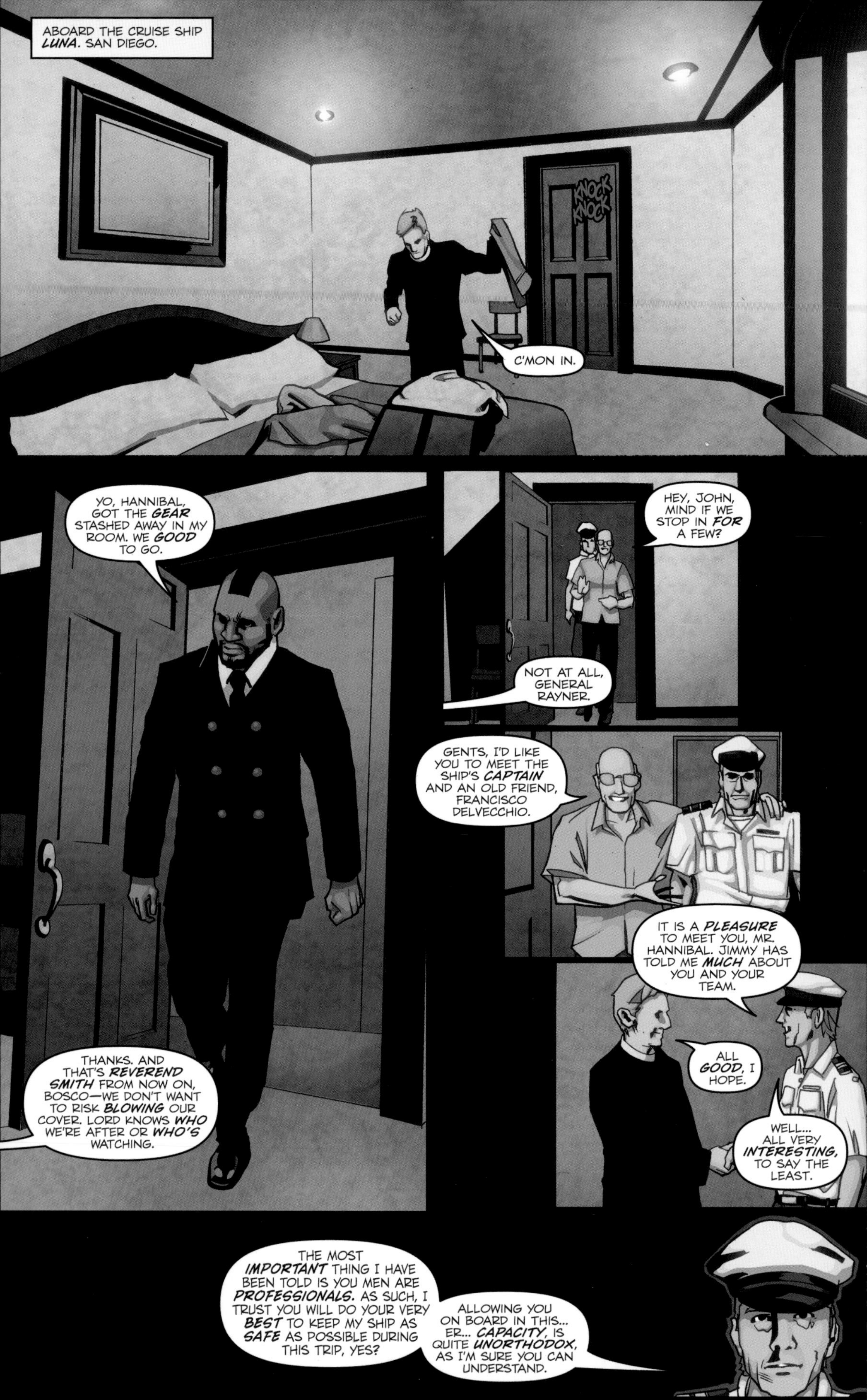
ABOARD THE CRUISE SHIP LUNA. SAN DIEGO.
KNOCK KNOCK
C'MON IN.
YO, HANNIBAL, GOT THE GEAR STASHED AWAY IN MY ROOM. WE GOOD TO GO.
THANKS. AND THAT'S REVEREND SMITH FROM NOW ON, BOSCO—WE DON'T WANT TO RISK BLOWING OUR COVER. LORD KNOWS WHO WE'RE AFTER OR WHO'S WATCHING.
HEY, JOHN, MIND IF WE STOP IN FOR A FEW?
NOT AT ALL, GENERAL RAYNER.
GENTS, I'D LIKE YOU TO MEET THE SHIP'S CAPTAIN AND AN OLD FRIEND, FRANCISCO DELVECCHIO.
IT IS A PLEASURE TO MEET YOU, MR. HANNIBAL. JIMMY HAS TOLD ME MUCH ABOUT YOU AND YOUR TEAM.
ALL GOOD, I HOPE.
WELL... ALL VERY INTERESTING, TO SAY THE LEAST.
THE MOST IMPORTANT THING I HAVE BEEN TOLD IS YOU MEN ARE PROFESSIONALS. AS SUCH, I TRUST YOU WILL DO YOUR VERY BEST TO KEEP MY SHIP AS SAFE AS POSSIBLE DURING THIS TRIP, YES?
ALLOWING YOU ON BOARD IN THIS... ER... CAPACITY, IS QUITE UNORTHODOX, AS I'M SURE YOU CAN UNDERSTAND.

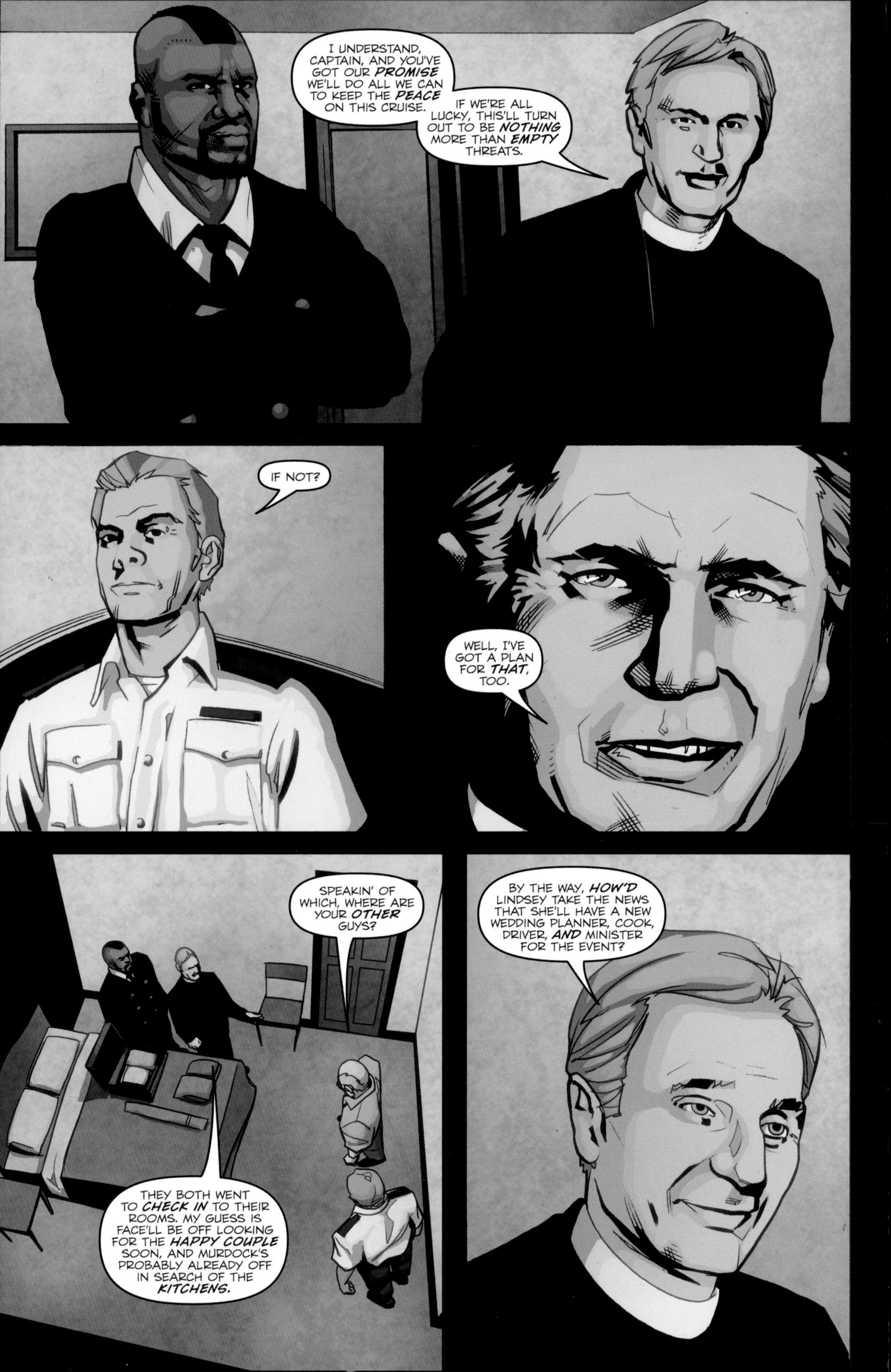
I UNDERSTAND, CAPTAIN, AND YOU'VE GOT OUR PROMISE WE'LL DO ALL WE CAN TO KEEP THE PEACE ON THIS CRUISE.
IF WE'RE ALL LUCKY, THIS'LL TURN OUT TO BE NOTHING MORE THAN EMPTY THREATS.
IF NOT?
WELL, I'VE GOT A PLAN FOR THAT, TOO.
SPEAKIN' OF WHICH, WHERE ARE YOUR OTHER GUYS?
THEY BOTH WENT TO CHECK IN TO THEIR ROOMS. MY GUESS IS FACE'LL BE OFF LOOKING FOR THE HAPPY COUPLE SOON, AND MURDOCK'S PROBABLY ALREADY OFF IN SEARCH OF THE KITCHENS.
BY THE WAY, HOW'D LINDSEY TAKE THE NEWS THAT SHE'LL HAVE A NEW WEDDING PLANNER, COOK, DRIVER, AND MINISTER FOR THE EVENT?

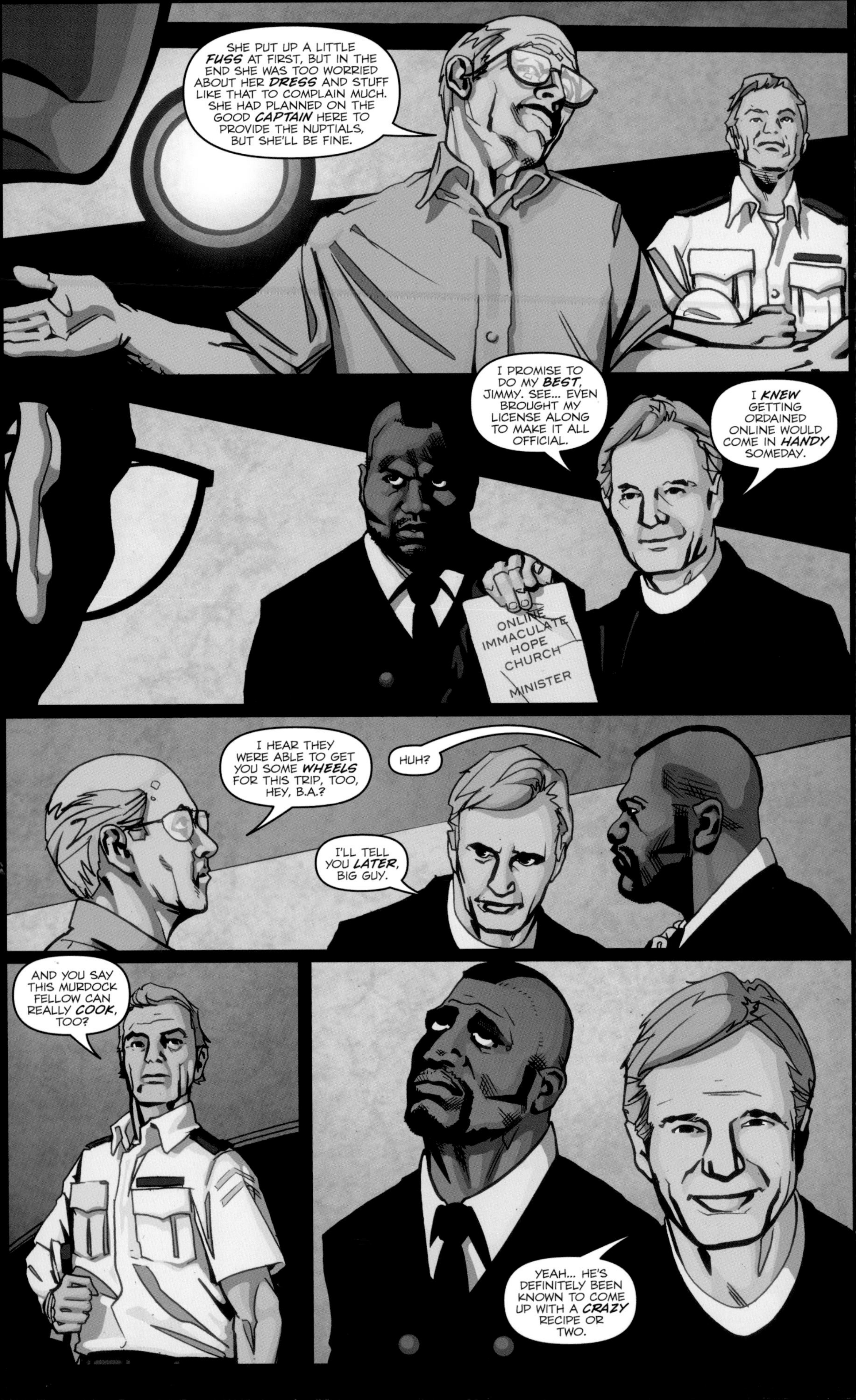
SHE PUT UP A LITTLE FUSS AT FIRST, BUT IN THE END SHE WAS TOO WORRIED ABOUT HER DRESS AND STUFF LIKE THAT TO COMPLAIN MUCH. SHE HAD PLANNED ON THE GOOD CAPTAIN HERE TO PROVIDE THE NUPTIALS, BUT SHE'LL BE FINE.
I PROMISE TO DO MY BEST, JIMMY. SEE... EVEN BROUGHT MY LICENSE ALONG TO MAKE IT ALL OFFICIAL.
I KNEW GETTING ORDAINED ONLINE WOULD COME IN HANDY SOMEDAY.
ONLINE IMMACULATE HOPE CHURCH
MINISTER
I HEAR THEY WERE ABLE TO GET YOU SOME WHEELS FOR THIS TRIP, TOO, HEY, B.A.?
HUH?
I'LL TELL YOU LATER, BIG GUY.
AND YOU SAY THIS MURDOCK FELLOW CAN REALLY COOK, TOO?
YEAH... HE'S DEFINITELY BEEN KNOWN TO COME UP WITH A CRAZY RECIPE OR TWO.

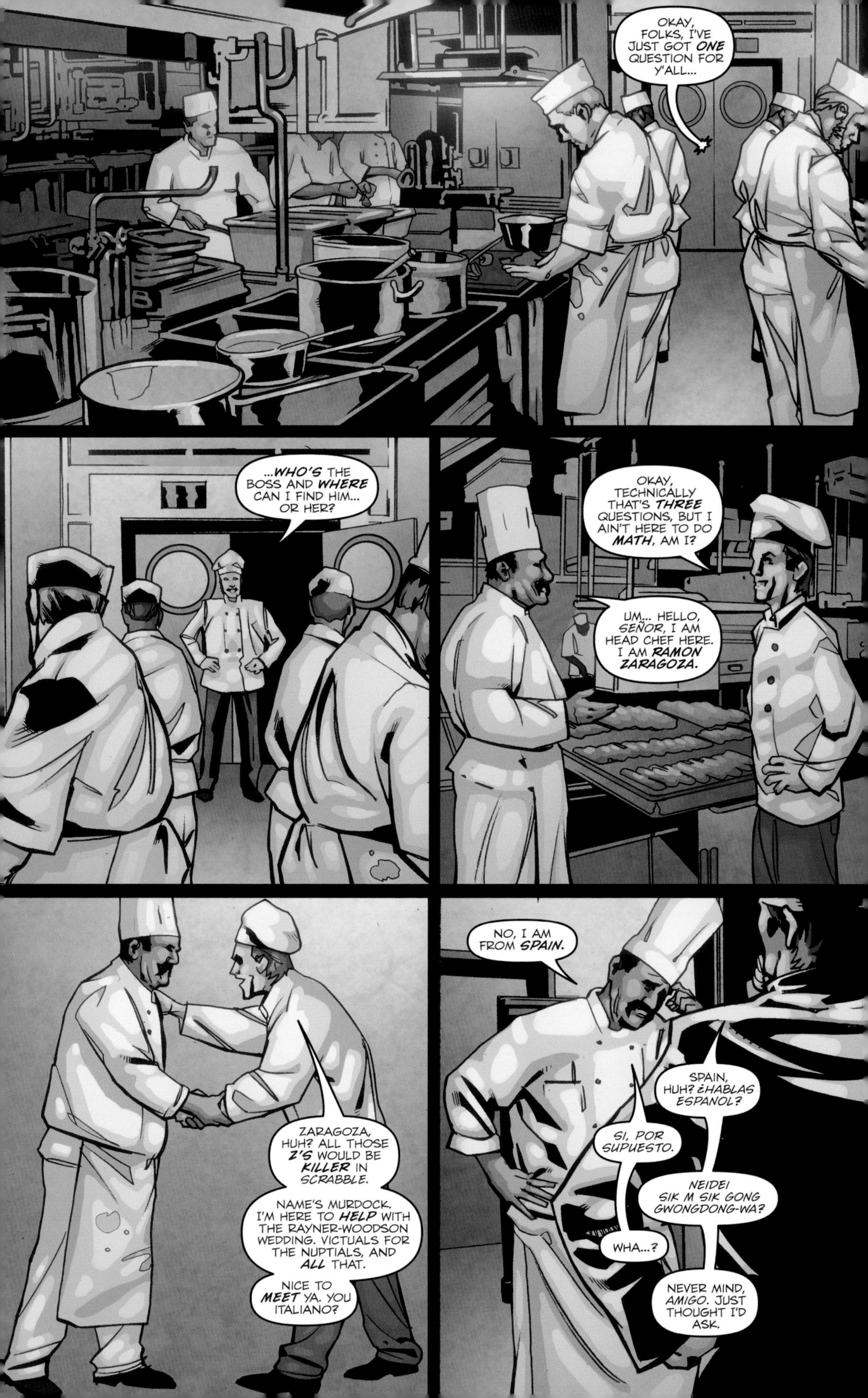
OKAY, FOLKS, I'VE JUST GOT ONE QUESTION FOR Y'ALL...
...WHO'S THE BOSS AND WHERE CAN I FIND HIM... OR HER?
OKAY, TECHNICALLY THAT'S THREE QUESTIONS, BUT I AIN'T HERE TO DO MATH, AM I?
UM... HELLO, SEÑOR, I AM HEAD CHEF HERE. I AM RAMON ZARAGOZA.
ZARAGOZA, HUH? ALL THOSE Z'S WOULD BE KILLER IN SCRABBLE.
NAME'S MURDOCK. I'M HERE TO HELP WITH THE RAYNER-WOODSON WEDDING. VICTUALS FOR THE NUPTIALS, AND ALL THAT.
NICE TO MEET YA. YOU ITALIANO?
NO, I AM FROM SPAIN.
SPAIN, HUH? ¿HABLAS ESPANOL?
SI, POR SUPUESTO.
NEIDEI SIK M SIK GONG GWONGDONG-WA?
WHA...?
NEVER MIND, AMIGO. JUST THOUGHT I'D ASK.

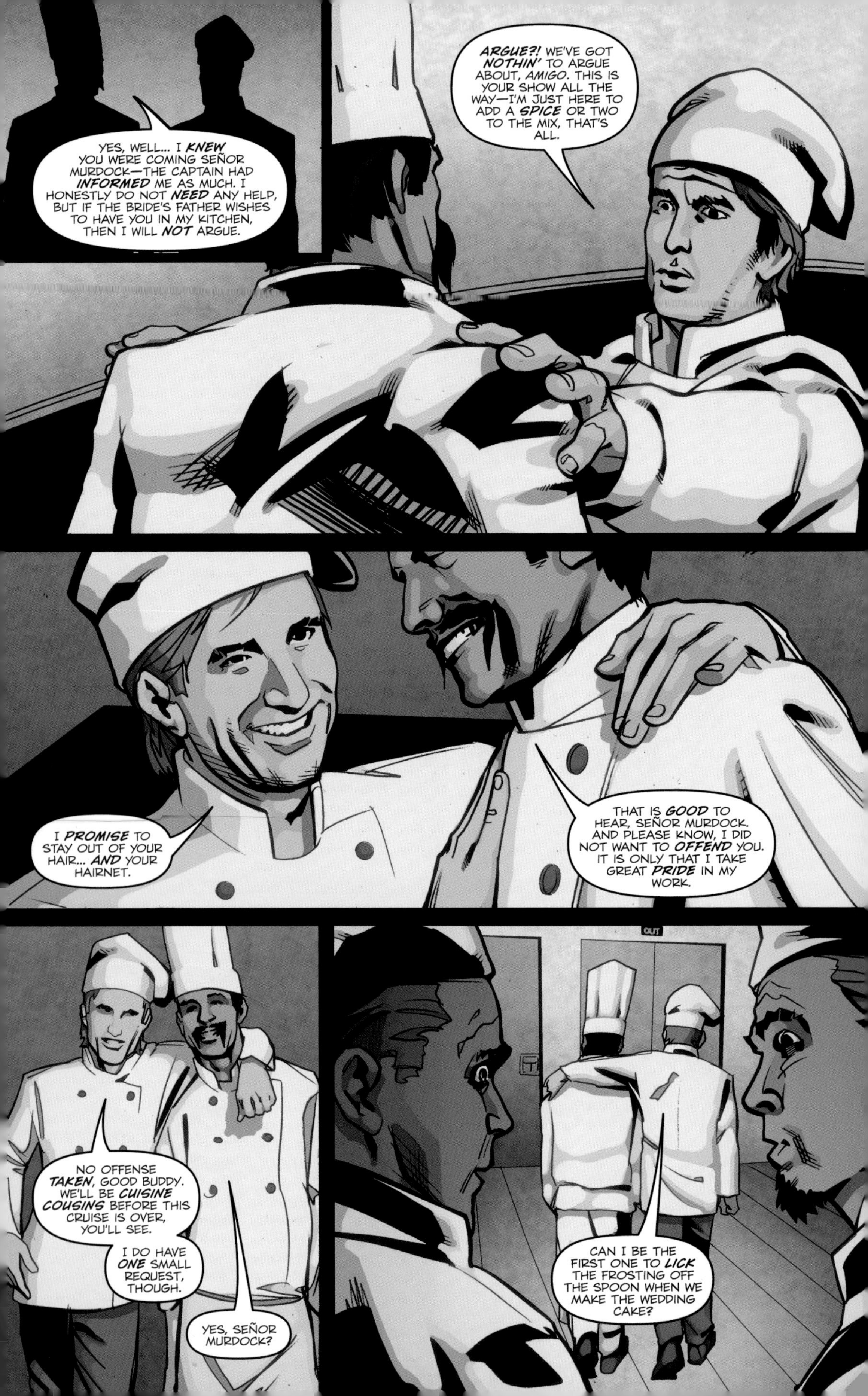
YES, WELL... I KNEW YOU WERE COMING SEÑOR MURDOCK—THE CAPTAIN HAD INFORMED ME AS MUCH. I HONESTLY DO NOT NEED ANY HELP, BUT IF THE BRIDE'S FATHER WISHES TO HAVE YOU IN MY KITCHEN, THEN I WILL NOT ARGUE.
ARGUE?! WE'VE GOT NOTHIN' TO ARGUE ABOUT, AMIGO. THIS IS YOUR SHOW ALL THE WAY—I'M JUST HERE TO ADD A SPICE OR TWO TO THE MIX, THAT'S ALL.
I PROMISE TO STAY OUT OF YOUR HAIR... AND YOUR HAIRNET.
THAT IS GOOD TO HEAR, SEÑOR MURDOCK. AND PLEASE KNOW, I DID NOT WANT TO OFFEND YOU. IT IS ONLY THAT I TAKE GREAT PRIDE IN MY WORK.
NO OFFENSE TAKEN, GOOD BUDDY. WE'LL BE CUISINE COUSINS BEFORE THIS CRUISE IS OVER, YOU'LL SEE.
I DO HAVE ONE SMALL REQUEST, THOUGH.
YES, SEÑOR MURDOCK?
OUT
CAN I BE THE FIRST ONE TO LICK THE FROSTING OFF THE SPOON WHEN WE MAKE THE WEDDING CAKE?

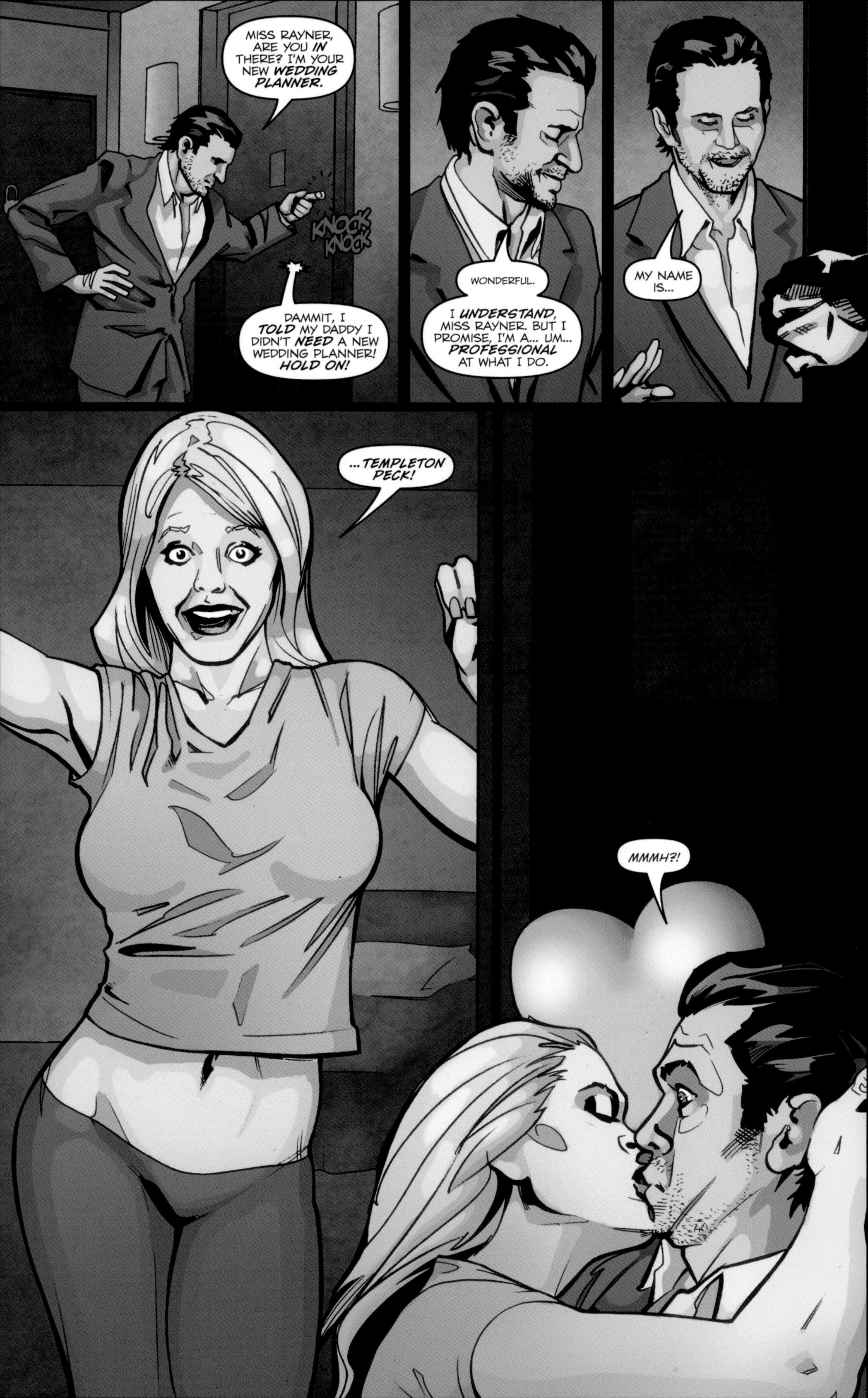
MISS RAYNER, ARE YOU IN THERE? I'M YOUR NEW WEDDING PLANNER.
KNOCK KNOCK
DAMMIT, I TOLD MY DADDY I DIDN'T NEED A NEW WEDDING PLANNER! HOLD ON!
WONDERFUL.
I UNDERSTAND, MISS RAYNER. BUT I PROMISE, I'M A... UM... PROFESSIONAL AT WHAT I DO.
MY NAME IS...
...TEMPLETON PECK!
MMMH?!

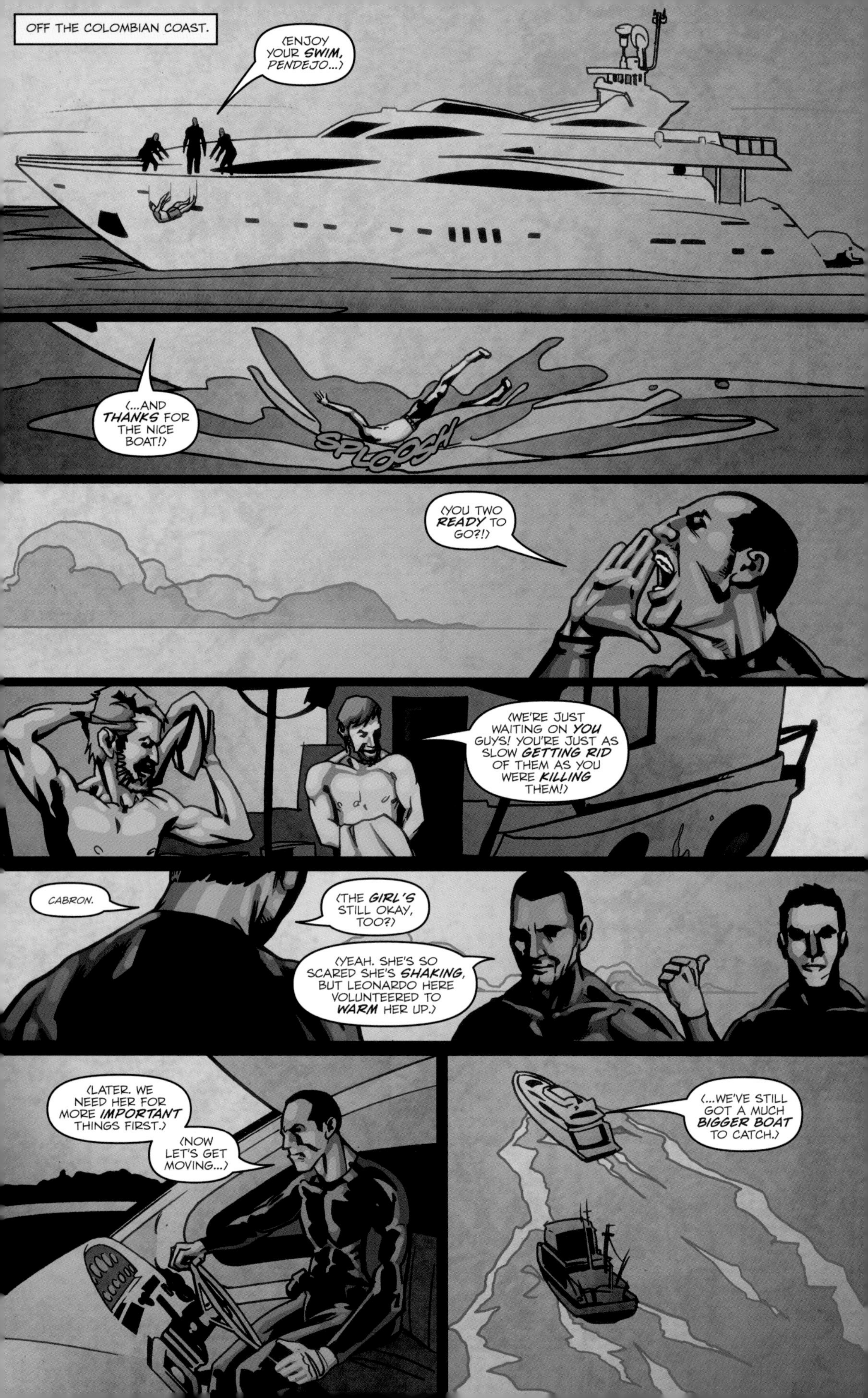
OFF THE COLOMBIAN COAST.
(ENJOY YOUR SWIM, PENDEJO...)
(...AND THANKS FOR THE NICE BOAT!)
SPLOOSH
(YOU TWO READY TO GO?!)
(WE'RE JUST WAITING ON YOU GUYS! YOU'RE JUST AS SLOW GETTING RID OF THEM AS YOU WERE KILLING THEM!)
CABRON.
(THE GIRL'S STILL OKAY, TOO?)
(YEAH. SHE'S SO SCARED SHE'S SHAKING, BUT LEONARDO HERE VOLUNTEERED TO WARM HER UP.)
(LATER. WE NEED HER FOR MORE IMPORTANT THINGS FIRST.)
(NOW LET'S GET MOVING...)
(...WE'VE STILL GOT A MUCH BIGGER BOAT TO CATCH.)

# CHAPTER THREE

CRUISE SHIP LUNA. PACIFIC OCEAN.

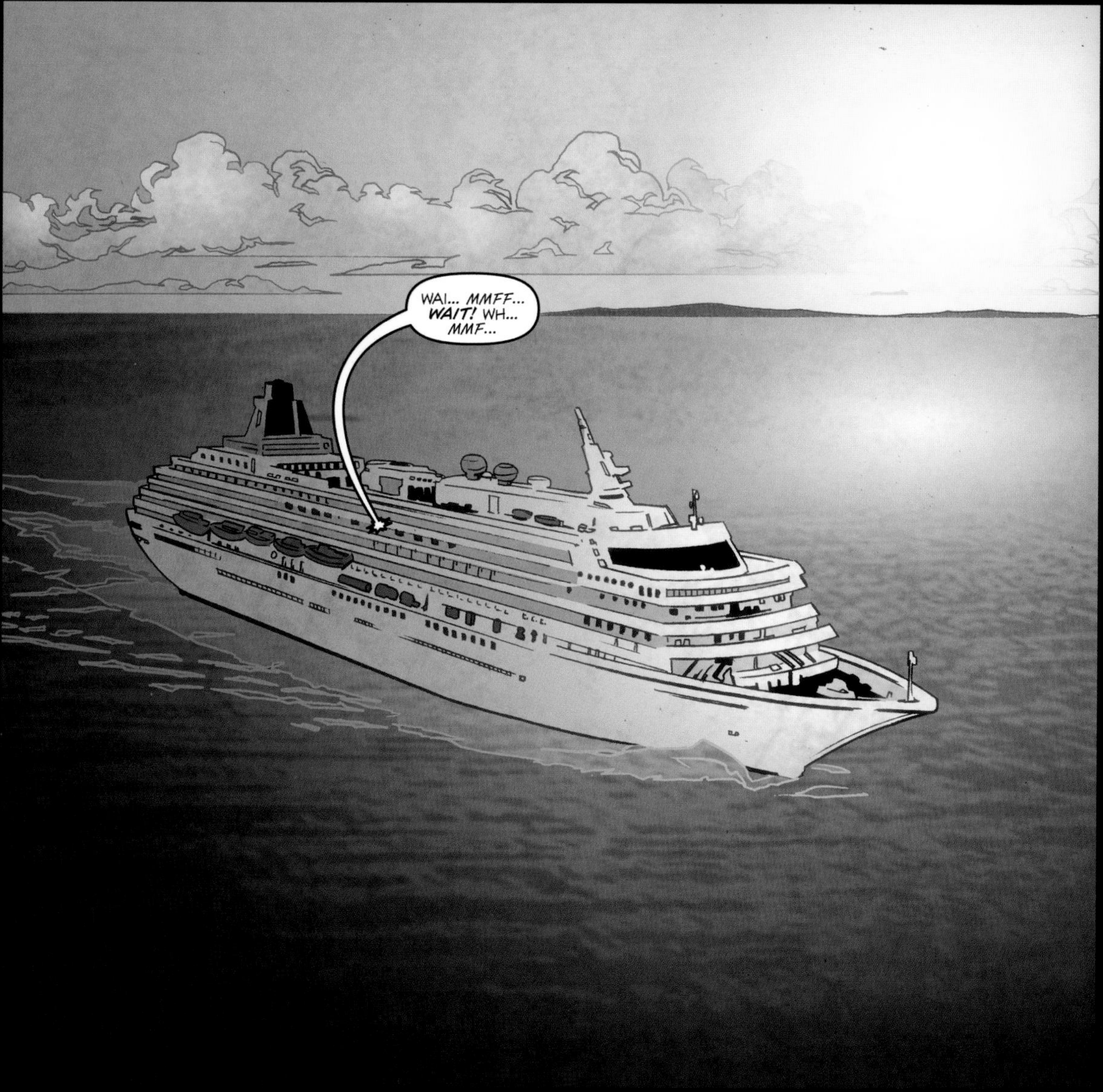
WAI... MMFF... WAIT! WH... MMF...

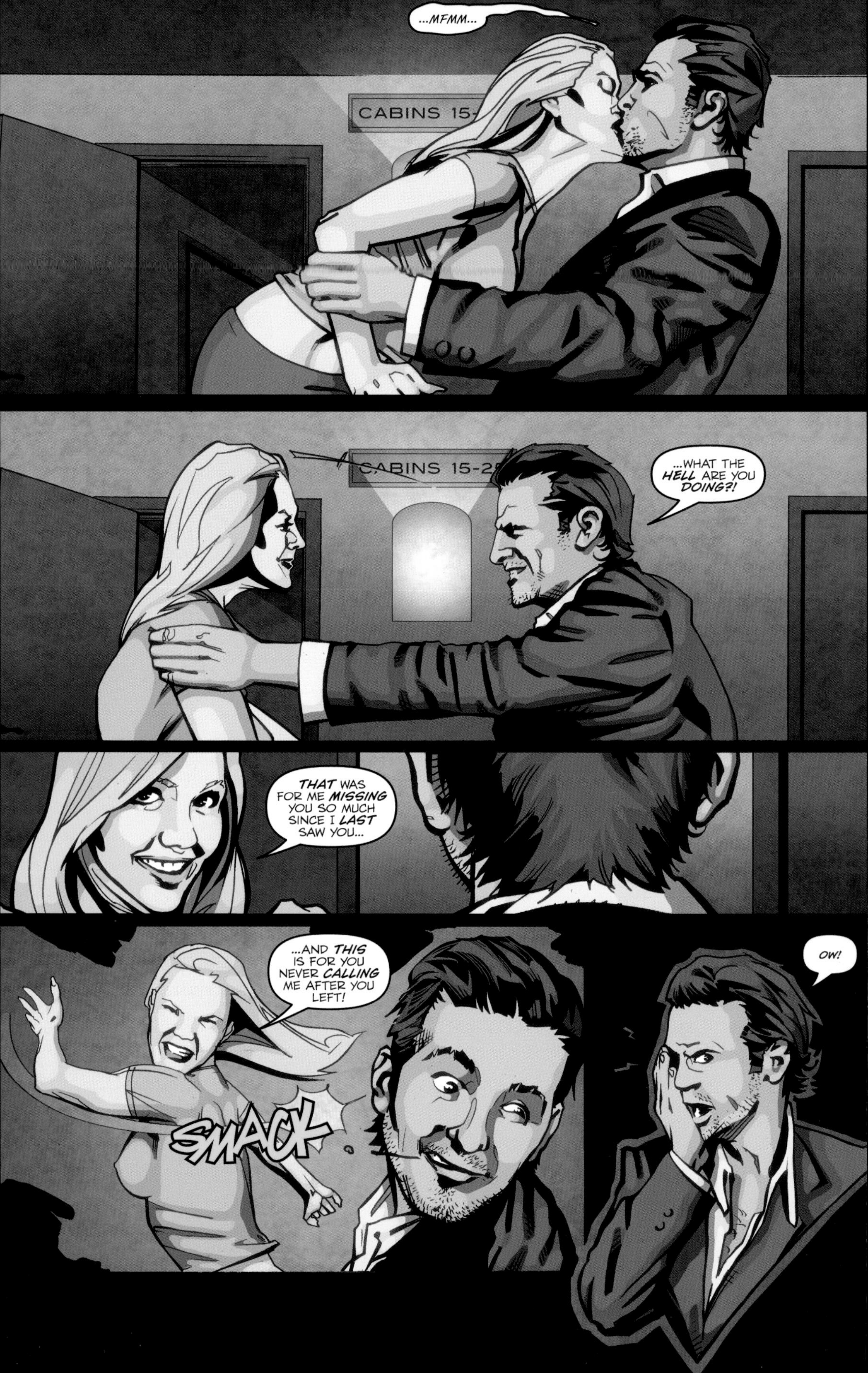
...MFMM...
CABINS 15-
CABINS 15-25
...WHAT THE HELL ARE YOU DOING?!
THAT WAS FOR ME MISSING YOU SO MUCH SINCE I LAST SAW YOU...
...AND THIS IS FOR YOU NEVER CALLING ME AFTER YOU LEFT!
SMACK
OW!

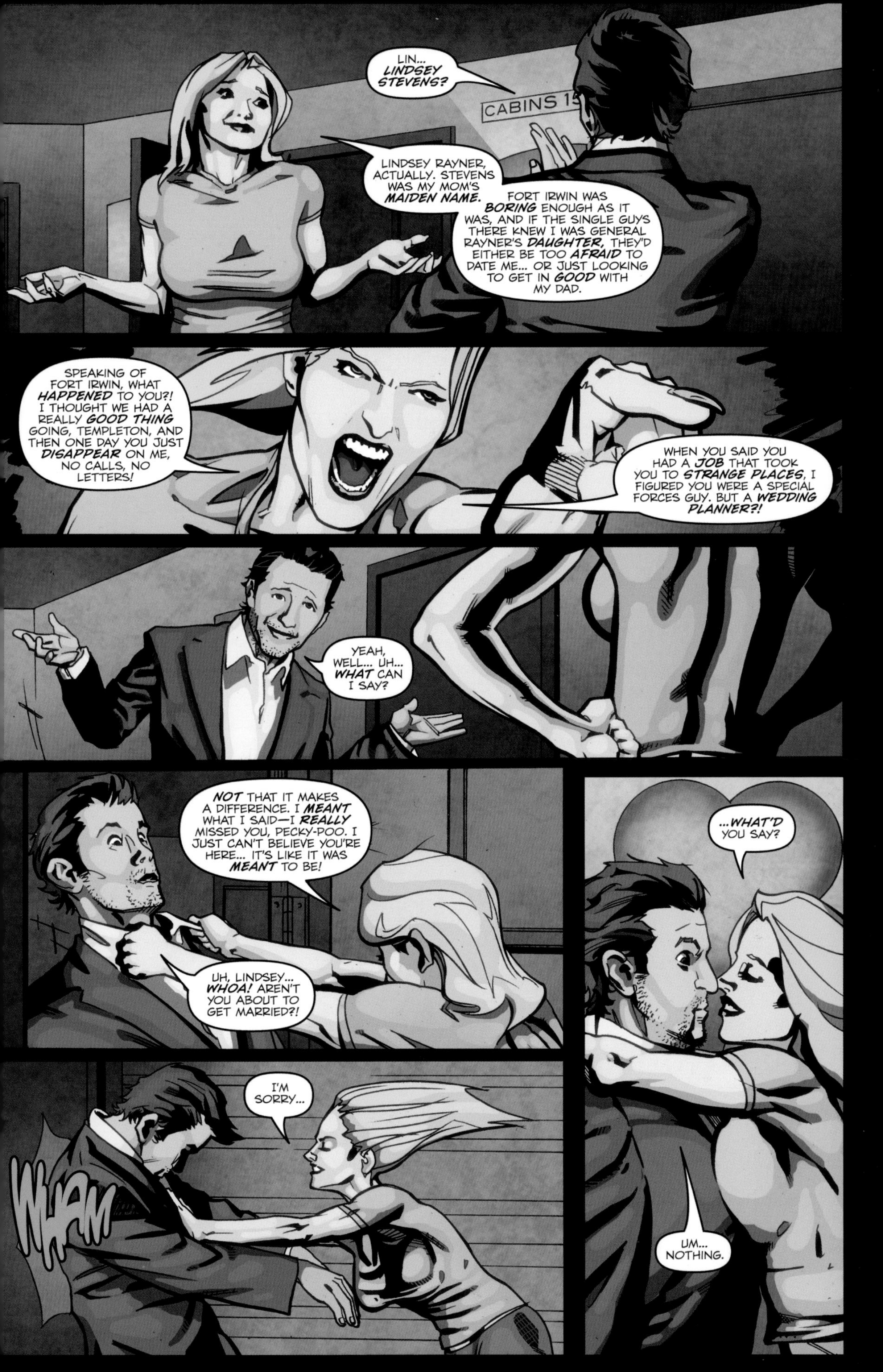
LIN... LINDSEY STEVENS?
CABINS 15
LINDSEY RAYNER, ACTUALLY. STEVENS WAS MY MOM'S MAIDEN NAME.
FORT IRWIN WAS BORING ENOUGH AS IT WAS, AND IF THE SINGLE GUYS THERE KNEW I WAS GENERAL RAYNER'S DAUGHTER, THEY'D EITHER BE TOO AFRAID TO DATE ME... OR JUST LOOKING TO GET IN GOOD WITH MY DAD.
SPEAKING OF FORT IRWIN, WHAT HAPPENED TO YOU?! I THOUGHT WE HAD A REALLY GOOD THING GOING, TEMPLETON, AND THEN ONE DAY YOU JUST DISAPPEAR ON ME, NO CALLS, NO LETTERS!
WHEN YOU SAID YOU HAD A JOB THAT TOOK YOU TO STRANGE PLACES, I FIGURED YOU WERE A SPECIAL FORCES GUY. BUT A WEDDING PLANNER?!
YEAH, WELL... UH... WHAT CAN I SAY?
NOT THAT IT MAKES A DIFFERENCE. I MEANT WHAT I SAID—I REALLY MISSED YOU, PECKY-POO. I JUST CAN'T BELIEVE YOU'RE HERE... IT'S LIKE IT WAS MEANT TO BE!
UH, LINDSEY... WHOA! AREN'T YOU ABOUT TO GET MARRIED?!
I'M SORRY...
WHAM
...WHAT'D YOU SAY?
UM... NOTHING.

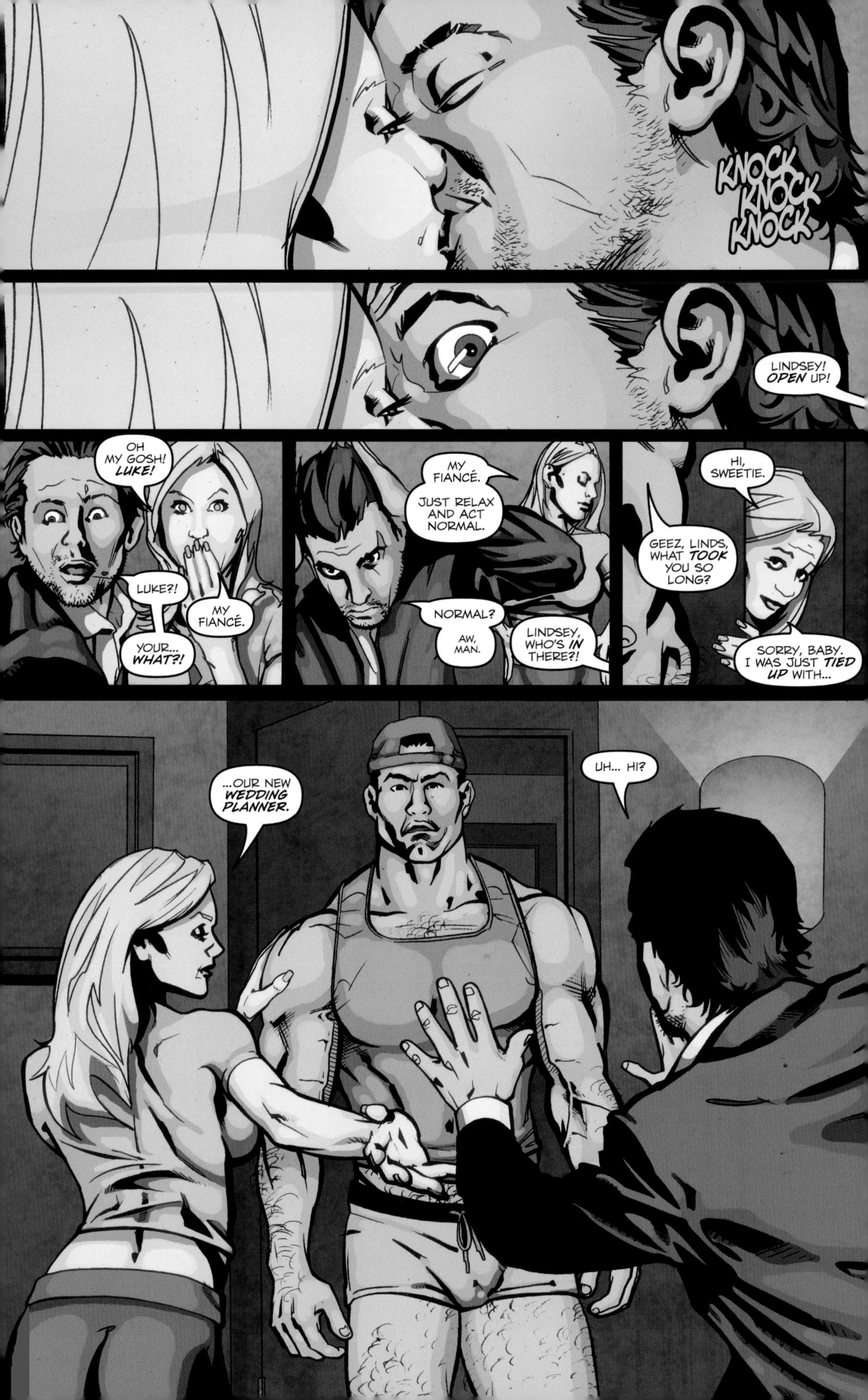
KNOCK KNOCK KNOCK
LINDSEY! OPEN UP!
OH MY GOSH! LUKE!
LUKE?!
MY FIANCÉ.
YOUR... WHAT?!
MY FIANCÉ.
JUST RELAX AND ACT NORMAL.
NORMAL?
AW, MAN.
LINDSEY, WHO'S IN THERE?!
HI, SWEETIE.
GEEZ, LINDS, WHAT TOOK YOU SO LONG?
SORRY, BABY. I WAS JUST TIED UP WITH...
...OUR NEW WEDDING PLANNER.
UH... HI?

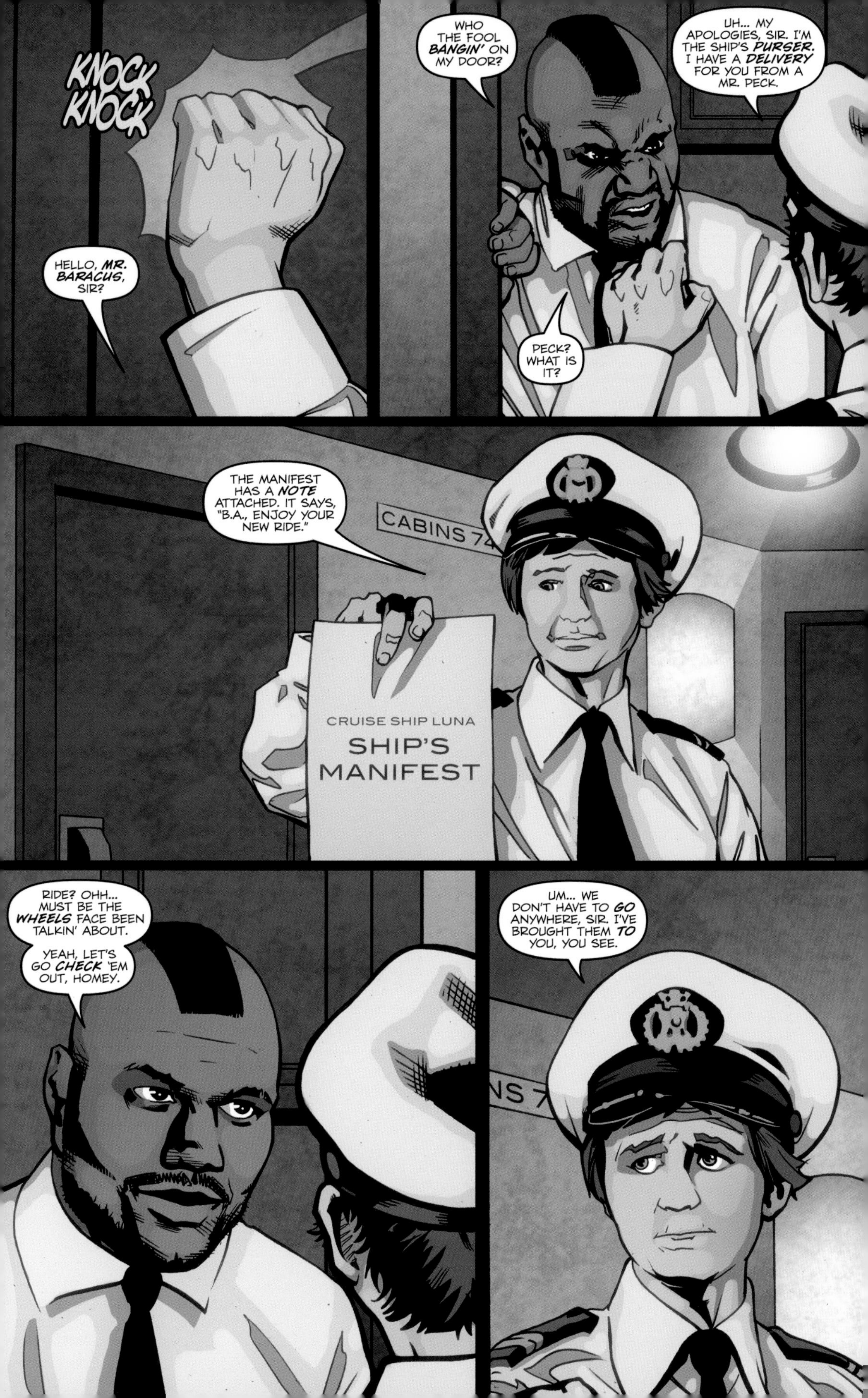
KNOCK KNOCK
HELLO, MR. BARACUS, SIR?
WHO THE FOOL BANGIN' ON MY DOOR?
UH... MY APOLOGIES, SIR. I'M THE SHIP'S PURSER. I HAVE A DELIVERY FOR YOU FROM A MR. PECK.
PECK? WHAT IS IT?
THE MANIFEST HAS A NOTE ATTACHED. IT SAYS, "B.A., ENJOY YOUR NEW RIDE."
CABINS 74
CRUISE SHIP LUNA
SHIP'S MANIFEST
RIDE? OHH... MUST BE THE WHEELS FACE BEEN TALKIN' ABOUT.
YEAH, LET'S GO CHECK 'EM OUT, HOMEY.
UM... WE DON'T HAVE TO GO ANYWHERE, SIR. I'VE BROUGHT THEM TO YOU, YOU SEE.

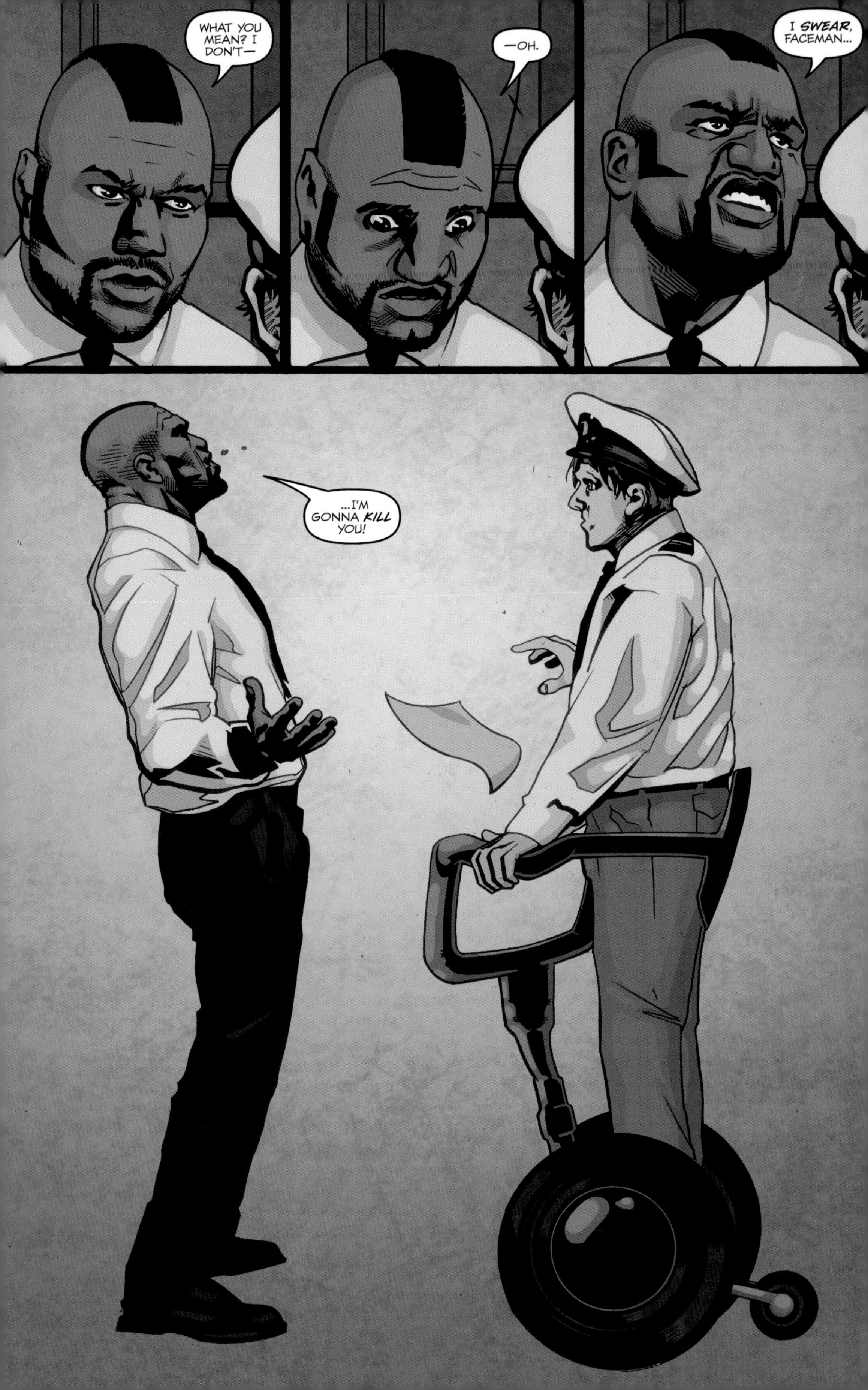
WHAT YOU MEAN? I DON'T—
—OH.
I SWEAR, FACEMAN...
...I'M GONNA KILL YOU!

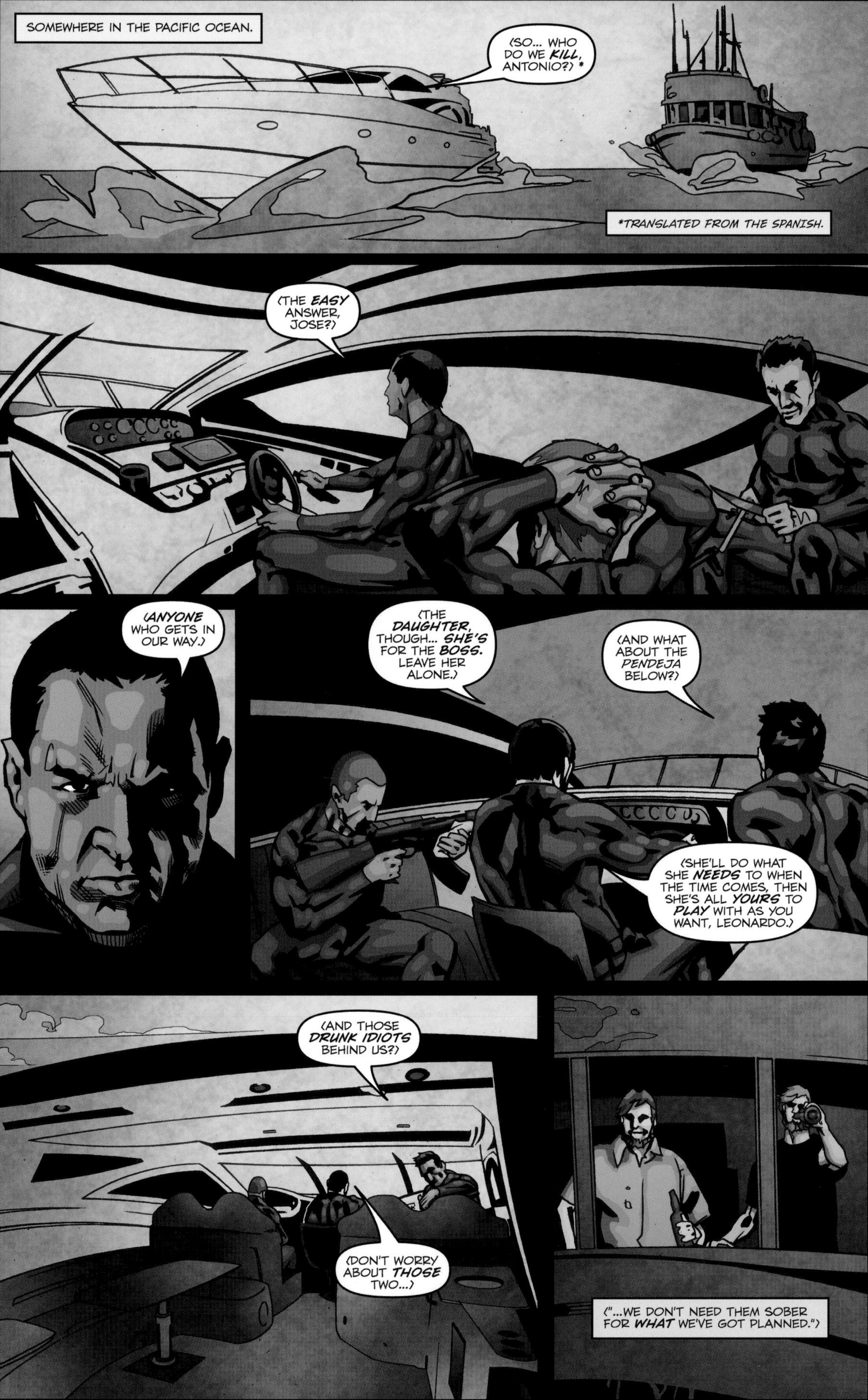
SOMEWHERE IN THE PACIFIC OCEAN.
(SO... WHO DO WE KILL, ANTONIO?) *
*TRANSLATED FROM THE SPANISH.
(THE EASY ANSWER, JOSE?)
(ANYONE WHO GETS IN OUR WAY.)
(THE DAUGHTER, THOUGH... SHE'S FOR THE BOSS. LEAVE HER ALONE.)
(AND WHAT ABOUT THE PENDEJA BELOW?)
(SHE'LL DO WHAT SHE NEEDS TO WHEN THE TIME COMES, THEN SHE'S ALL YOURS TO PLAY WITH AS YOU WANT, LEONARDO.)
(AND THOSE DRUNK IDIOTS BEHIND US?)
(DON'T WORRY ABOUT THOSE TWO...)
("...WE DON'T NEED THEM SOBER FOR WHAT WE'VE GOT PLANNED.")

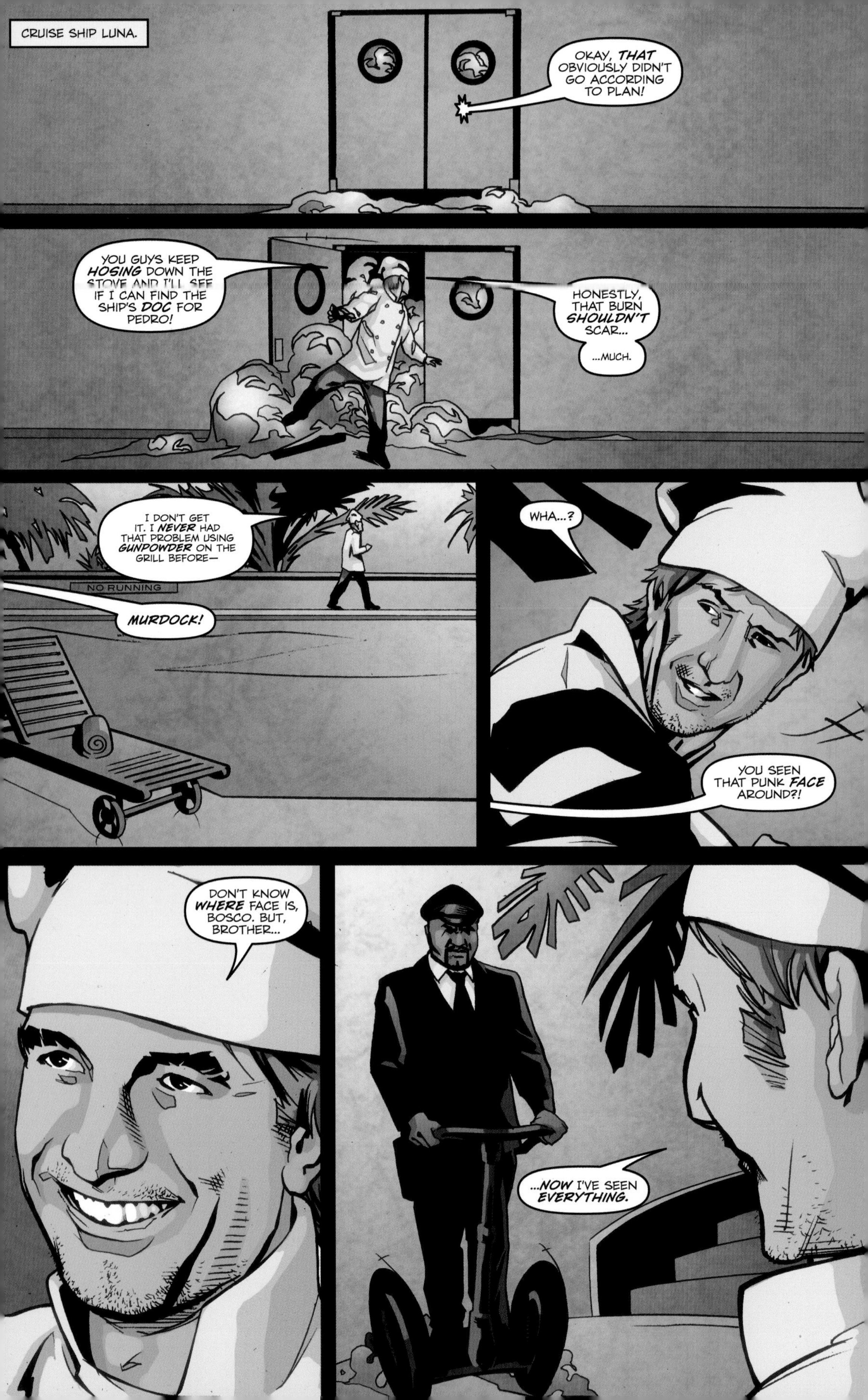
CRUISE SHIP LUNA.
OKAY, THAT OBVIOUSLY DIDN'T GO ACCORDING TO PLAN!
YOU GUYS KEEP HOSING DOWN THE STOVE AND I'LL SEE IF I CAN FIND THE SHIP'S DOC FOR PEDRO!
HONESTLY, THAT BURN SHOULDN'T SCAR...
...MUCH.
I DON'T GET IT. I NEVER HAD THAT PROBLEM USING GUNPOWDER ON THE GRILL BEFORE—
NO RUNNING
MURDOCK!
WHA...?
YOU SEEN THAT PUNK FACE AROUND?!
DON'T KNOW WHERE FACE IS, BOSCO. BUT, BROTHER...
...NOW I'VE SEEN EVERYTHING.

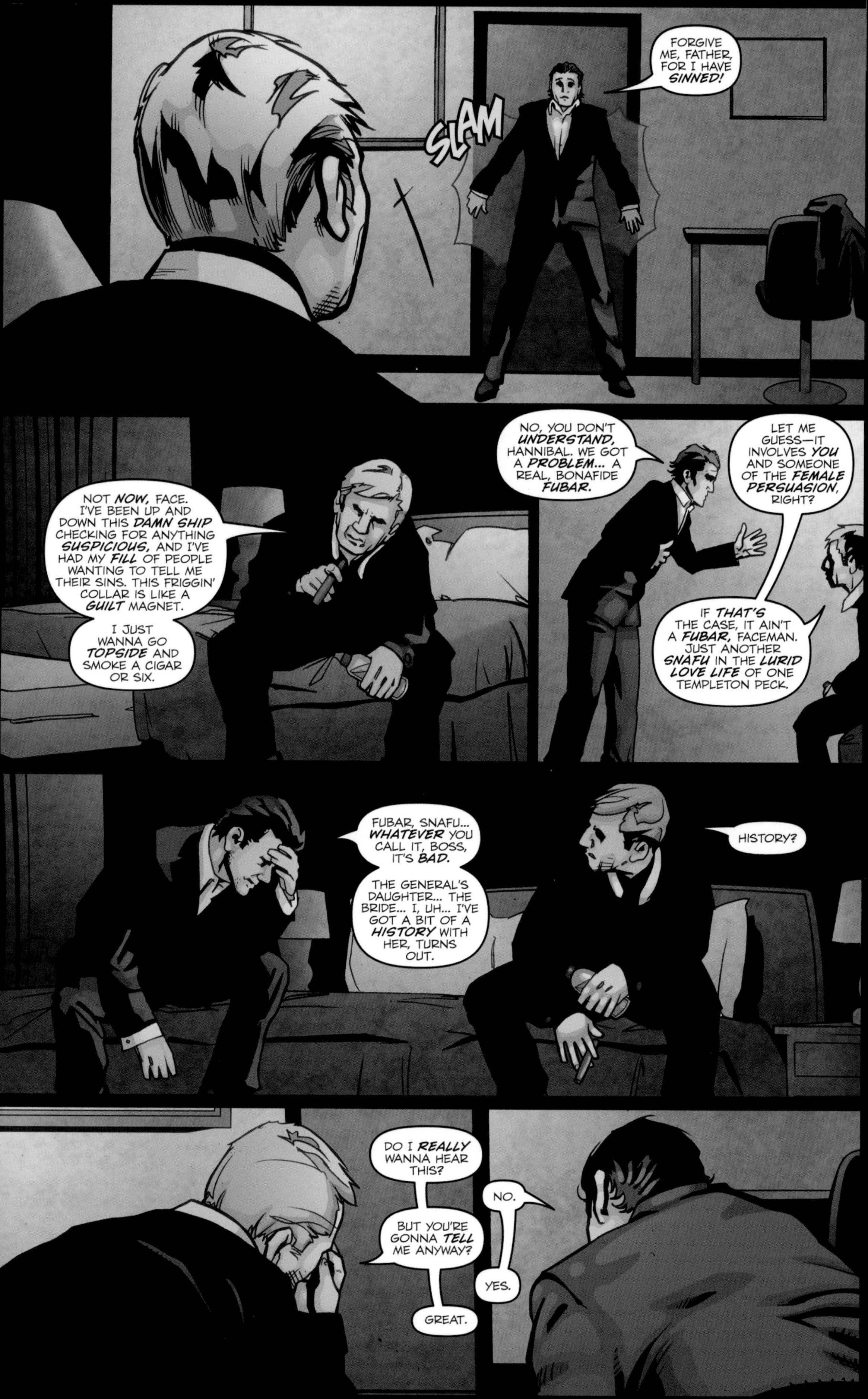
FORGIVE ME, FATHER, FOR I HAVE SINNED!
SLAM
NOT NOW, FACE. I'VE BEEN UP AND DOWN THIS DAMN SHIP CHECKING FOR ANYTHING SUSPICIOUS, AND I'VE HAD MY FILL OF PEOPLE WANTING TO TELL ME THEIR SINS. THIS FRIGGIN' COLLAR IS LIKE A GUILT MAGNET.
I JUST WANNA GO TOPSIDE AND SMOKE A CIGAR OR SIX.
NO, YOU DON'T UNDERSTAND, HANNIBAL. WE GOT A PROBLEM... A REAL, BONAFIDE FUBAR.
LET ME GUESS—IT INVOLVES YOU AND SOMEONE OF THE FEMALE PERSUASION, RIGHT?
IF THAT'S THE CASE, IT AIN'T A FUBAR, FACEMAN. JUST ANOTHER SNAFU IN THE LURID LOVE LIFE OF ONE TEMPLETON PECK.
FUBAR, SNAFU... WHATEVER YOU CALL IT, BOSS, IT'S BAD.
THE GENERAL'S DAUGHTER... THE BRIDE... I, UH... I'VE GOT A BIT OF A HISTORY WITH HER, TURNS OUT.
HISTORY?
DO I REALLY WANNA HEAR THIS?
NO.
BUT YOU'RE GONNA TELL ME ANYWAY?
YES.
GREAT.

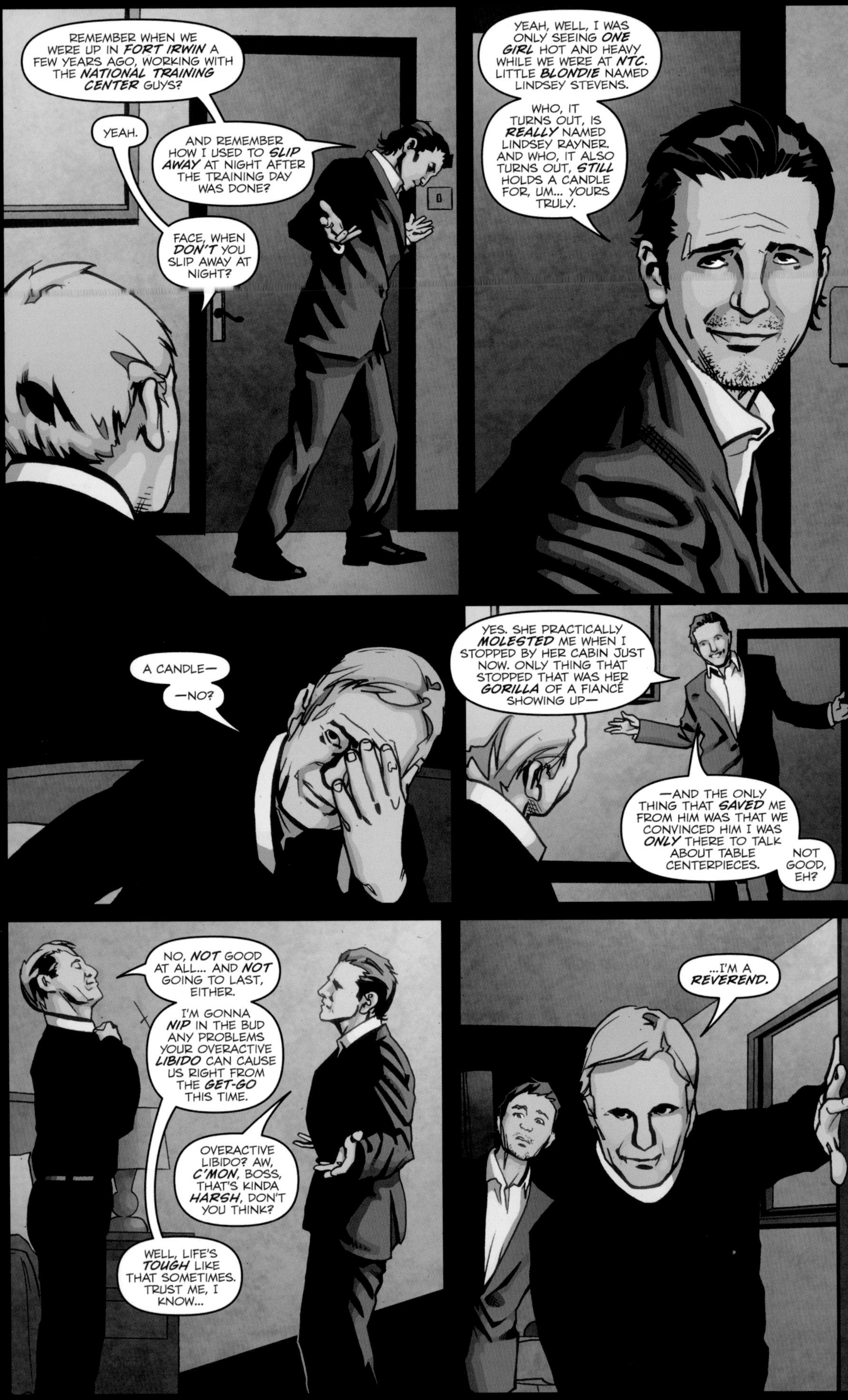
REMEMBER WHEN WE WERE UP IN FORT IRWIN A FEW YEARS AGO, WORKING WITH THE NATIONAL TRAINING CENTER GUYS?
YEAH.
AND REMEMBER HOW I USED TO SLIP AWAY AT NIGHT AFTER THE TRAINING DAY WAS DONE?
FACE, WHEN DON'T YOU SLIP AWAY AT NIGHT?
YEAH, WELL, I WAS ONLY SEEING ONE GIRL HOT AND HEAVY WHILE WE WERE AT NTC. LITTLE BLONDIE NAMED LINDSEY STEVENS.
WHO, IT TURNS OUT, IS REALLY NAMED LINDSEY RAYNER. AND WHO, IT ALSO TURNS OUT, STILL HOLDS A CANDLE FOR, UM... YOURS TRULY.
A CANDLE—
—NO?
YES. SHE PRACTICALLY MOLESTED ME WHEN I STOPPED BY HER CABIN JUST NOW. ONLY THING THAT STOPPED THAT WAS HER GORILLA OF A FIANCÉ SHOWING UP—
—AND THE ONLY THING THAT SAVED ME FROM HIM WAS THAT WE CONVINCED HIM I WAS ONLY THERE TO TALK ABOUT TABLE CENTERPIECES.
NOT GOOD, EH?
NO, NOT GOOD AT ALL... AND NOT GOING TO LAST, EITHER.
I'M GONNA NIP IN THE BUD ANY PROBLEMS YOUR OVERACTIVE LIBIDO CAN CAUSE US RIGHT FROM THE GET-GO THIS TIME.
OVERACTIVE LIBIDO? AW, C'MON, BOSS, THAT'S KINDA HARSH, DON'T YOU THINK?
WELL, LIFE'S TOUGH LIKE THAT SOMETIMES. TRUST ME, I KNOW...
...I'M A REVEREND.

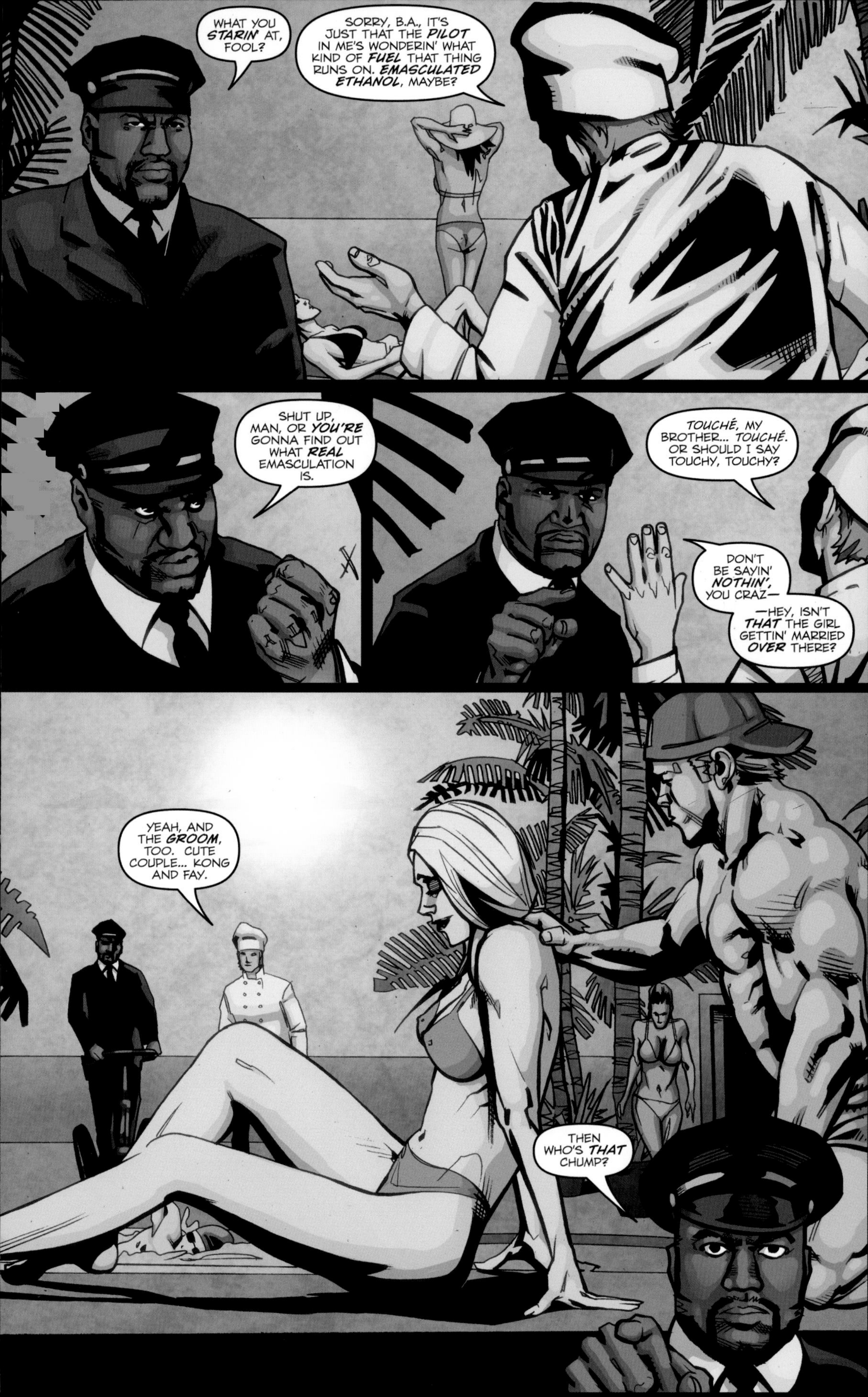

WHAT YOU STARIN' AT, FOOL?
SORRY, B.A., IT'S JUST THAT THE PILOT IN ME'S WONDERIN' WHAT KIND OF FUEL THAT THING RUNS ON. EMASCULATED ETHANOL, MAYBE?
SHUT UP, MAN, OR YOU'RE GONNA FIND OUT WHAT REAL EMASCULATION IS.
TOUCHÉ, MY BROTHER... TOUCHÉ. OR SHOULD I SAY TOUCHY, TOUCHY?
DON'T BE SAYIN' NOTHIN', YOU CRAZ—
—HEY, ISN'T THAT THE GIRL GETTIN' MARRIED OVER THERE?
YEAH, AND THE GROOM, TOO. CUTE COUPLE... KONG AND FAY.
THEN WHO'S THAT CHUMP?

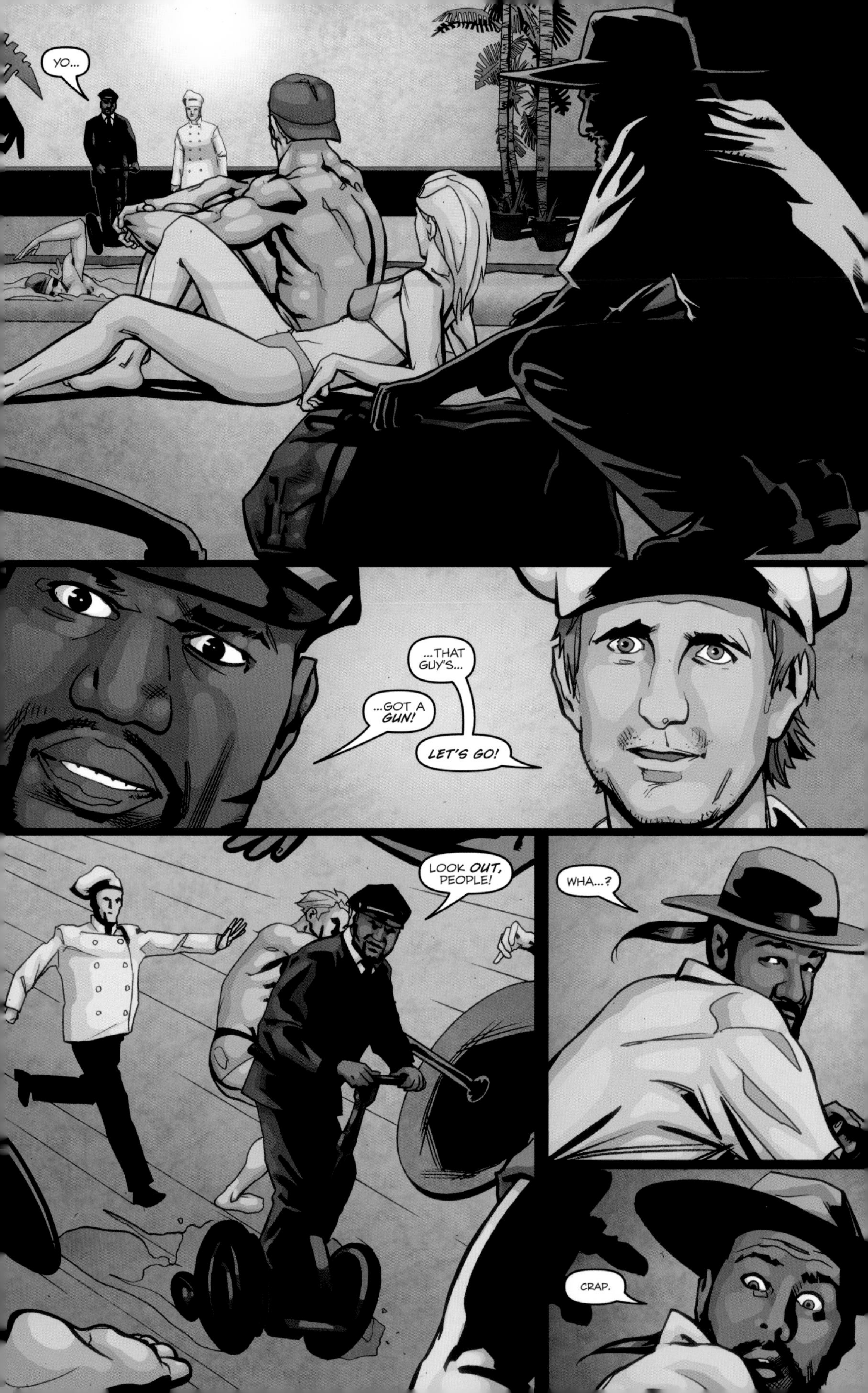
YO...
...THAT GUY'S...
...GOT A GUN!
LET'S GO!
LOOK OUT, PEOPLE!
WHA...?
CRAP.

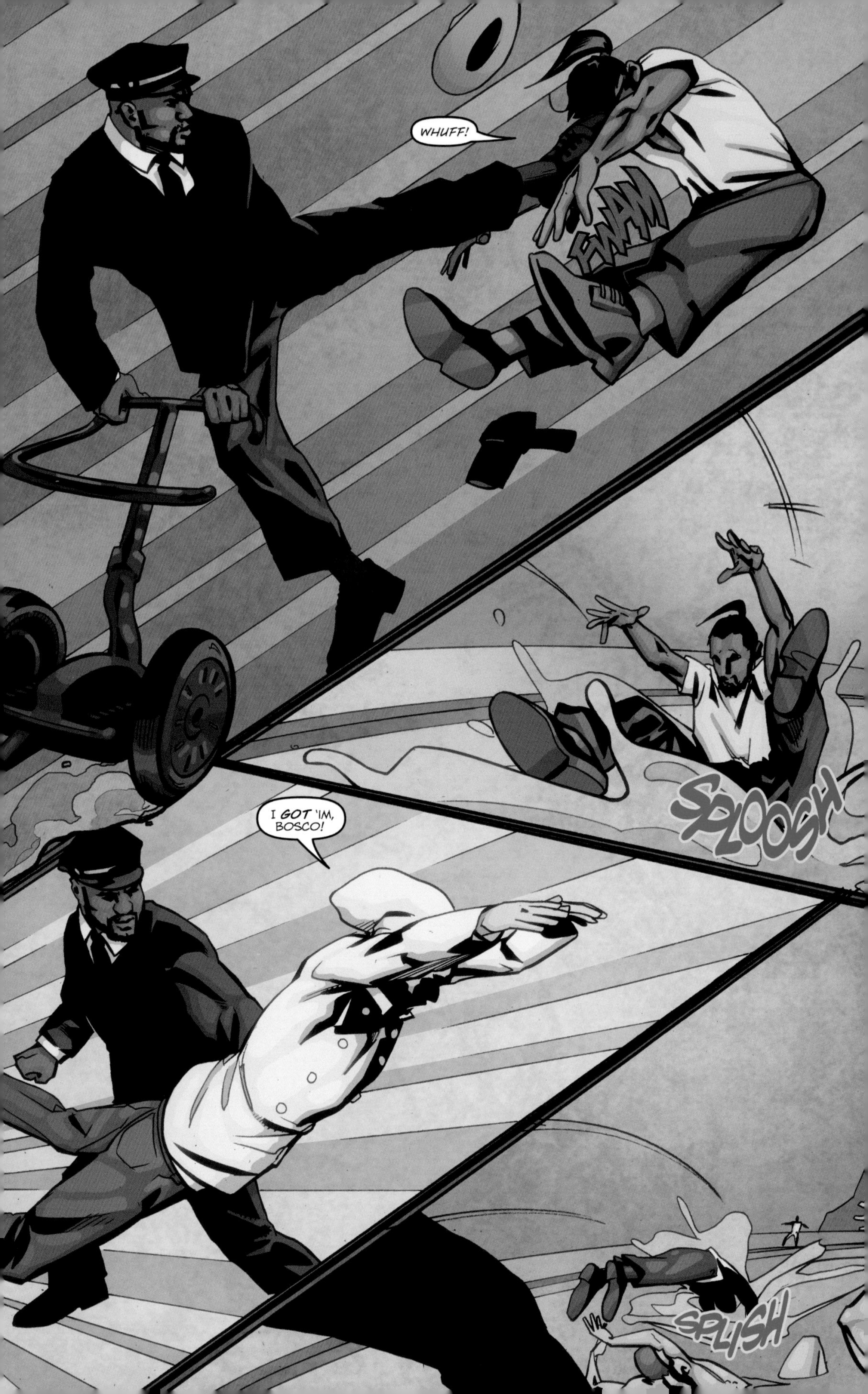
WHUFF!
WHAM
SPLOOSH
I GOT 'IM, BOSCO!
SPLISH

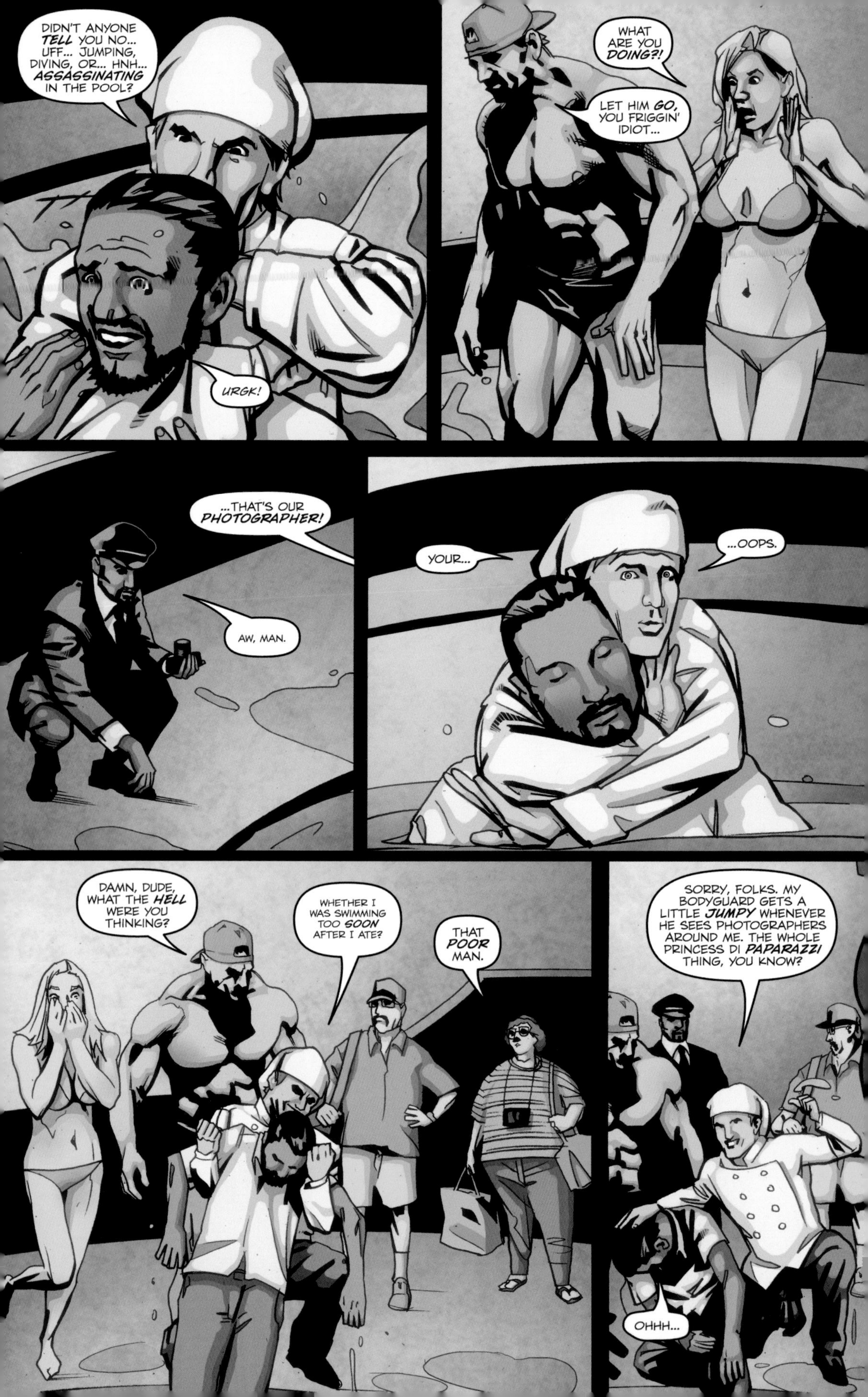
DIDN'T ANYONE TELL YOU NO... UFF... JUMPING, DIVING, OR... HNH... ASSASSINATING IN THE POOL?
URGK!
WHAT ARE YOU DOING?!
LET HIM GO, YOU FRIGGIN' IDIOT...
...THAT'S OUR PHOTOGRAPHER!
AW, MAN.
YOUR...
...OOPS.
DAMN, DUDE, WHAT THE HELL WERE YOU THINKING?
WHETHER I WAS SWIMMING TOO SOON AFTER I ATE?
THAT POOR MAN.
SORRY, FOLKS. MY BODYGUARD GETS A LITTLE JUMPY WHENEVER HE SEES PHOTOGRAPHERS AROUND ME. THE WHOLE PRINCESS DI PAPARAZZI THING, YOU KNOW?
OHHH...

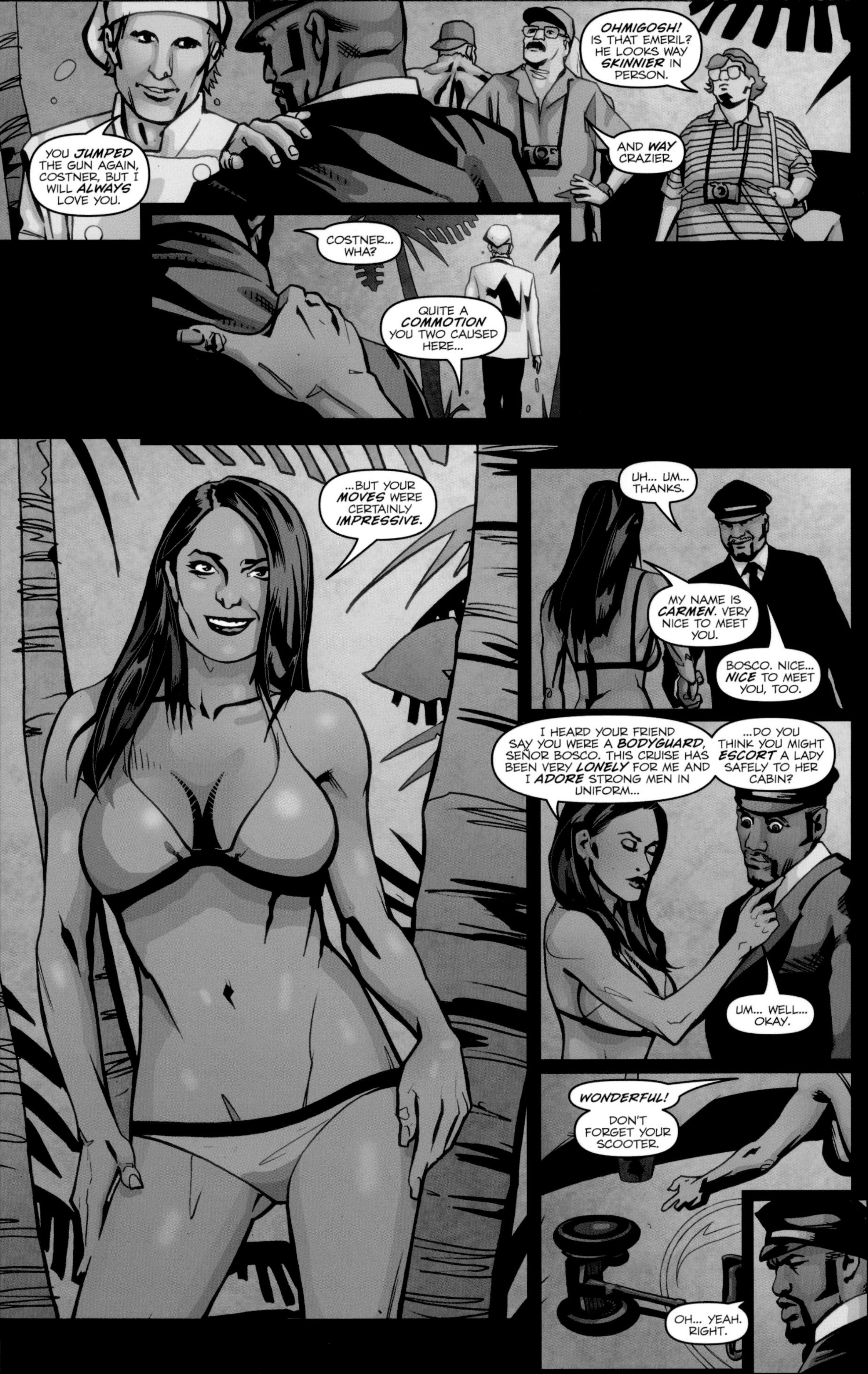
OHMIGOSH! IS THAT EMERIL? HE LOOKS WAY SKINNIER IN PERSON.
YOU JUMPED THE GUN AGAIN, COSTNER, BUT I WILL ALWAYS LOVE YOU.
AND WAY CRAZIER.
COSTNER... WHA?
QUITE A COMMOTION YOU TWO CAUSED HERE...
...BUT YOUR MOVES WERE CERTAINLY IMPRESSIVE.
UH... UM... THANKS.
MY NAME IS CARMEN. VERY NICE TO MEET YOU.
BOSCO. NICE... NICE TO MEET YOU, TOO.
I HEARD YOUR FRIEND SAY YOU WERE A BODYGUARD, SEÑOR BOSCO. THIS CRUISE HAS BEEN VERY LONELY FOR ME AND I ADORE STRONG MEN IN UNIFORM...
...DO YOU THINK YOU MIGHT ESCORT A LADY SAFELY TO HER CABIN?
UM... WELL... OKAY.
WONDERFUL! DON'T FORGET YOUR SCOOTER.
OH... YEAH. RIGHT.

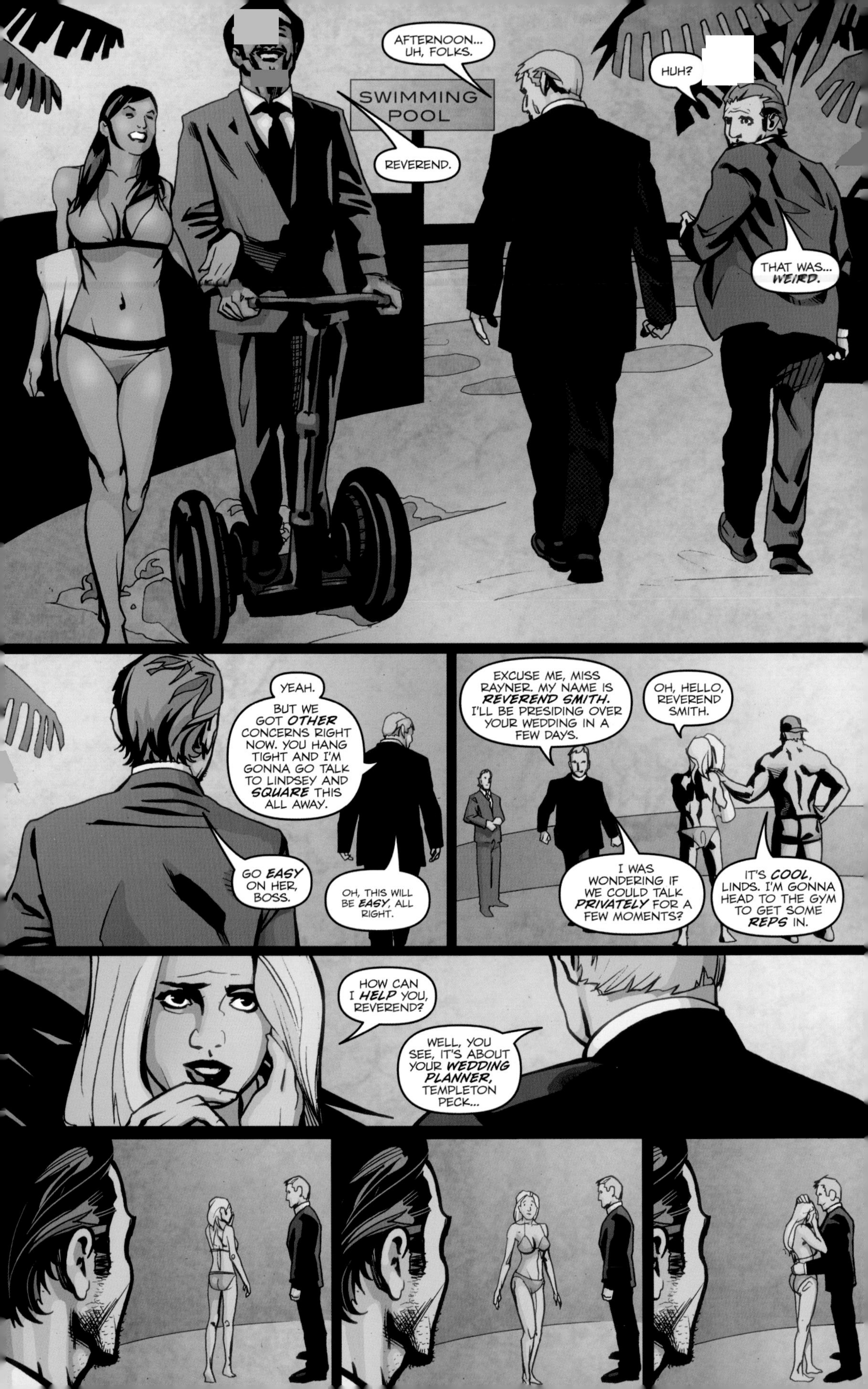
SWIMMING POOL
AFTERNOON... UH, FOLKS.
REVEREND.
HUH?
THAT WAS... *WEIRD.*
YEAH.
BUT WE GOT *OTHER* CONCERNS RIGHT NOW. YOU HANG TIGHT AND I'M GONNA GO TALK TO LINDSEY AND *SQUARE* THIS ALL AWAY.
GO *EASY* ON HER, BOSS.
OH, THIS WILL BE *EASY*, ALL RIGHT.
EXCUSE ME, MISS RAYNER. MY NAME IS *REVEREND SMITH.* I'LL BE PRESIDING OVER YOUR WEDDING IN A FEW DAYS.
OH, HELLO, REVEREND SMITH.
I WAS WONDERING IF WE COULD TALK *PRIVATELY* FOR A FEW MOMENTS?
IT'S *COOL*, LINDS. I'M GONNA HEAD TO THE GYM TO GET SOME *REPS* IN.
HOW CAN I *HELP* YOU, REVEREND?
WELL, YOU SEE, IT'S ABOUT YOUR *WEDDING PLANNER,* TEMPLETON PECK...

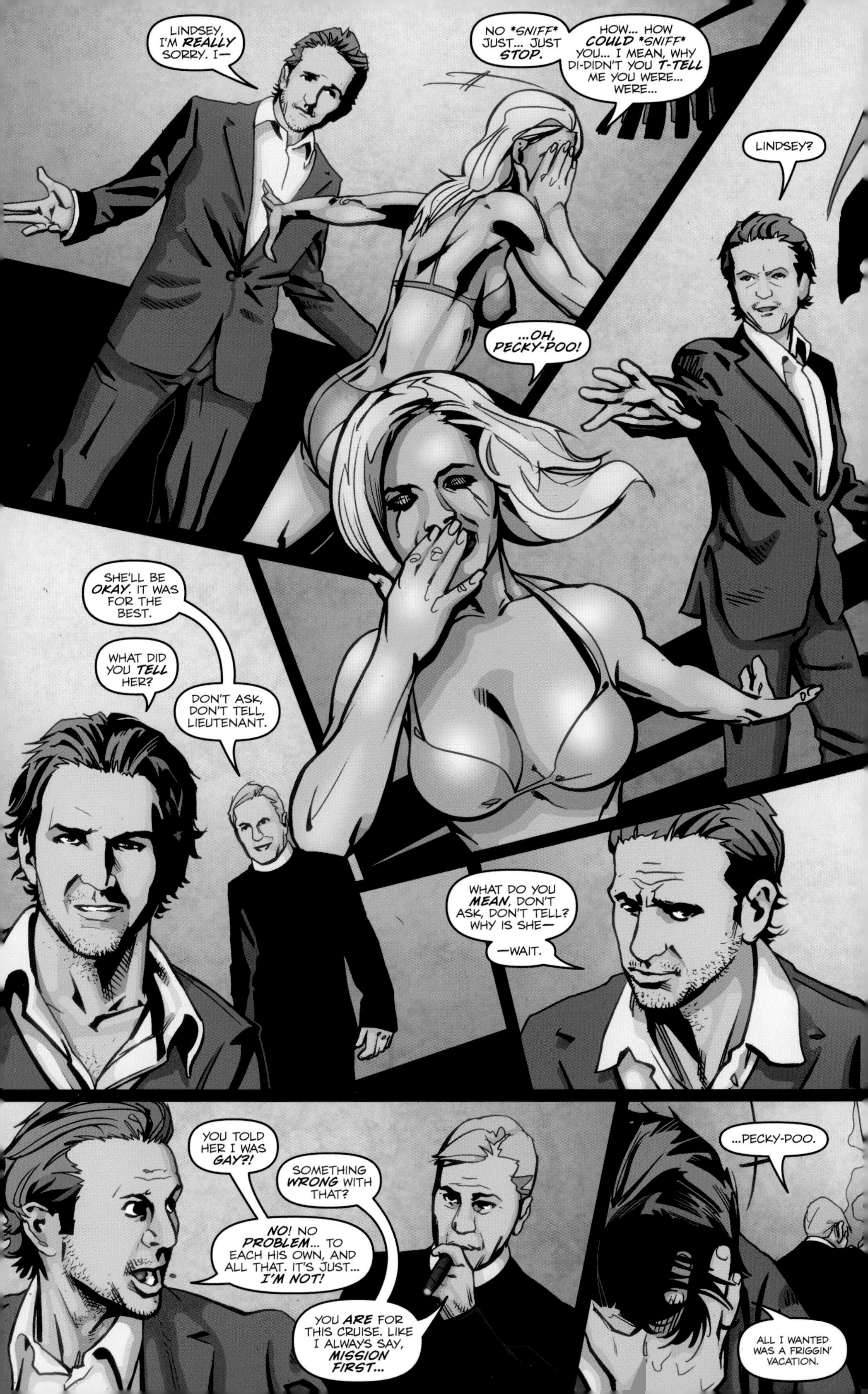
LINDSEY, I'M REALLY SORRY. I—
NO *SNIFF* JUST... JUST STOP.
HOW... HOW COULD *SNIFF* YOU... I MEAN, WHY DI-DIDN'T YOU T-TELL ME YOU WERE... WERE...
LINDSEY?
...OH, PECKY-POO!
SHE'LL BE OKAY. IT WAS FOR THE BEST.
WHAT DID YOU TELL HER?
DON'T ASK, DON'T TELL, LIEUTENANT.
WHAT DO YOU MEAN, DON'T ASK, DON'T TELL? WHY IS SHE—
—WAIT.
YOU TOLD HER I WAS GAY?!
SOMETHING WRONG WITH THAT?
NO! NO PROBLEM... TO EACH HIS OWN, AND ALL THAT. IT'S JUST... I'M NOT!
YOU ARE FOR THIS CRUISE. LIKE I ALWAYS SAY, MISSION FIRST...
...PECKY-POO.
ALL I WANTED WAS A FRIGGIN' VACATION.

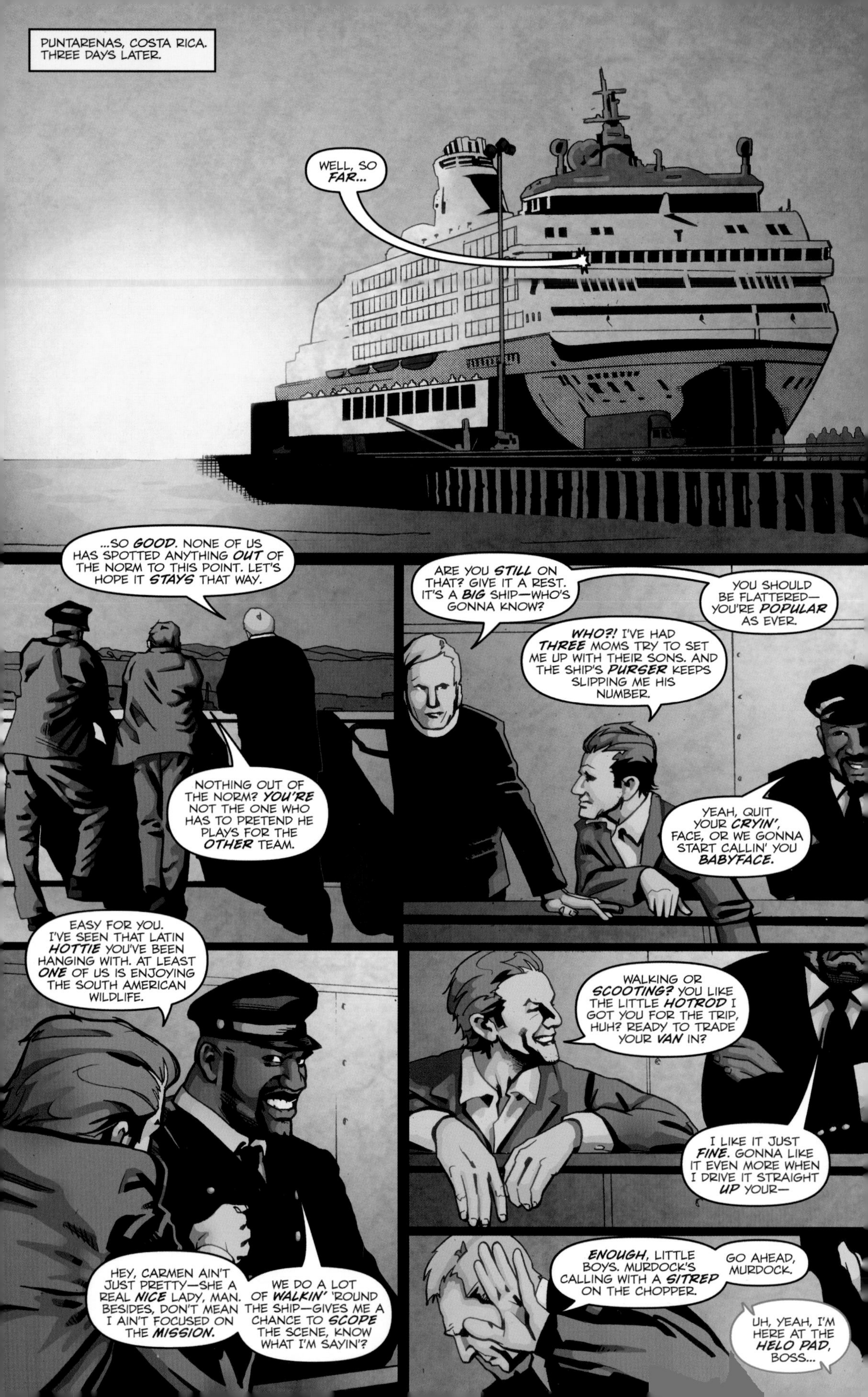
PUNTARENAS, COSTA RICA. THREE DAYS LATER.
WELL, SO FAR...
...SO GOOD. NONE OF US HAS SPOTTED ANYTHING OUT OF THE NORM TO THIS POINT. LET'S HOPE IT STAYS THAT WAY.
NOTHING OUT OF THE NORM? YOU'RE NOT THE ONE WHO HAS TO PRETEND HE PLAYS FOR THE OTHER TEAM.
ARE YOU STILL ON THAT? GIVE IT A REST. IT'S A BIG SHIP—WHO'S GONNA KNOW?
WHO?! I'VE HAD THREE MOMS TRY TO SET ME UP WITH THEIR SONS. AND THE SHIP'S PURSER KEEPS SLIPPING ME HIS NUMBER.
YOU SHOULD BE FLATTERED—YOU'RE POPULAR AS EVER.
YEAH, QUIT YOUR CRYIN', FACE, OR WE GONNA START CALLIN' YOU BABYFACE.
EASY FOR YOU. I'VE SEEN THAT LATIN HOTTIE YOU'VE BEEN HANGING WITH. AT LEAST ONE OF US IS ENJOYING THE SOUTH AMERICAN WILDLIFE.
HEY, CARMEN AIN'T JUST PRETTY—SHE A REAL NICE LADY, MAN. BESIDES, DON'T MEAN I AIN'T FOCUSED ON THE MISSION.
WE DO A LOT OF WALKIN' 'ROUND THE SHIP—GIVES ME A CHANCE TO SCOPE THE SCENE, KNOW WHAT I'M SAYIN'?
WALKING OR SCOOTING? YOU LIKE THE LITTLE HOTROD I GOT YOU FOR THE TRIP, HUH? READY TO TRADE YOUR VAN IN?
I LIKE IT JUST FINE. GONNA LIKE IT EVEN MORE WHEN I DRIVE IT STRAIGHT UP YOUR—
ENOUGH, LITTLE BOYS. MURDOCK'S CALLING WITH A SITREP ON THE CHOPPER.
GO AHEAD, MURDOCK.
UH, YEAH, I'M HERE AT THE HELO PAD, BOSS...

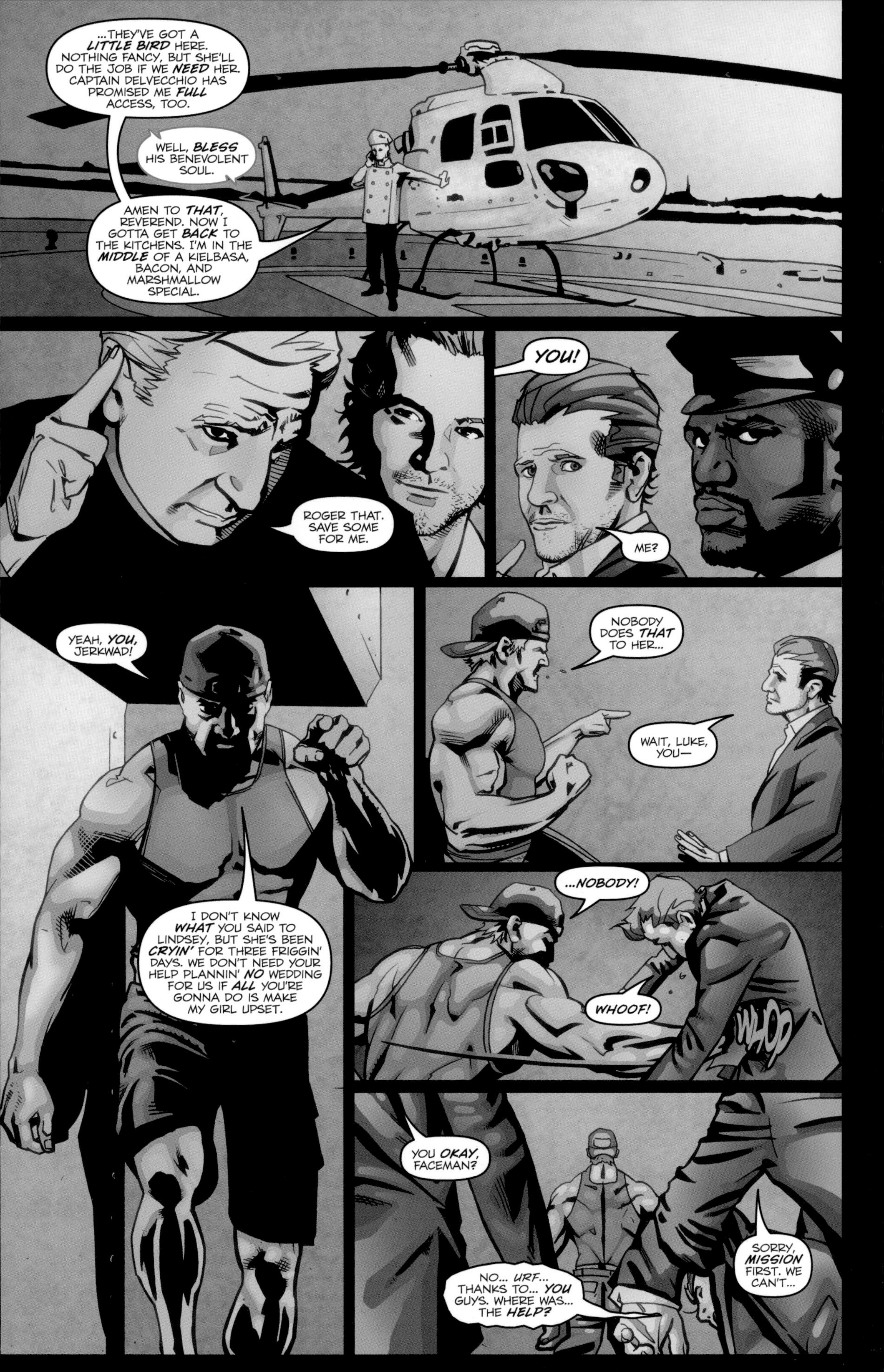
...THEY'VE GOT A LITTLE BIRD HERE. NOTHING FANCY, BUT SHE'LL DO THE JOB IF WE NEED HER. CAPTAIN DELVECCHIO HAS PROMISED ME FULL ACCESS, TOO.
WELL, BLESS HIS BENEVOLENT SOUL.
AMEN TO THAT, REVEREND. NOW I GOTTA GET BACK TO THE KITCHENS. I'M IN THE MIDDLE OF A KIELBASA, BACON, AND MARSHMALLOW SPECIAL.
ROGER THAT. SAVE SOME FOR ME.
YOU!
ME?
YEAH, YOU, JERKWAD!
I DON'T KNOW WHAT YOU SAID TO LINDSEY, BUT SHE'S BEEN CRYIN' FOR THREE FRIGGIN' DAYS. WE DON'T NEED YOUR HELP PLANNIN' NO WEDDING FOR US IF ALL YOU'RE GONNA DO IS MAKE MY GIRL UPSET.
NOBODY DOES THAT TO HER...
WAIT, LUKE, YOU—
...NOBODY!
WHOOF!
WHOP
YOU OKAY, FACEMAN?
SORRY, MISSION FIRST. WE CAN'T...
NO... URF... THANKS TO... YOU GUYS. WHERE WAS... THE HELP?

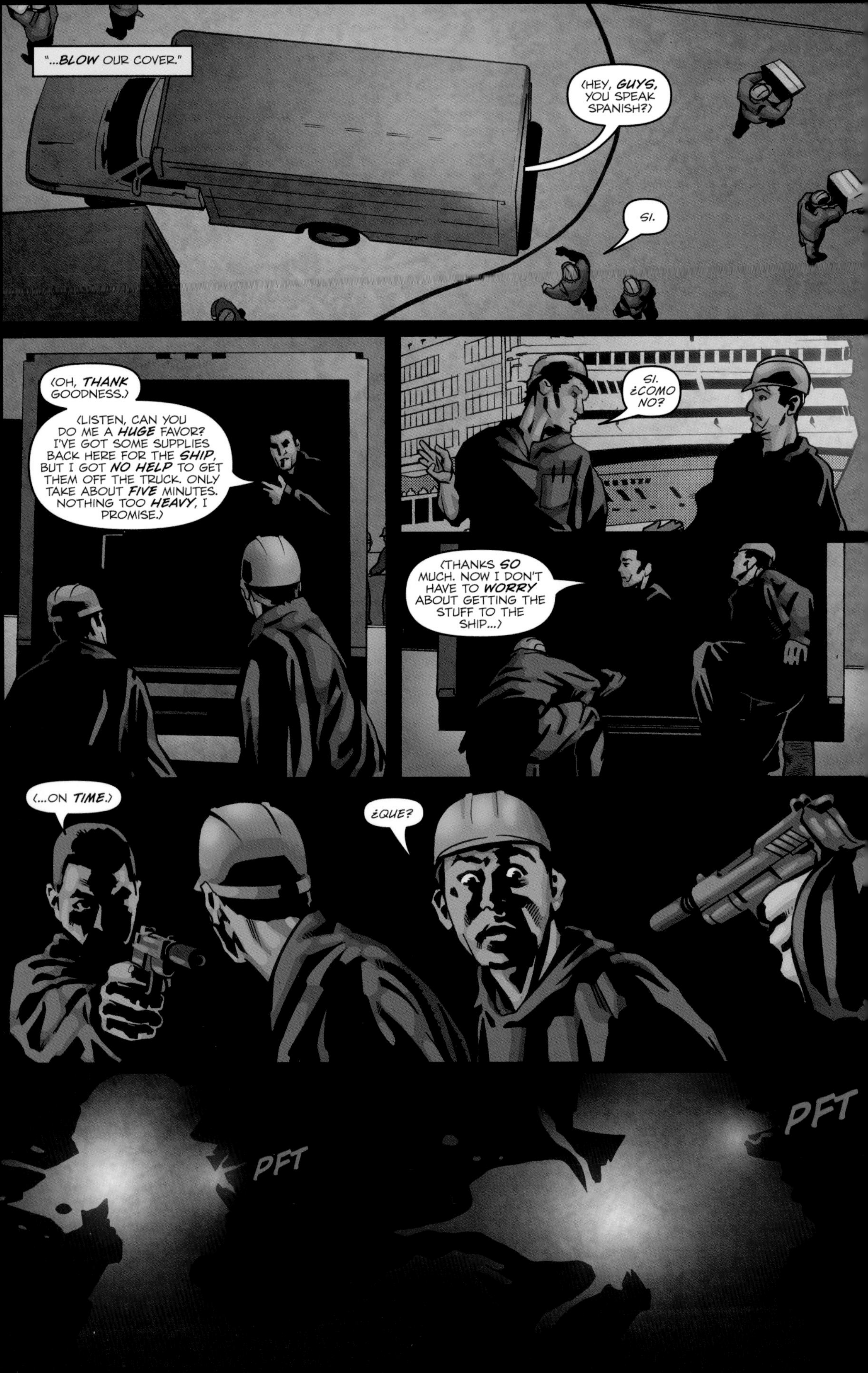
"...BLOW OUR COVER."
(HEY, GUYS, YOU SPEAK SPANISH?)
SI.
(OH, THANK GOODNESS.)
(LISTEN, CAN YOU DO ME A HUGE FAVOR? I'VE GOT SOME SUPPLIES BACK HERE FOR THE SHIP, BUT I GOT NO HELP TO GET THEM OFF THE TRUCK. ONLY TAKE ABOUT FIVE MINUTES. NOTHING TOO HEAVY, I PROMISE.)
SI. ¿COMO NO?
(THANKS SO MUCH. NOW I DON'T HAVE TO WORRY ABOUT GETTING THE STUFF TO THE SHIP...)
(...ON TIME.)
¿QUE?
PFT
PFT

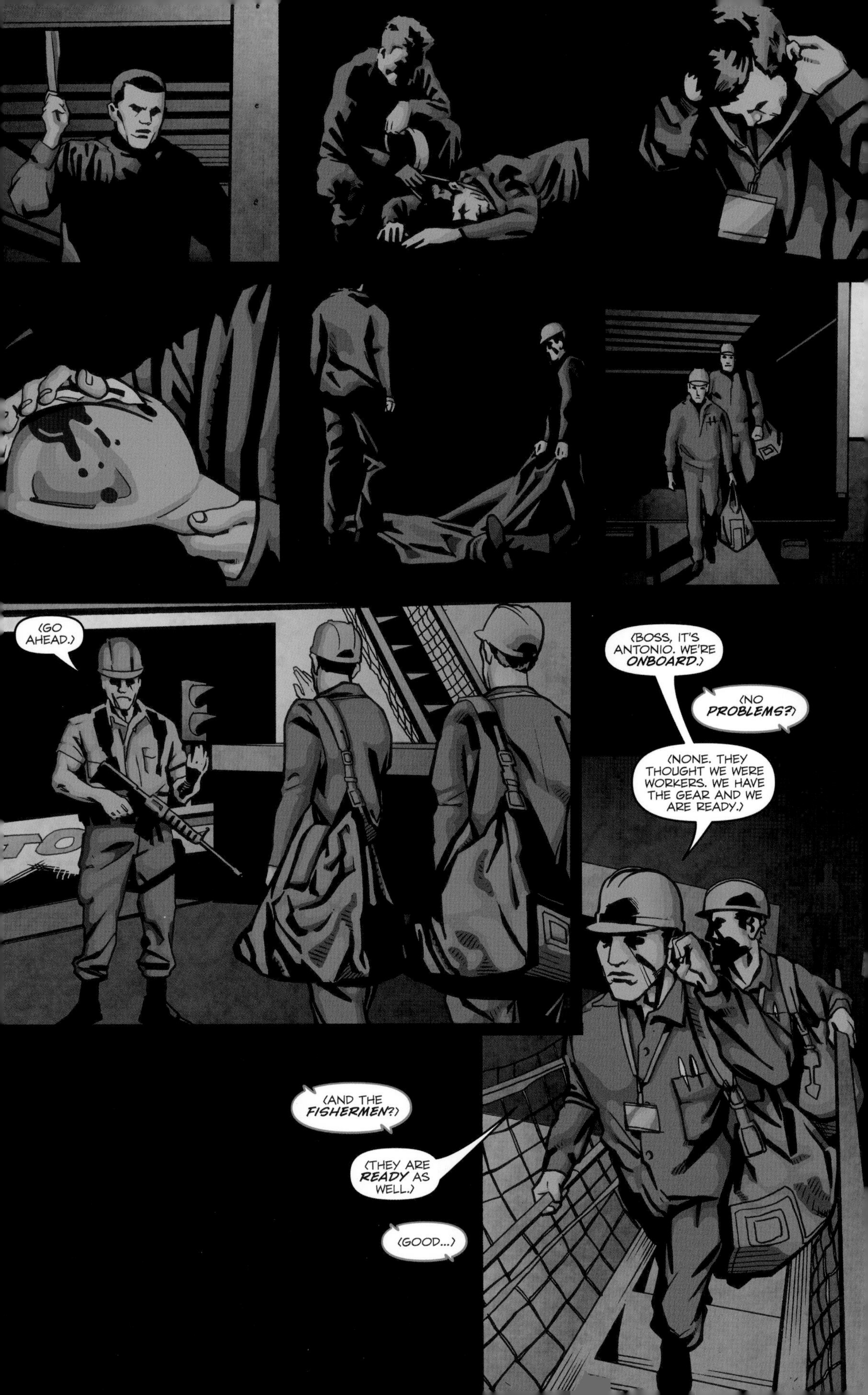

(GO AHEAD.)
(BOSS, IT'S ANTONIO. WE'RE ONBOARD.)
(NO PROBLEMS?)
(NONE. THEY THOUGHT WE WERE WORKERS. WE HAVE THE GEAR AND WE ARE READY.)
(AND THE FISHERMEN?)
(THEY ARE READY AS WELL.)
(GOOD...)

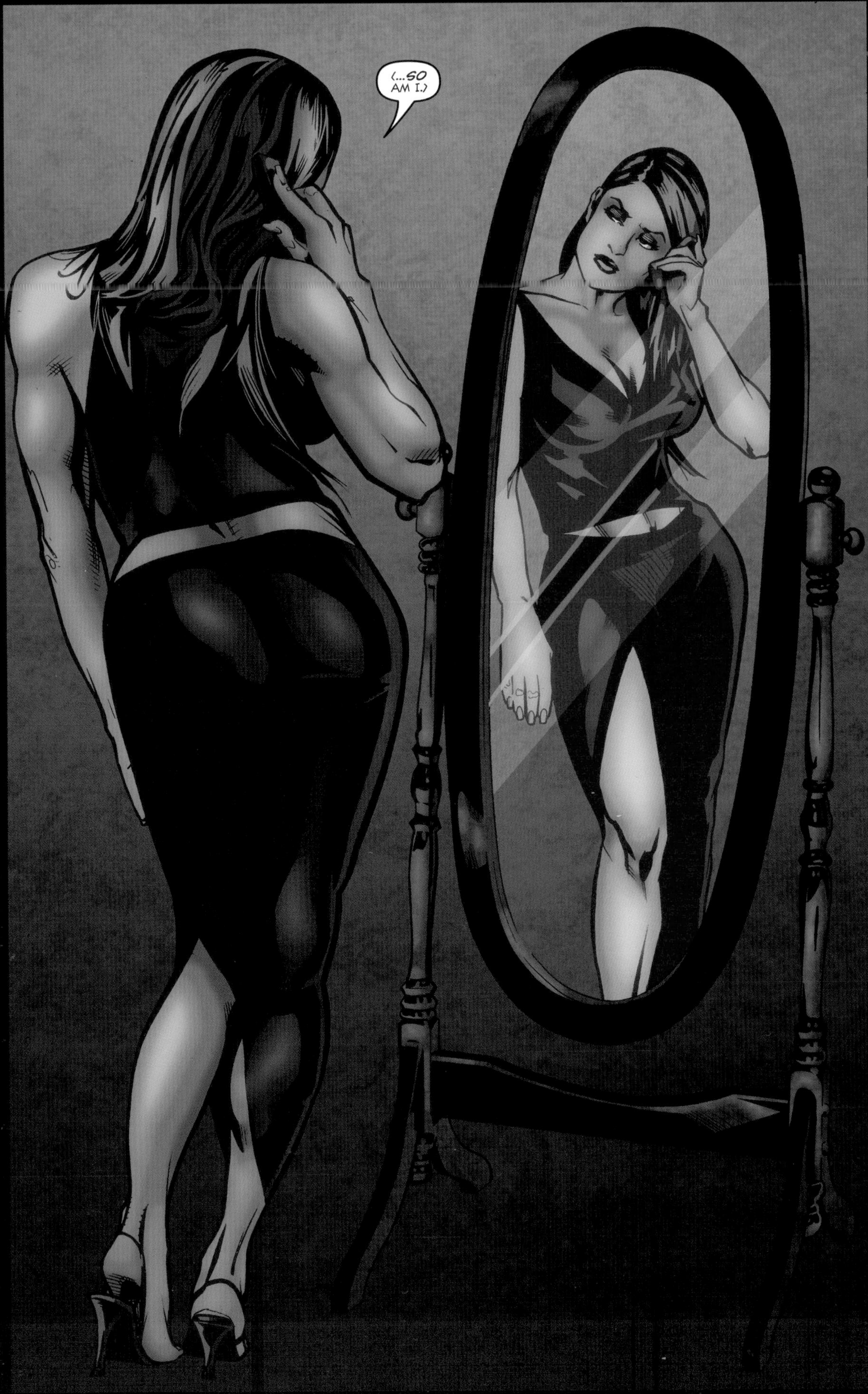
(...SO AM I.)

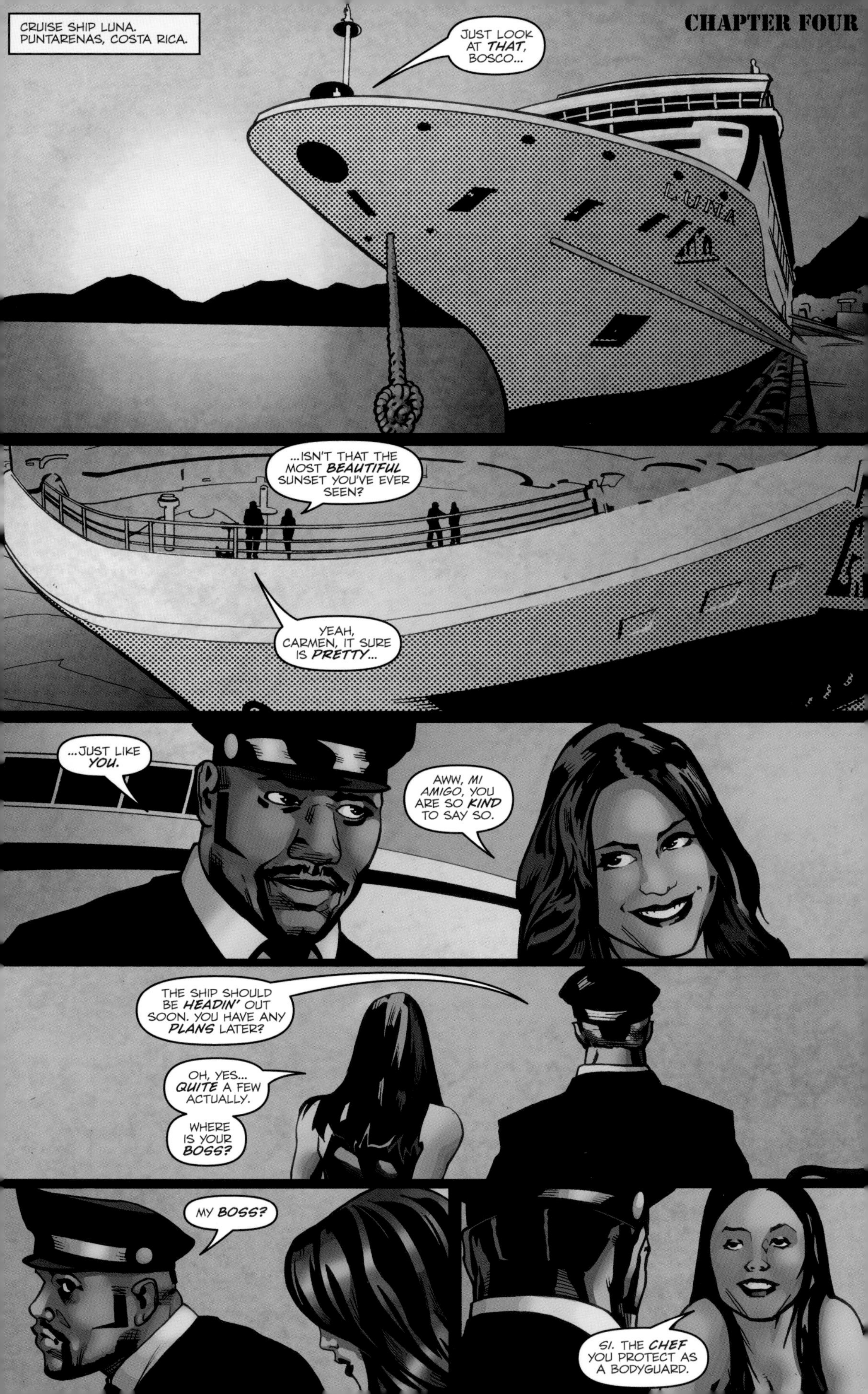
CHAPTER FOUR
CRUISE SHIP LUNA. PUNTARENAS, COSTA RICA.
JUST LOOK AT THAT, BOSCO...
LUNA
...ISN'T THAT THE MOST BEAUTIFUL SUNSET YOU'VE EVER SEEN?
YEAH, CARMEN, IT SURE IS PRETTY...
...JUST LIKE YOU.
AWW, MI AMIGO, YOU ARE SO KIND TO SAY SO.
THE SHIP SHOULD BE HEADIN' OUT SOON. YOU HAVE ANY PLANS LATER?
OH, YES... QUITE A FEW ACTUALLY.
WHERE IS YOUR BOSS?
MY BOSS?
SI. THE CHEF YOU PROTECT AS A BODYGUARD.

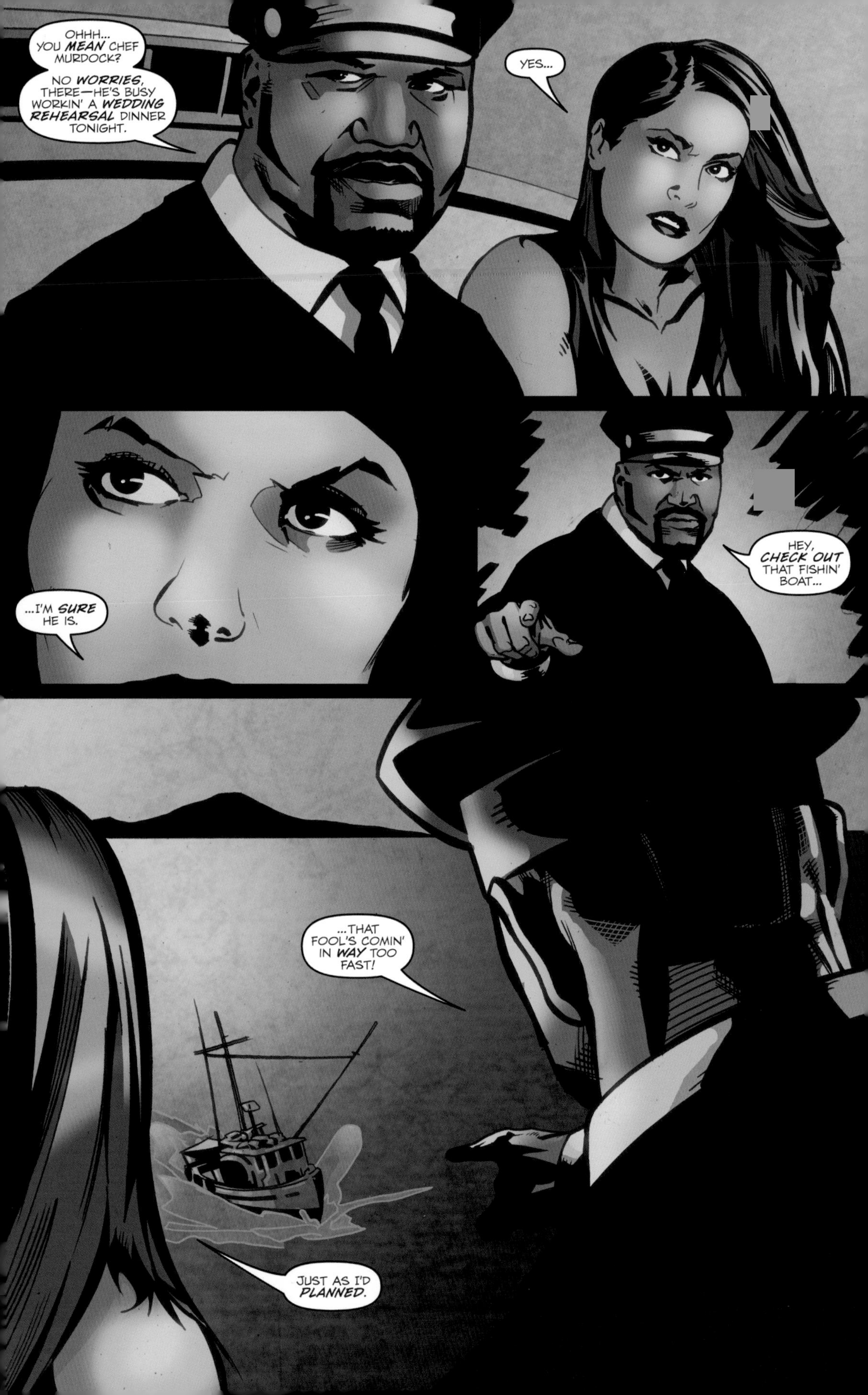
OHHH... YOU MEAN CHEF MURDOCK?
NO WORRIES, THERE—HE'S BUSY WORKIN' A WEDDING REHEARSAL DINNER TONIGHT.
YES...
...I'M SURE HE IS.
HEY, CHECK OUT THAT FISHIN' BOAT...
...THAT FOOL'S COMIN' IN WAY TOO FAST!
JUST AS I'D PLANNED.

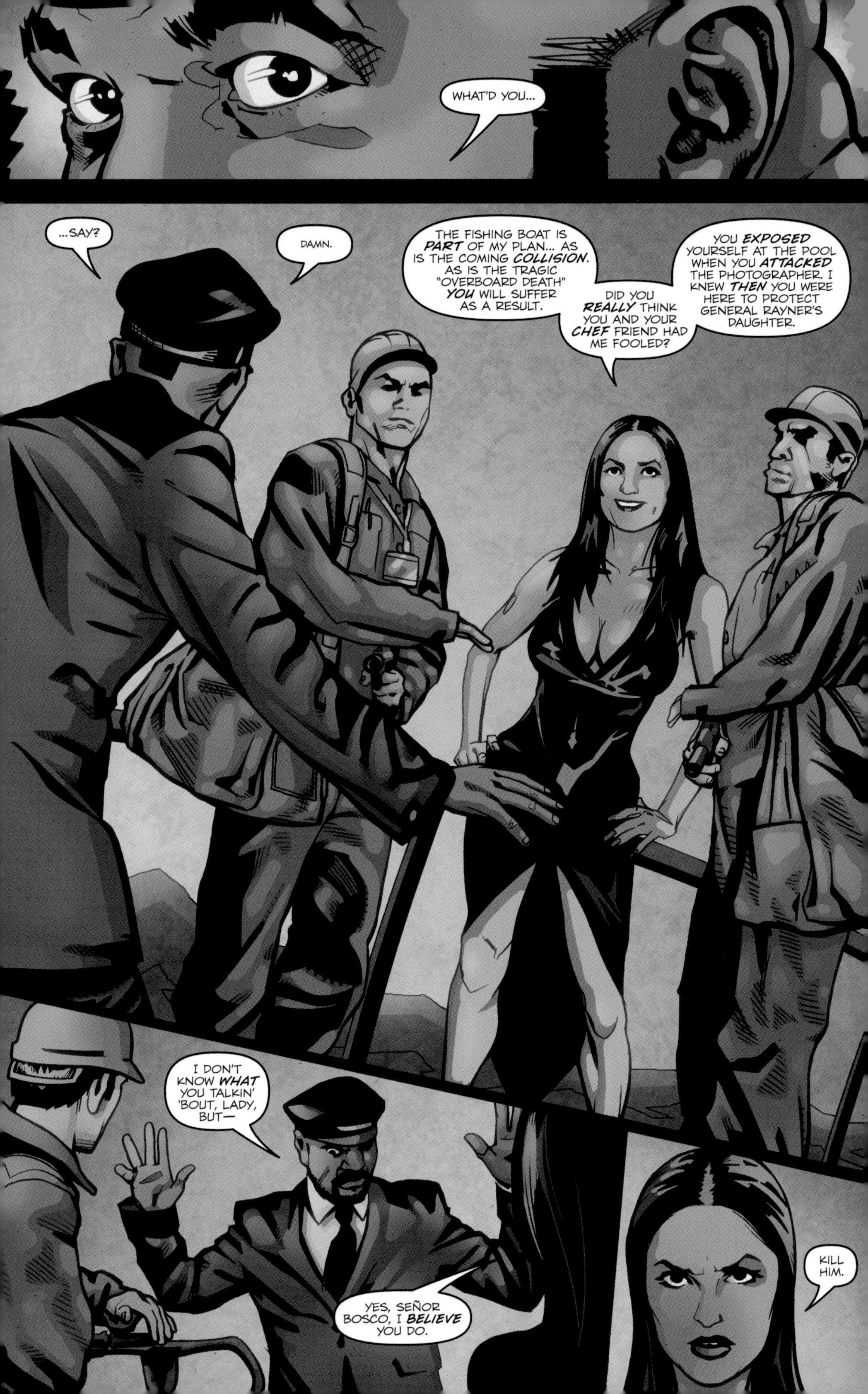

WHAT'D YOU...
...SAY?
DAMN.
THE FISHING BOAT IS PART OF MY PLAN... AS IS THE COMING COLLISION. AS IS THE TRAGIC "OVERBOARD DEATH" YOU WILL SUFFER AS A RESULT.
DID YOU REALLY THINK YOU AND YOUR CHEF FRIEND HAD ME FOOLED?
YOU EXPOSED YOURSELF AT THE POOL WHEN YOU ATTACKED THE PHOTOGRAPHER. I KNEW THEN YOU WERE HERE TO PROTECT GENERAL RAYNER'S DAUGHTER.
I DON'T KNOW WHAT YOU TALKIN' 'BOUT, LADY, BUT—
YES, SEÑOR BOSCO, I BELIEVE YOU DO.
KILL HIM.

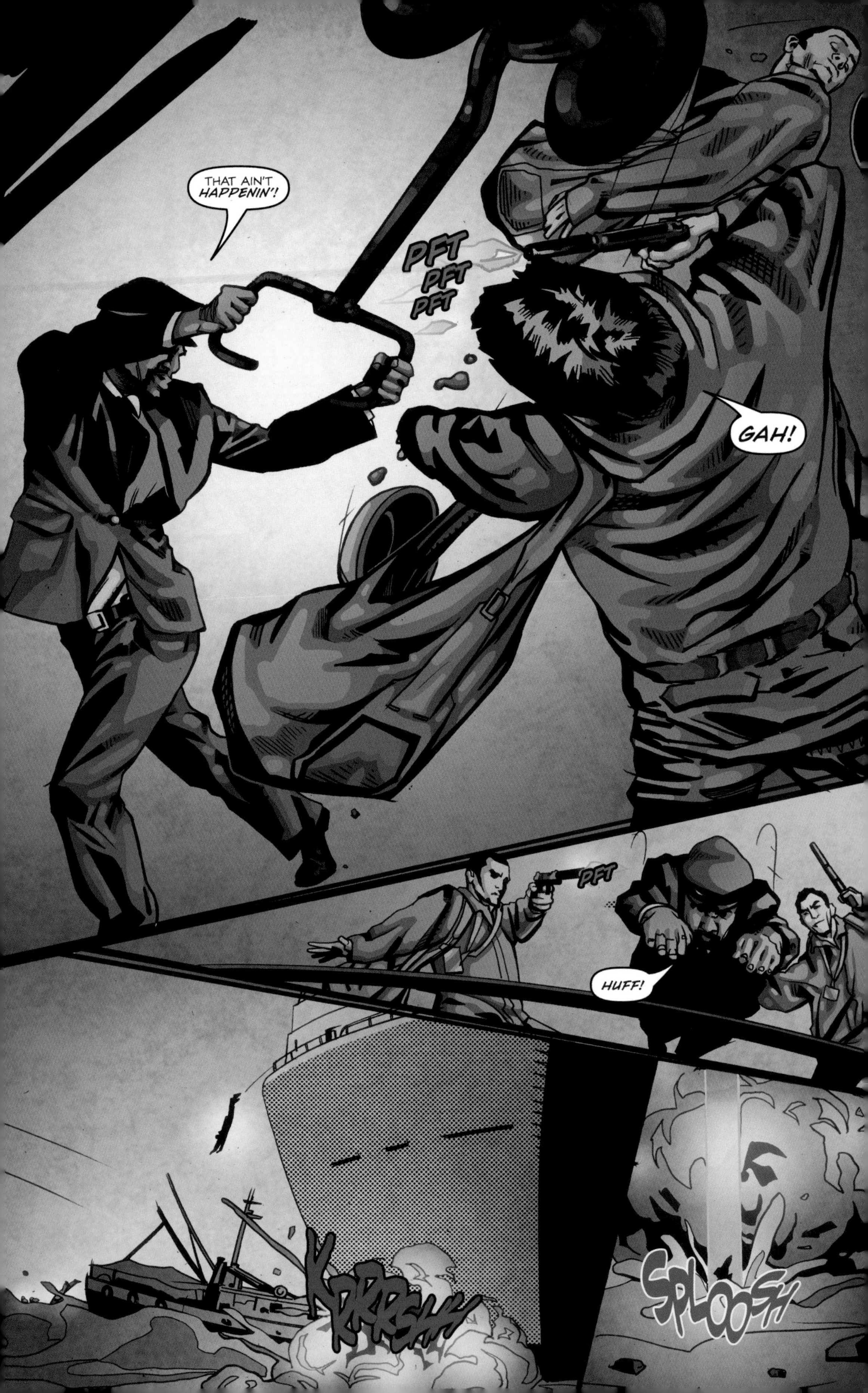
THAT AIN'T HAPPENIN'!
PFT PFT PFT
GAH!
PFT
HUFF!
KRRRSHH
SPLOOSH

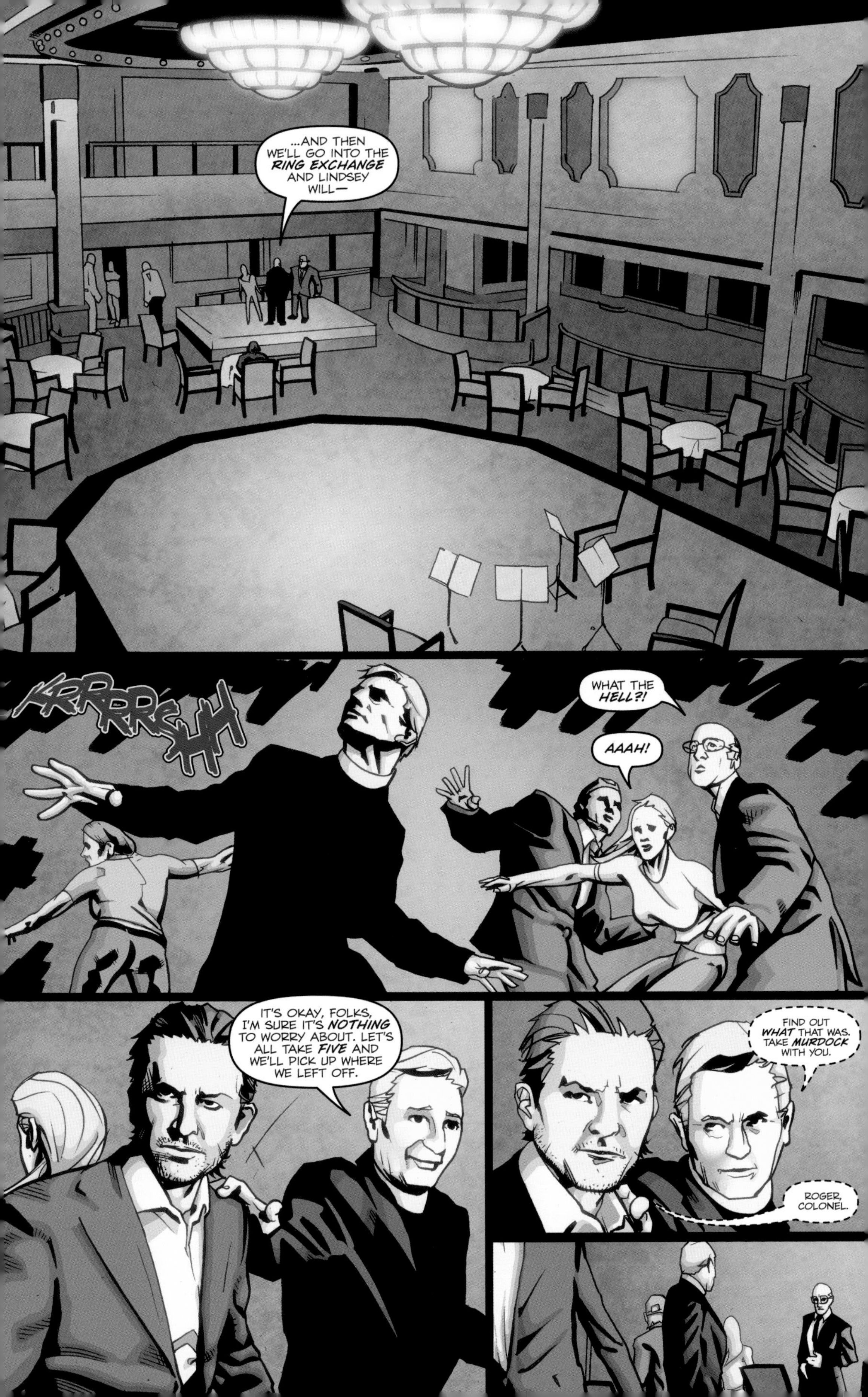
...AND THEN WE'LL GO INTO THE RING EXCHANGE AND LINDSEY WILL—
KRRRRRSHHH
WHAT THE HELL?!
AAAH!
IT'S OKAY, FOLKS, I'M SURE IT'S NOTHING TO WORRY ABOUT. LET'S ALL TAKE FIVE AND WE'LL PICK UP WHERE WE LEFT OFF.
FIND OUT WHAT THAT WAS. TAKE MURDOCK WITH YOU.
ROGER, COLONEL.

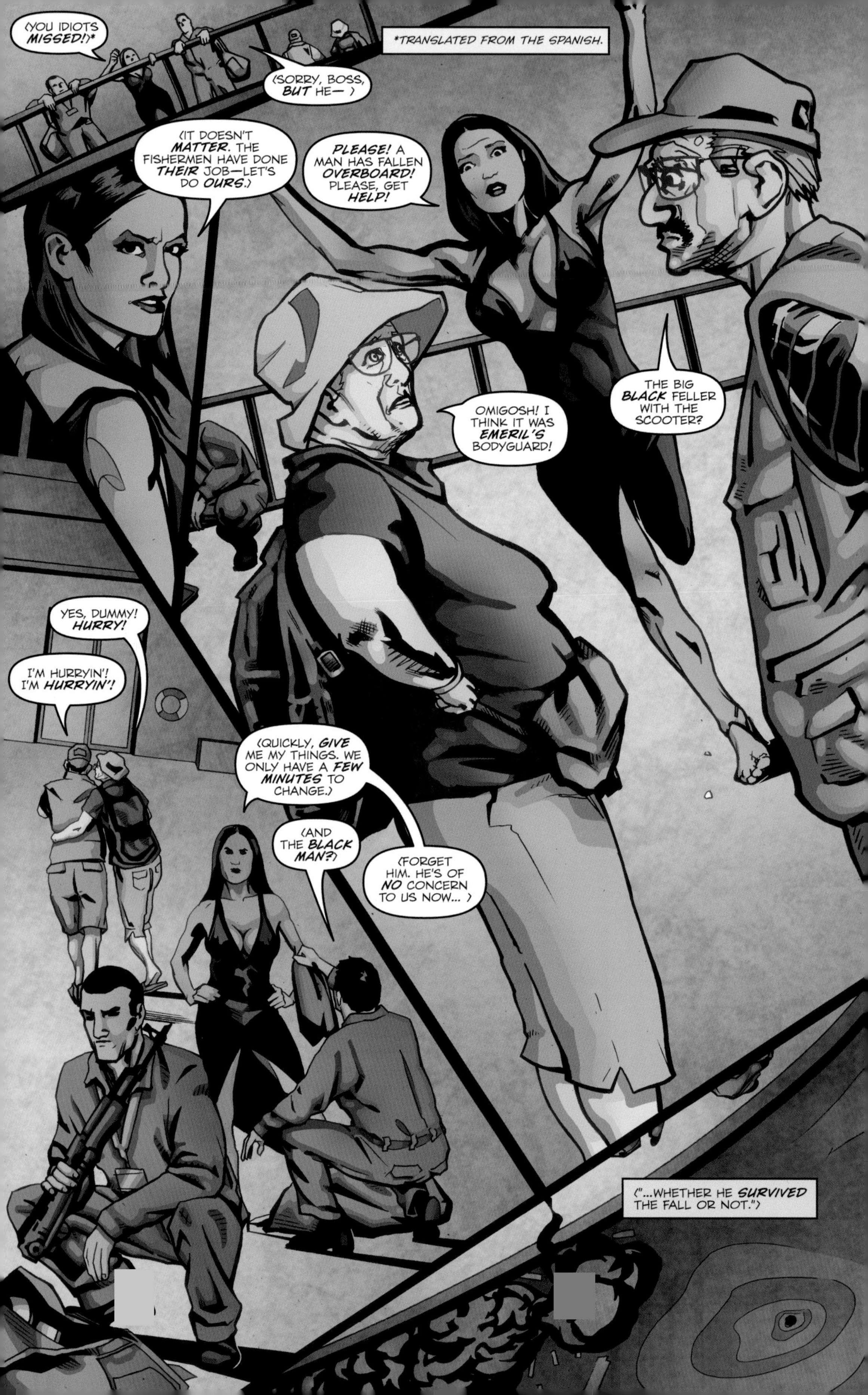
(YOU IDIOTS MISSED!)*
*TRANSLATED FROM THE SPANISH.
(SORRY, BOSS, BUT HE— )
(IT DOESN'T MATTER. THE FISHERMEN HAVE DONE THEIR JOB—LET'S DO OURS.)
PLEASE! A MAN HAS FALLEN OVERBOARD! PLEASE, GET HELP!
THE BIG BLACK FELLER WITH THE SCOOTER?
OMIGOSH! I THINK IT WAS EMERIL'S BODYGUARD!
YES, DUMMY! HURRY!
I'M HURRYIN'! I'M HURRYIN'!
(QUICKLY, GIVE ME MY THINGS. WE ONLY HAVE A FEW MINUTES TO CHANGE.)
(AND THE BLACK MAN?)
(FORGET HIM. HE'S OF NO CONCERN TO US NOW... )
("...WHETHER HE SURVIVED THE FALL OR NOT.")

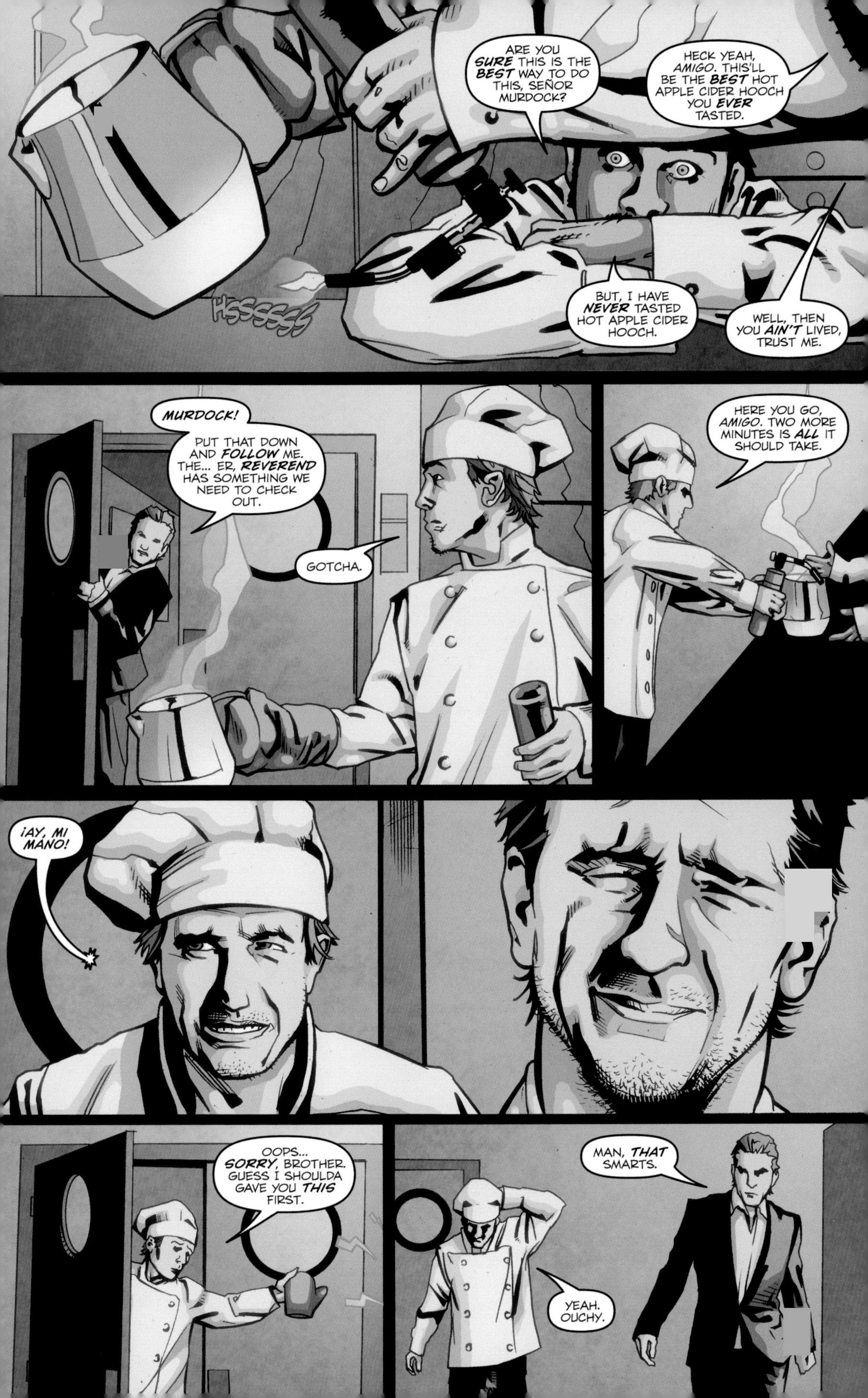
ARE YOU SURE THIS IS THE BEST WAY TO DO THIS, SEÑOR MURDOCK?
HECK YEAH, AMIGO. THIS'LL BE THE BEST HOT APPLE CIDER HOOCH YOU EVER TASTED.
HSSSSSS
BUT, I HAVE NEVER TASTED HOT APPLE CIDER HOOCH.
WELL, THEN YOU AIN'T LIVED, TRUST ME.
MURDOCK!
PUT THAT DOWN AND FOLLOW ME. THE... ER, REVEREND HAS SOMETHING WE NEED TO CHECK OUT.
GOTCHA.
HERE YOU GO, AMIGO. TWO MORE MINUTES IS ALL IT SHOULD TAKE.
¡AY, MI MANO!
OOPS... SORRY, BROTHER. GUESS I SHOULDA GAVE YOU THIS FIRST.
MAN, THAT SMARTS.
YEAH. OUCHY.

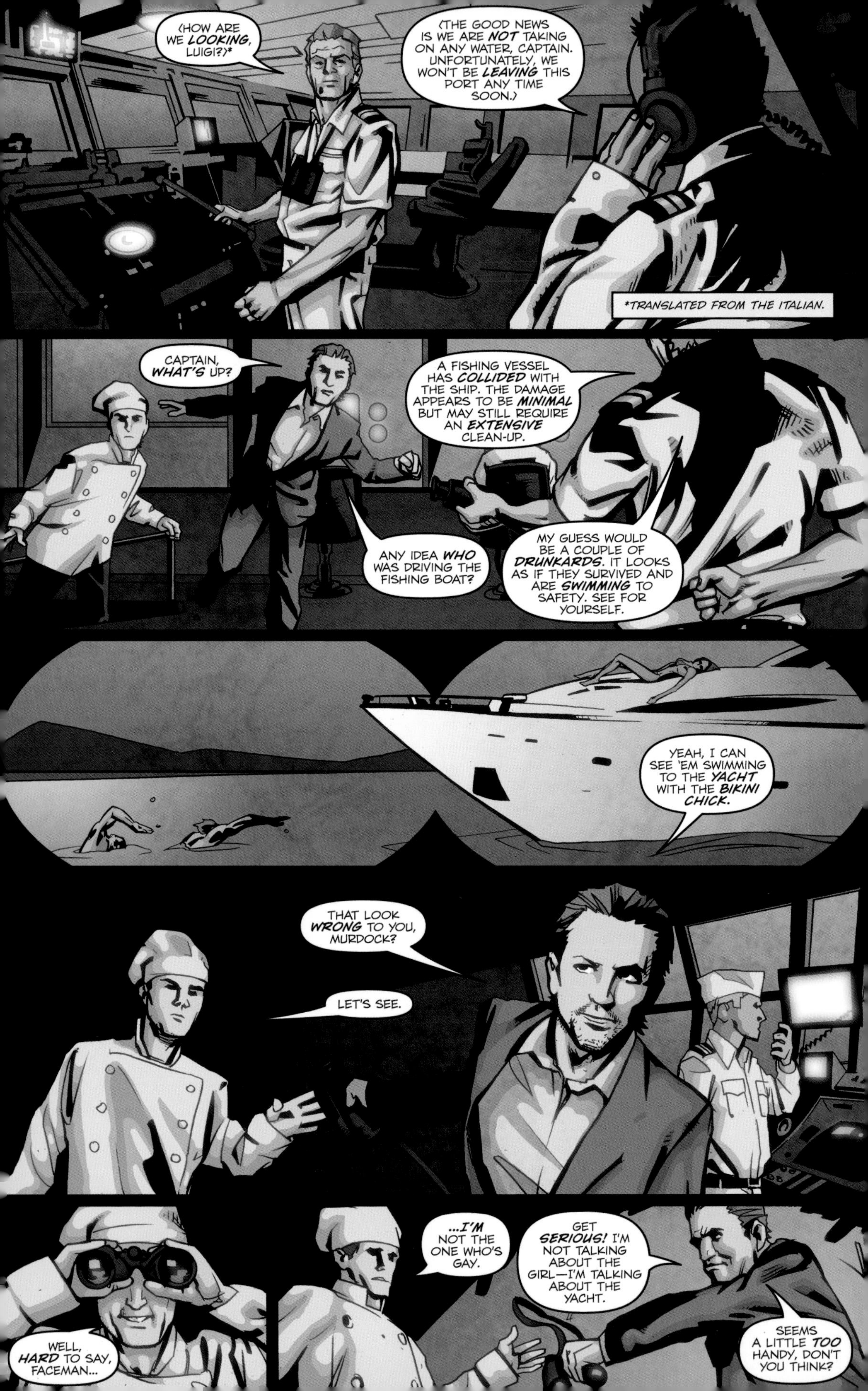
‹HOW ARE WE LOOKING, LUIGI?›*
‹THE GOOD NEWS IS WE ARE NOT TAKING ON ANY WATER, CAPTAIN. UNFORTUNATELY, WE WON'T BE LEAVING THIS PORT ANY TIME SOON.›
*TRANSLATED FROM THE ITALIAN.
CAPTAIN, WHAT'S UP?
A FISHING VESSEL HAS COLLIDED WITH THE SHIP. THE DAMAGE APPEARS TO BE MINIMAL BUT MAY STILL REQUIRE AN EXTENSIVE CLEAN-UP.
ANY IDEA WHO WAS DRIVING THE FISHING BOAT?
MY GUESS WOULD BE A COUPLE OF DRUNKARDS. IT LOOKS AS IF THEY SURVIVED AND ARE SWIMMING TO SAFETY. SEE FOR YOURSELF.
YEAH, I CAN SEE 'EM SWIMMING TO THE YACHT WITH THE BIKINI CHICK.
THAT LOOK WRONG TO YOU, MURDOCK?
LET'S SEE.
WELL, HARD TO SAY, FACEMAN...
...I'M NOT THE ONE WHO'S GAY.
GET SERIOUS! I'M NOT TALKING ABOUT THE GIRL—I'M TALKING ABOUT THE YACHT.
SEEMS A LITTLE TOO HANDY, DON'T YOU THINK?

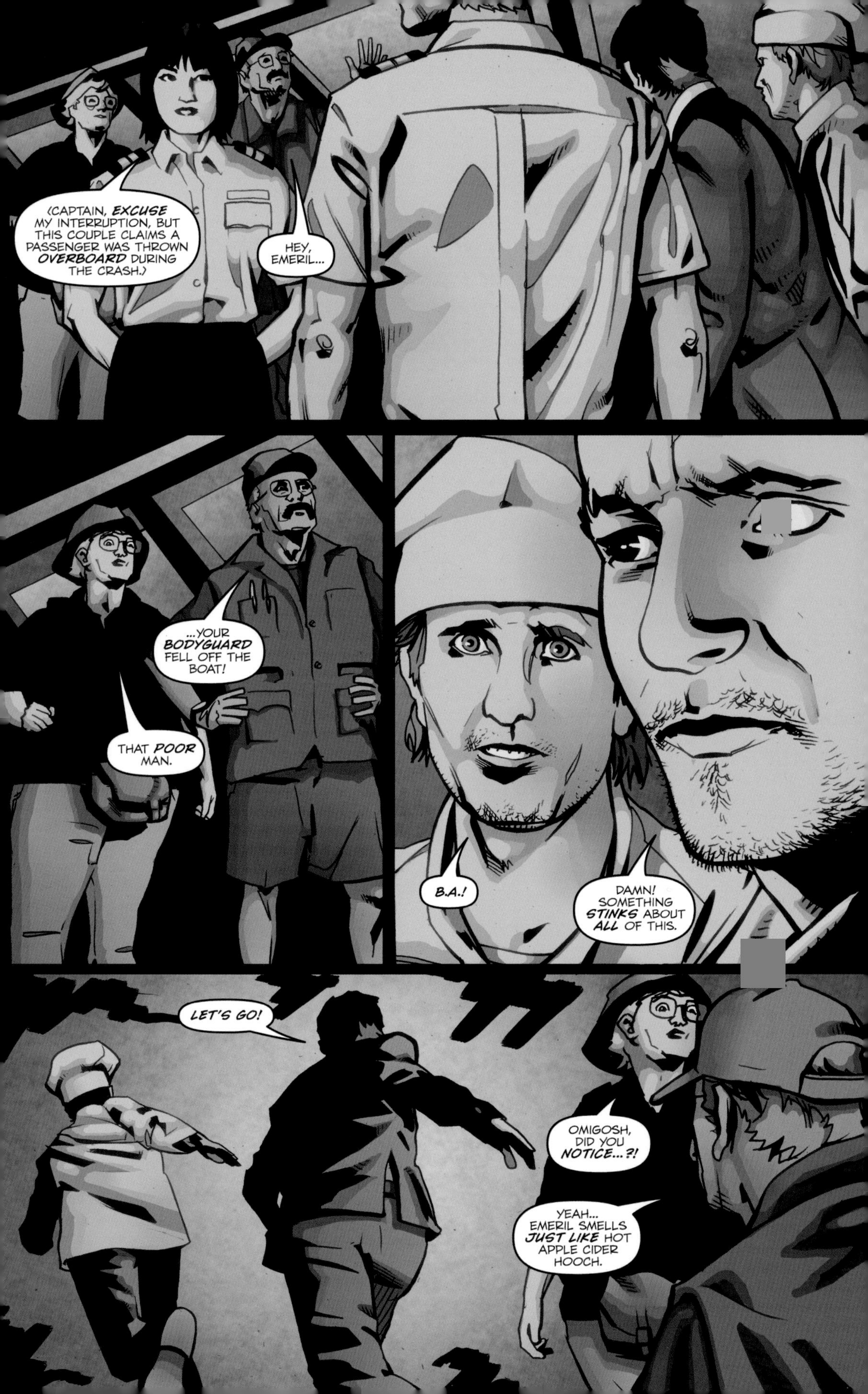

⟨CAPTAIN, EXCUSE MY INTERRUPTION, BUT THIS COUPLE CLAIMS A PASSENGER WAS THROWN OVERBOARD DURING THE CRASH.⟩
HEY, EMERIL...
...YOUR BODYGUARD FELL OFF THE BOAT!
THAT POOR MAN.
B.A.!
DAMN! SOMETHING STINKS ABOUT ALL OF THIS.
LET'S GO!
OMIGOSH, DID YOU NOTICE...?!
YEAH... EMERIL SMELLS JUST LIKE HOT APPLE CIDER HOOCH.

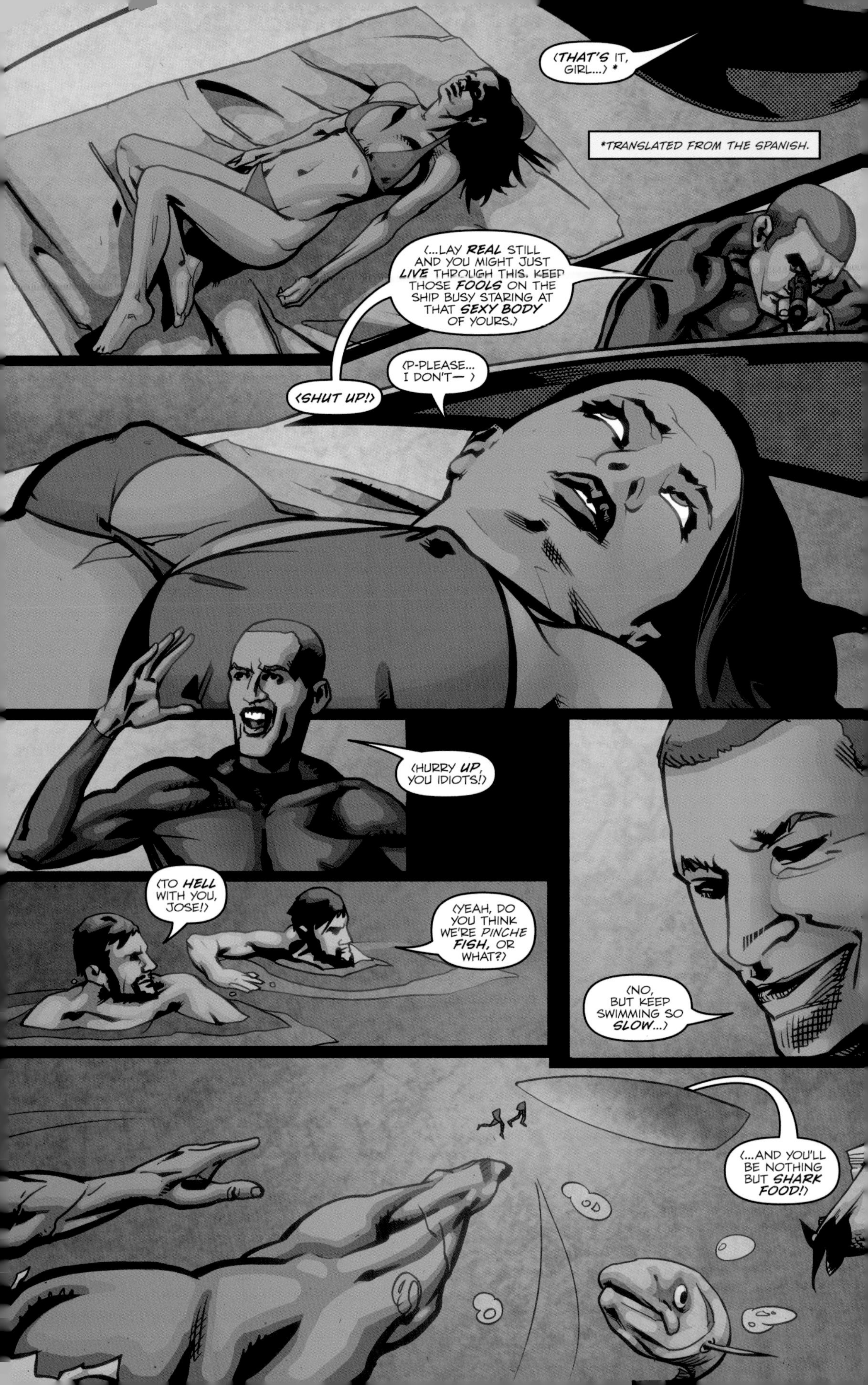

(THAT'S IT, GIRL...) *
*TRANSLATED FROM THE SPANISH.
(...LAY REAL STILL AND YOU MIGHT JUST LIVE THROUGH THIS. KEEP THOSE FOOLS ON THE SHIP BUSY STARING AT THAT SEXY BODY OF YOURS.)
(P-PLEASE... I DON'T— )
(SHUT UP!)
(HURRY UP, YOU IDIOTS!)
(TO HELL WITH YOU, JOSE!)
(YEAH, DO YOU THINK WE'RE PINCHE FISH, OR WHAT?)
(NO, BUT KEEP SWIMMING SO SLOW...)
(...AND YOU'LL BE NOTHING BUT SHARK FOOD!)

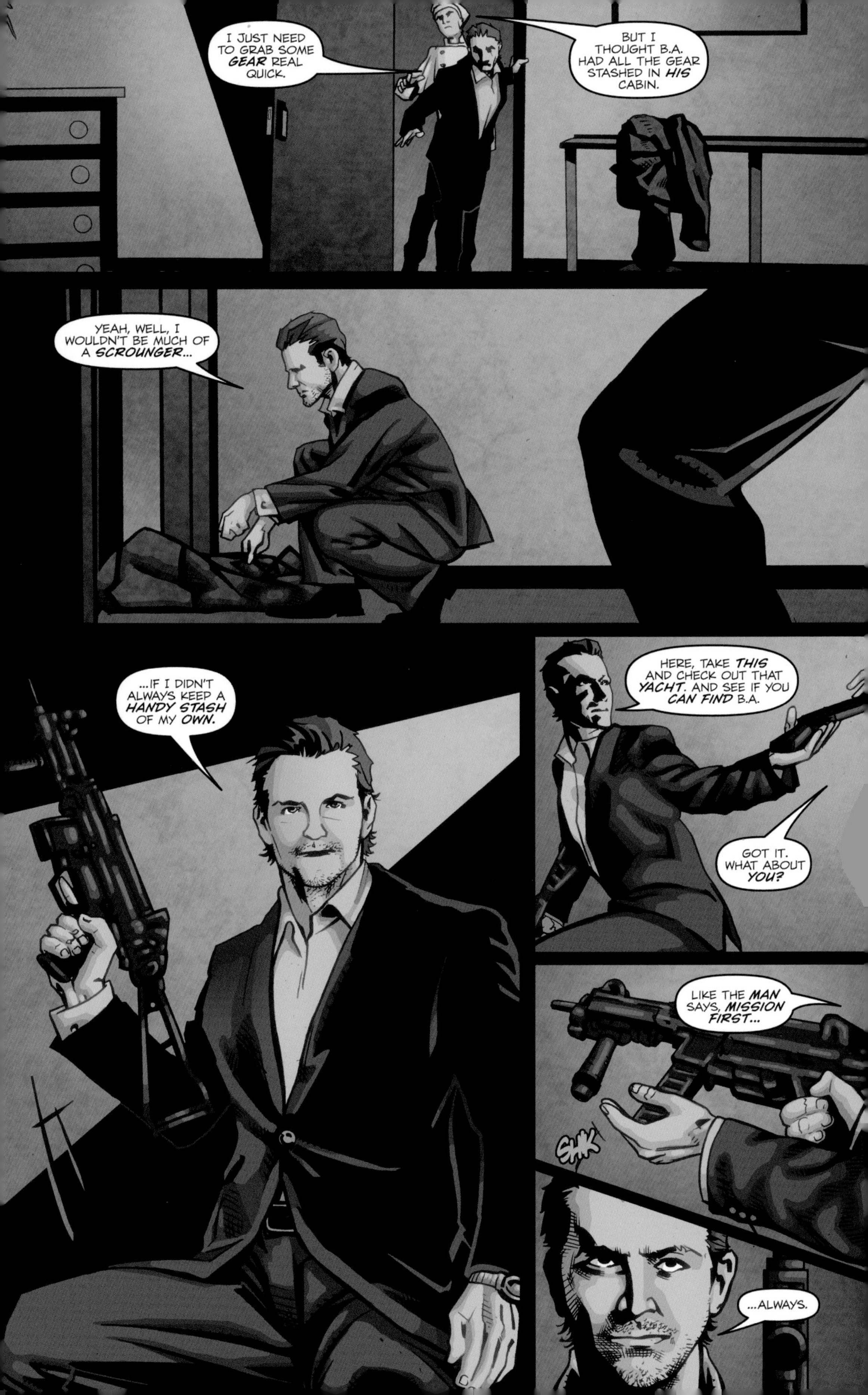
I JUST NEED TO GRAB SOME GEAR REAL QUICK.
BUT I THOUGHT B.A. HAD ALL THE GEAR STASHED IN HIS CABIN.
YEAH, WELL, I WOULDN'T BE MUCH OF A SCROUNGER...
...IF I DIDN'T ALWAYS KEEP A HANDY STASH OF MY OWN.
HERE, TAKE THIS AND CHECK OUT THAT YACHT. AND SEE IF YOU CAN FIND B.A.
GOT IT. WHAT ABOUT YOU?
LIKE THE MAN SAYS, MISSION FIRST...
SHK
...ALWAYS.

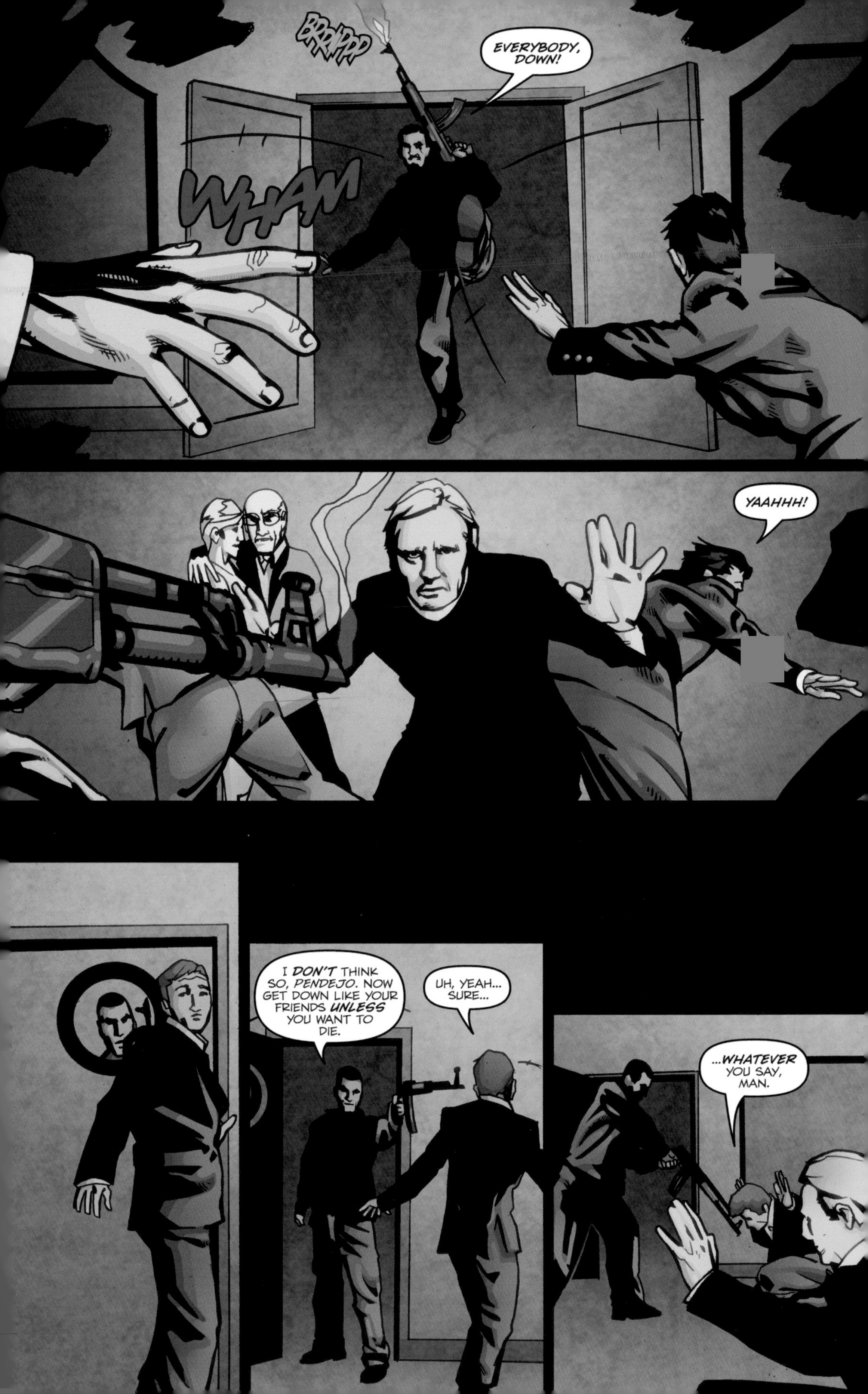
BRRAPPP
EVERYBODY, DOWN!
WHAM
YAAHHH!
I DON'T THINK SO, PENDEJO. NOW GET DOWN LIKE YOUR FRIENDS UNLESS YOU WANT TO DIE.
UH, YEAH... SURE...
...WHATEVER YOU SAY, MAN.

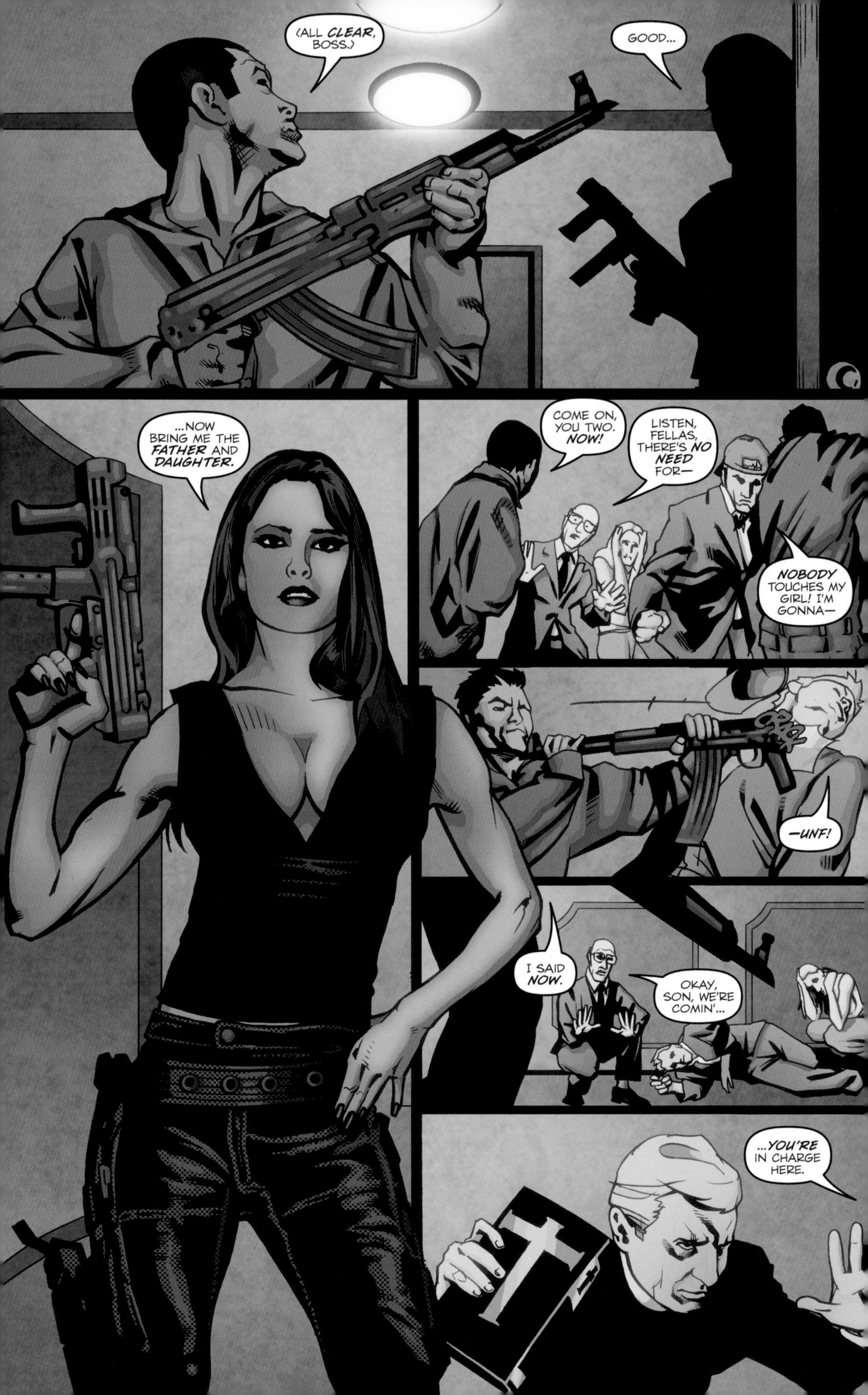

(ALL CLEAR, BOSS.)
GOOD...
...NOW BRING ME THE FATHER AND DAUGHTER.
COME ON, YOU TWO. NOW!
LISTEN, FELLAS, THERE'S NO NEED FOR—
NOBODY TOUCHES MY GIRL! I'M GONNA—
—UNF!
I SAID NOW.
OKAY, SON, WE'RE COMIN'...
...YOU'RE IN CHARGE HERE.

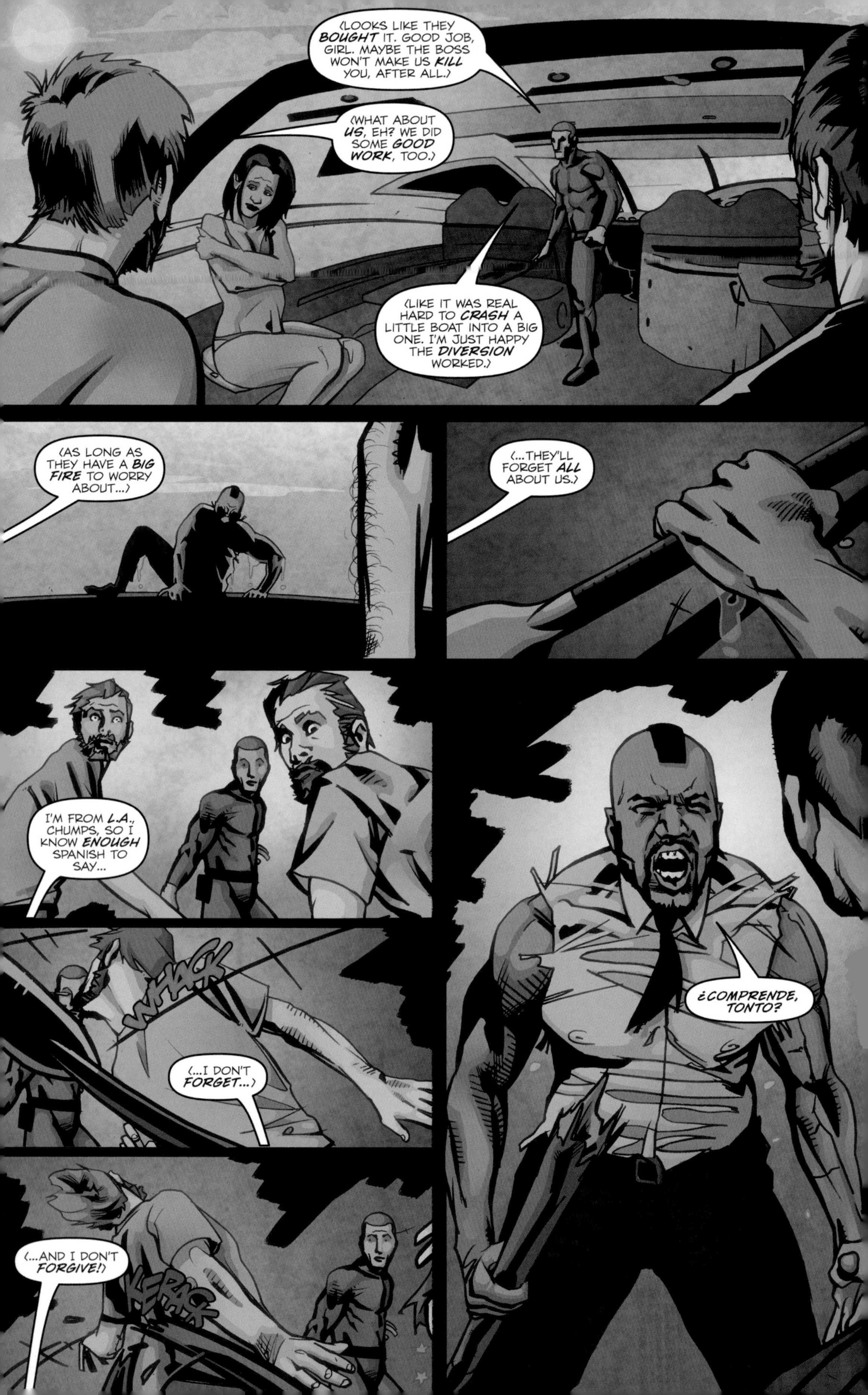

‹LOOKS LIKE THEY BOUGHT IT. GOOD JOB, GIRL. MAYBE THE BOSS WON'T MAKE US KILL YOU, AFTER ALL.›
‹WHAT ABOUT US, EH? WE DID SOME GOOD WORK, TOO.›
‹LIKE IT WAS REAL HARD TO CRASH A LITTLE BOAT INTO A BIG ONE. I'M JUST HAPPY THE DIVERSION WORKED.›
‹AS LONG AS THEY HAVE A BIG FIRE TO WORRY ABOUT...›
‹...THEY'LL FORGET ALL ABOUT US.›
I'M FROM L.A., CHUMPS, SO I KNOW ENOUGH SPANISH TO SAY...
WHACK
‹...I DON'T FORGET...›
‹...AND I DON'T FORGIVE!›
¿COMPRENDE, TONTO?

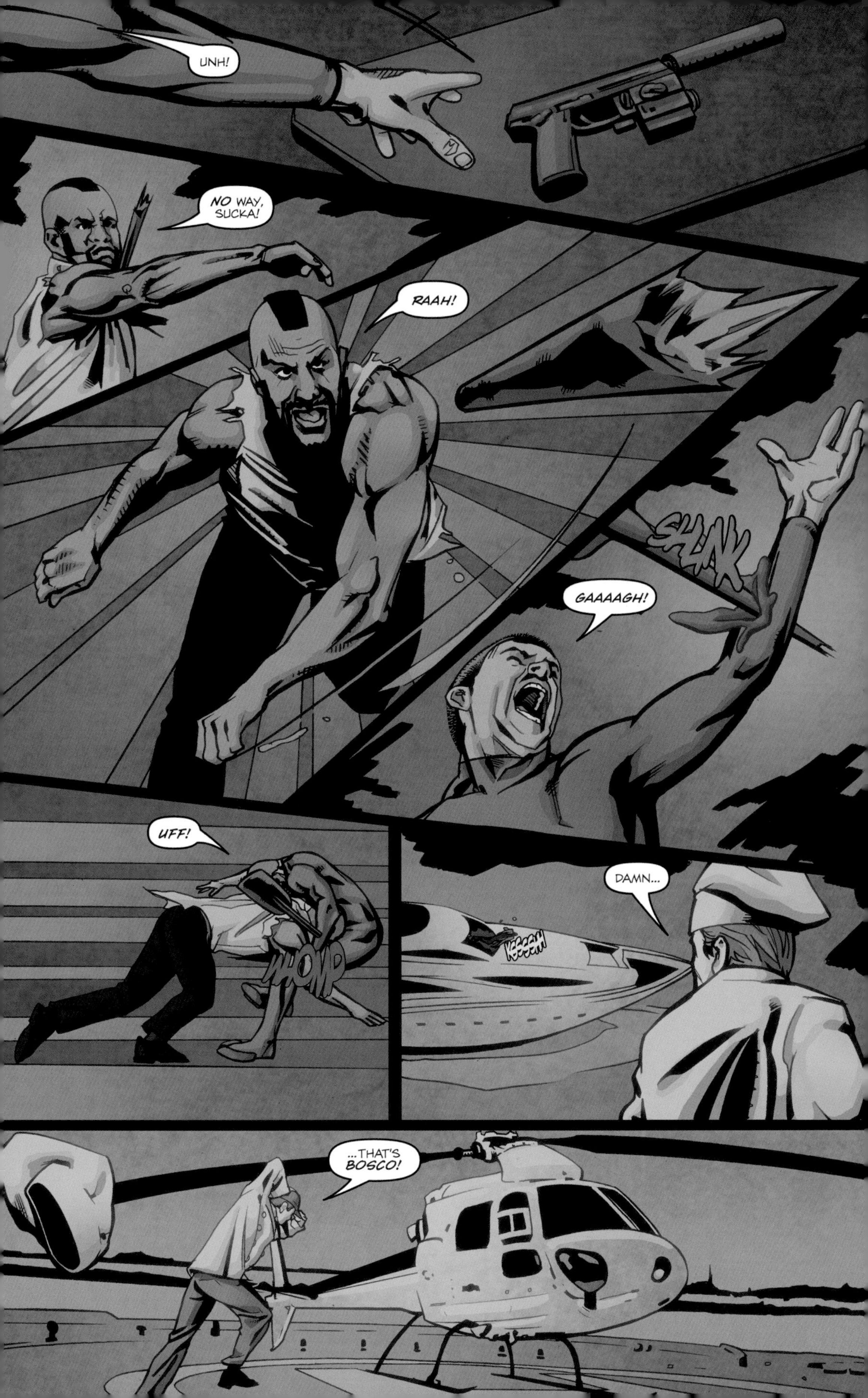
UNH!
NO WAY, SUCKA!
RAAH!
SHUNK
GAAAAGH!
UFF!
WHOMP
DAMN...
KSSSSH
...THAT'S BOSCO!

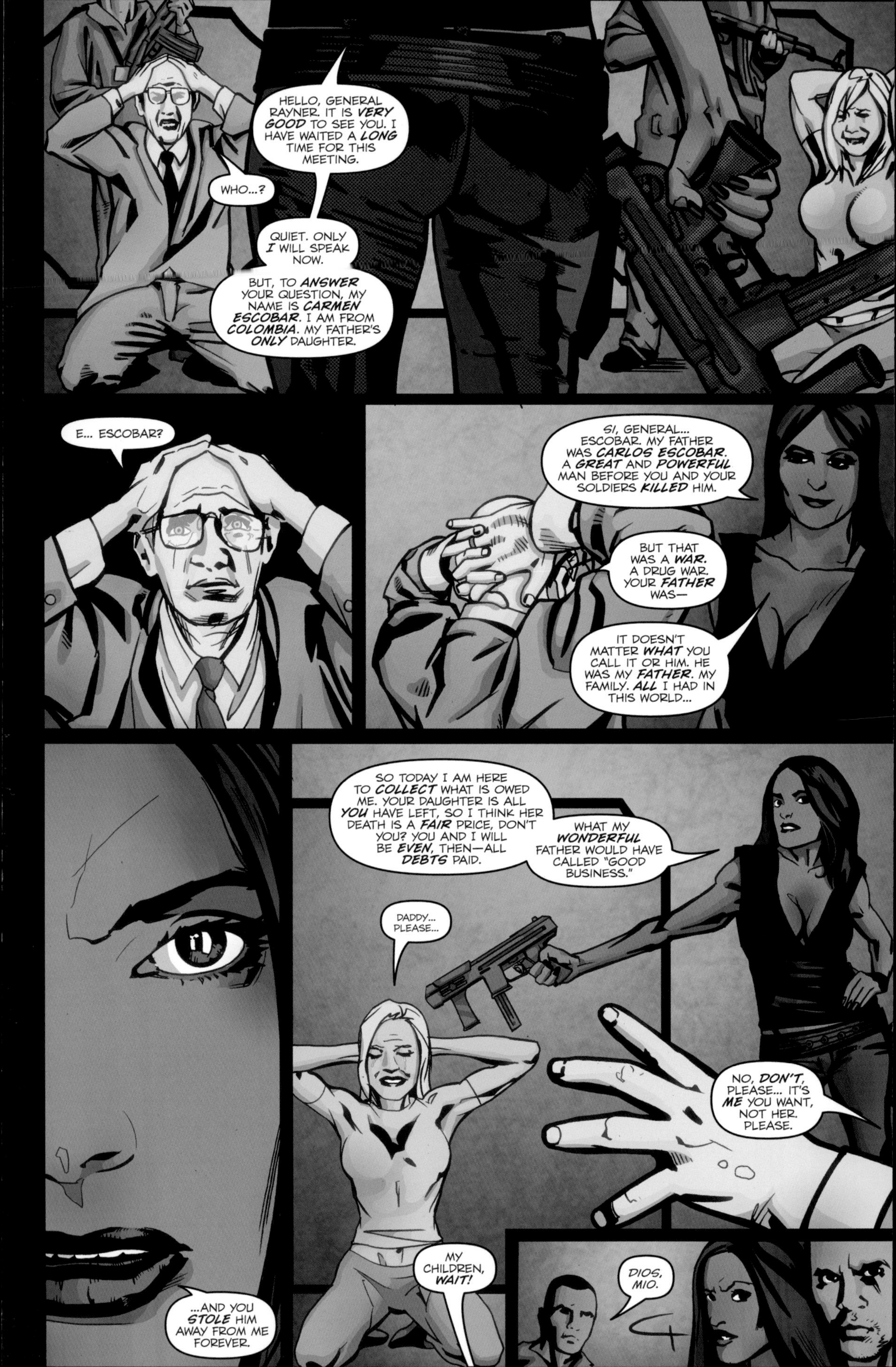
HELLO, GENERAL RAYNER. IT IS VERY GOOD TO SEE YOU. I HAVE WAITED A LONG TIME FOR THIS MEETING.
WHO...?
QUIET. ONLY I WILL SPEAK NOW.
BUT, TO ANSWER YOUR QUESTION, MY NAME IS CARMEN ESCOBAR. I AM FROM COLOMBIA. MY FATHER'S ONLY DAUGHTER.
E... ESCOBAR?
SÍ, GENERAL... ESCOBAR. MY FATHER WAS CARLOS ESCOBAR. A GREAT AND POWERFUL MAN BEFORE YOU AND YOUR SOLDIERS KILLED HIM.
BUT THAT WAS A WAR. A DRUG WAR. YOUR FATHER WAS—
IT DOESN'T MATTER WHAT YOU CALL IT OR HIM. HE WAS MY FATHER. MY FAMILY. ALL I HAD IN THIS WORLD...
...AND YOU STOLE HIM AWAY FROM ME FOREVER.
SO TODAY I AM HERE TO COLLECT WHAT IS OWED ME. YOUR DAUGHTER IS ALL YOU HAVE LEFT, SO I THINK HER DEATH IS A FAIR PRICE, DON'T YOU? YOU AND I WILL BE EVEN, THEN—ALL DEBTS PAID.
WHAT MY WONDERFUL FATHER WOULD HAVE CALLED "GOOD BUSINESS."
DADDY... PLEASE...
NO, DON'T, PLEASE... IT'S ME YOU WANT, NOT HER. PLEASE.
MY CHILDREN, WAIT!
DIOS, MIO.

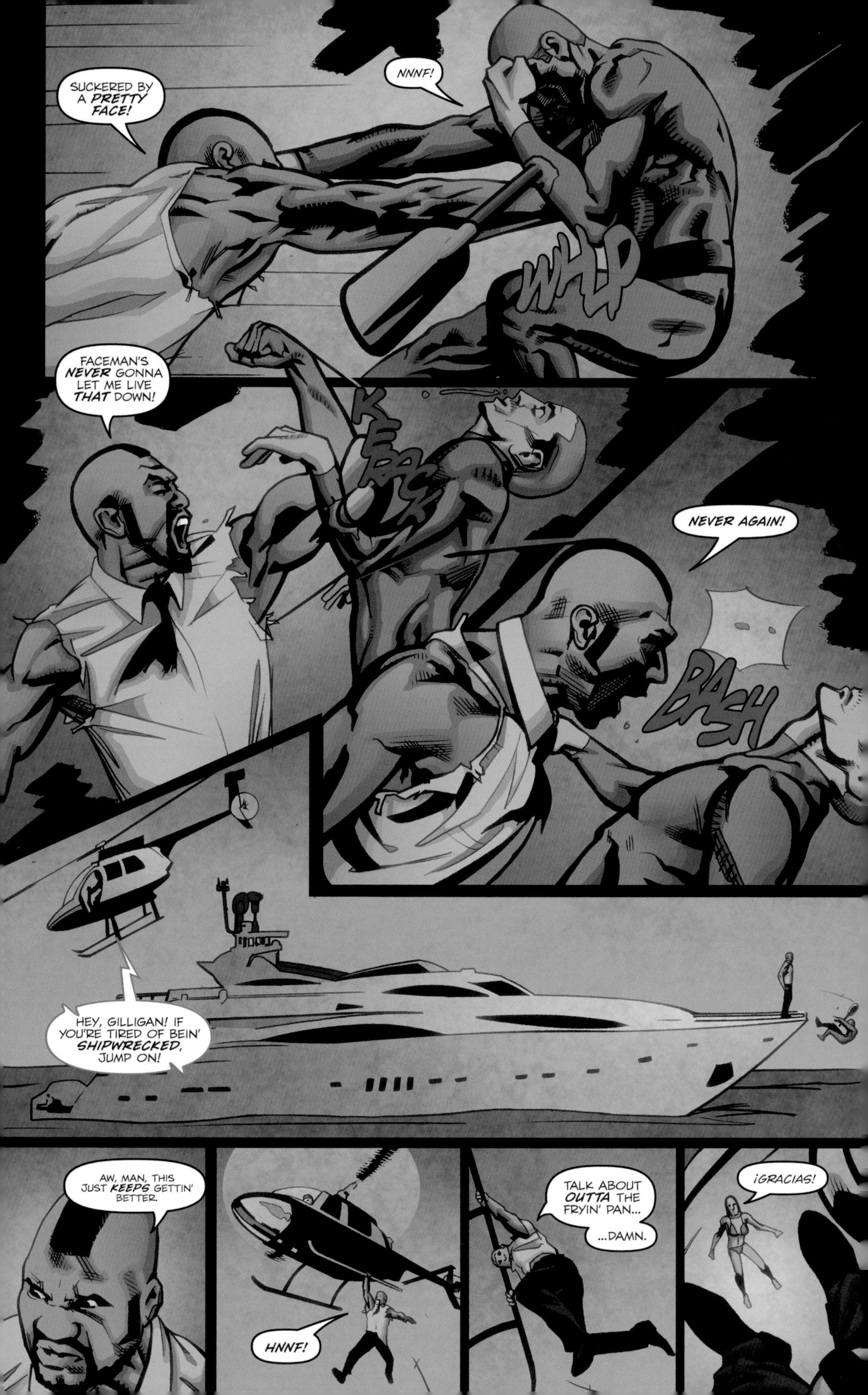
SUCKERED BY A PRETTY FACE!
NNNF!
WHLP
FACEMAN'S NEVER GONNA LET ME LIVE THAT DOWN!
KERACK
NEVER AGAIN!
BASH
HEY, GILLIGAN! IF YOU'RE TIRED OF BEIN' SHIPWRECKED, JUMP ON!
AW, MAN, THIS JUST KEEPS GETTIN' BETTER.
HNNF!
TALK ABOUT OUTTA THE FRYIN' PAN...
...DAMN.
¡GRACIAS!

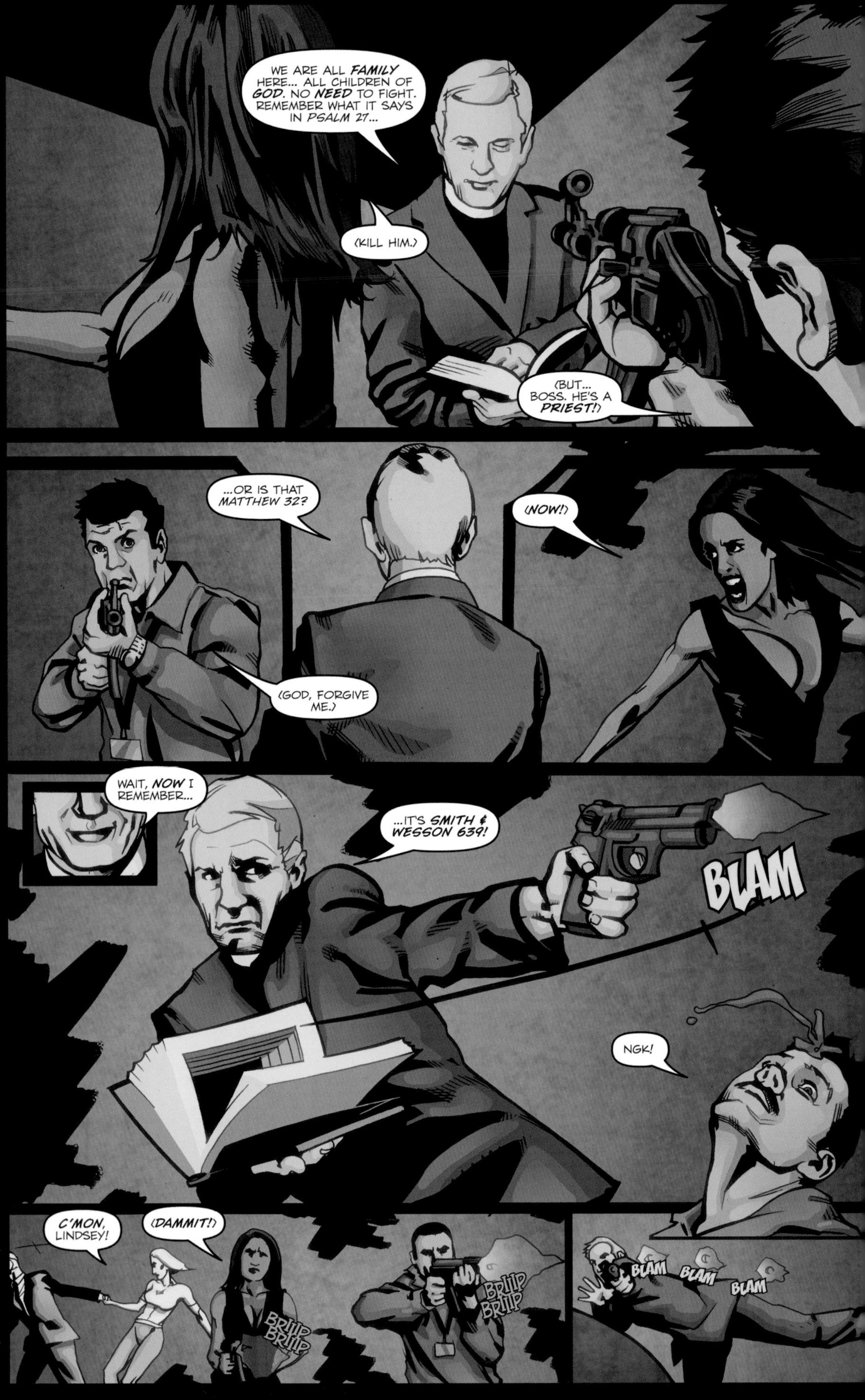
WE ARE ALL FAMILY HERE... ALL CHILDREN OF GOD. NO NEED TO FIGHT. REMEMBER WHAT IT SAYS IN PSALM 27...
(KILL HIM.)
(BUT... BOSS. HE'S A PRIEST!)
...OR IS THAT MATTHEW 32?
(NOW!)
(GOD, FORGIVE ME.)
WAIT, NOW I REMEMBER...
...IT'S SMITH & WESSON 639!
BLAM
NGK!
C'MON, LINDSEY!
(DAMMIT!)
BRIIIP BRIIIP
BRIIIP BRIIIP
BLAM
BLAM
BLAM

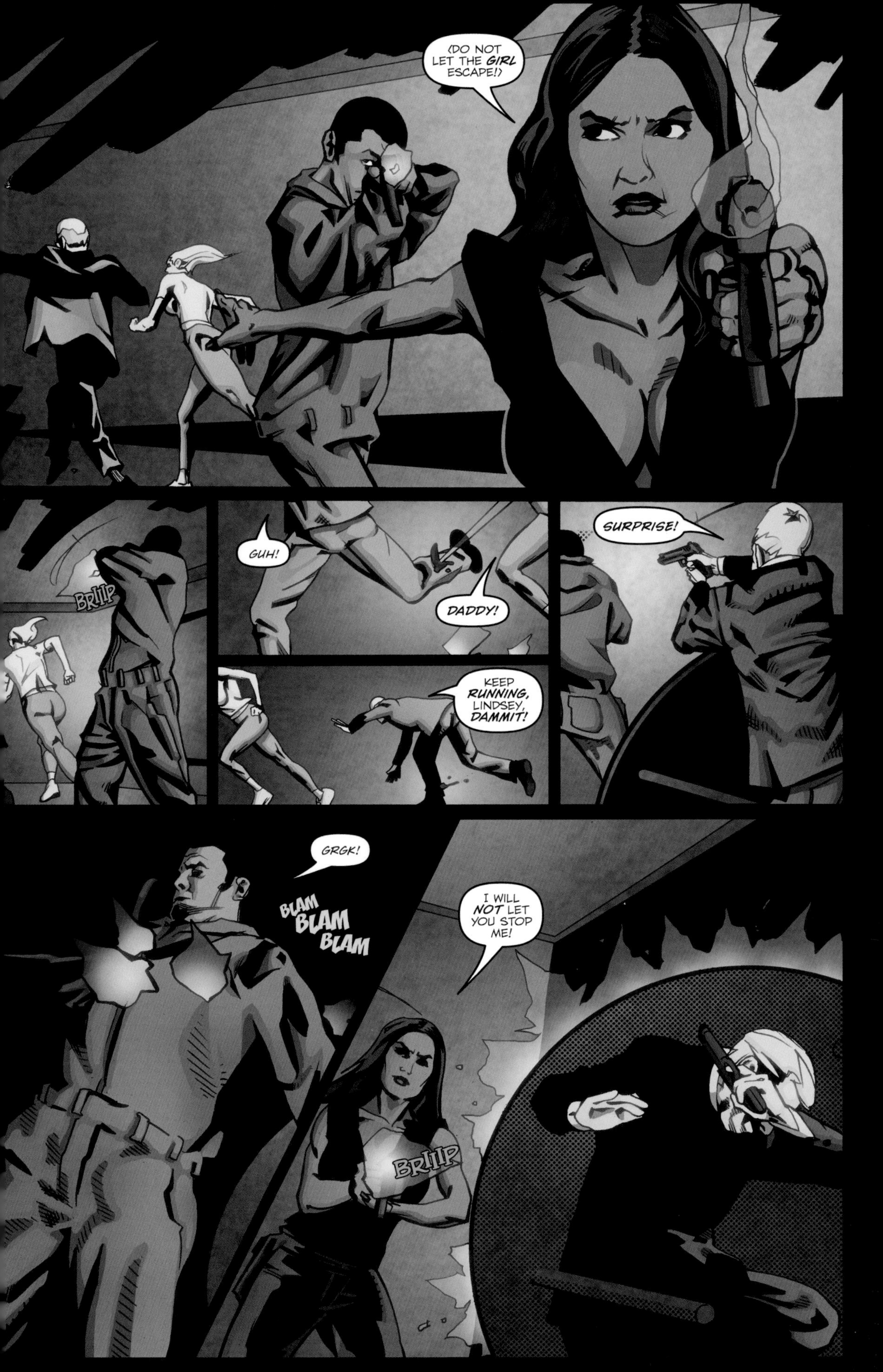
(DO NOT LET THE GIRL ESCAPE!)
BRIIP
GUH!
DADDY!
KEEP RUNNING, LINDSEY, DAMMIT!
SURPRISE!
GRGK!
BLAM BLAM BLAM
I WILL NOT LET YOU STOP ME!
BRIIP

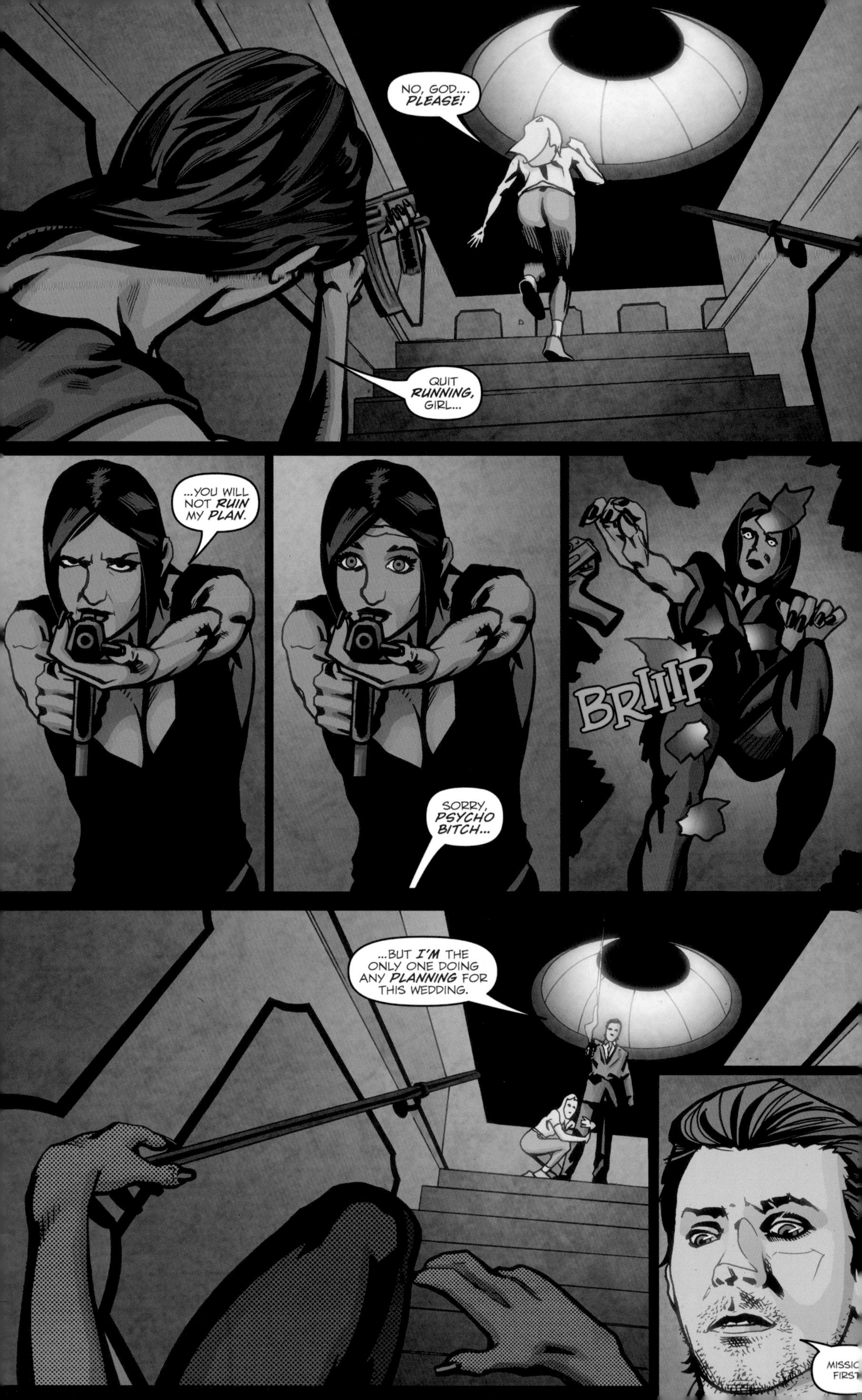
NO, GOD.... PLEASE!
QUIT RUNNING, GIRL...
...YOU WILL NOT RUIN MY PLAN.
SORRY, PSYCHO BITCH...
BRIIIP
...BUT I'M THE ONLY ONE DOING ANY PLANNING FOR THIS WEDDING.
MISSIC FIRST

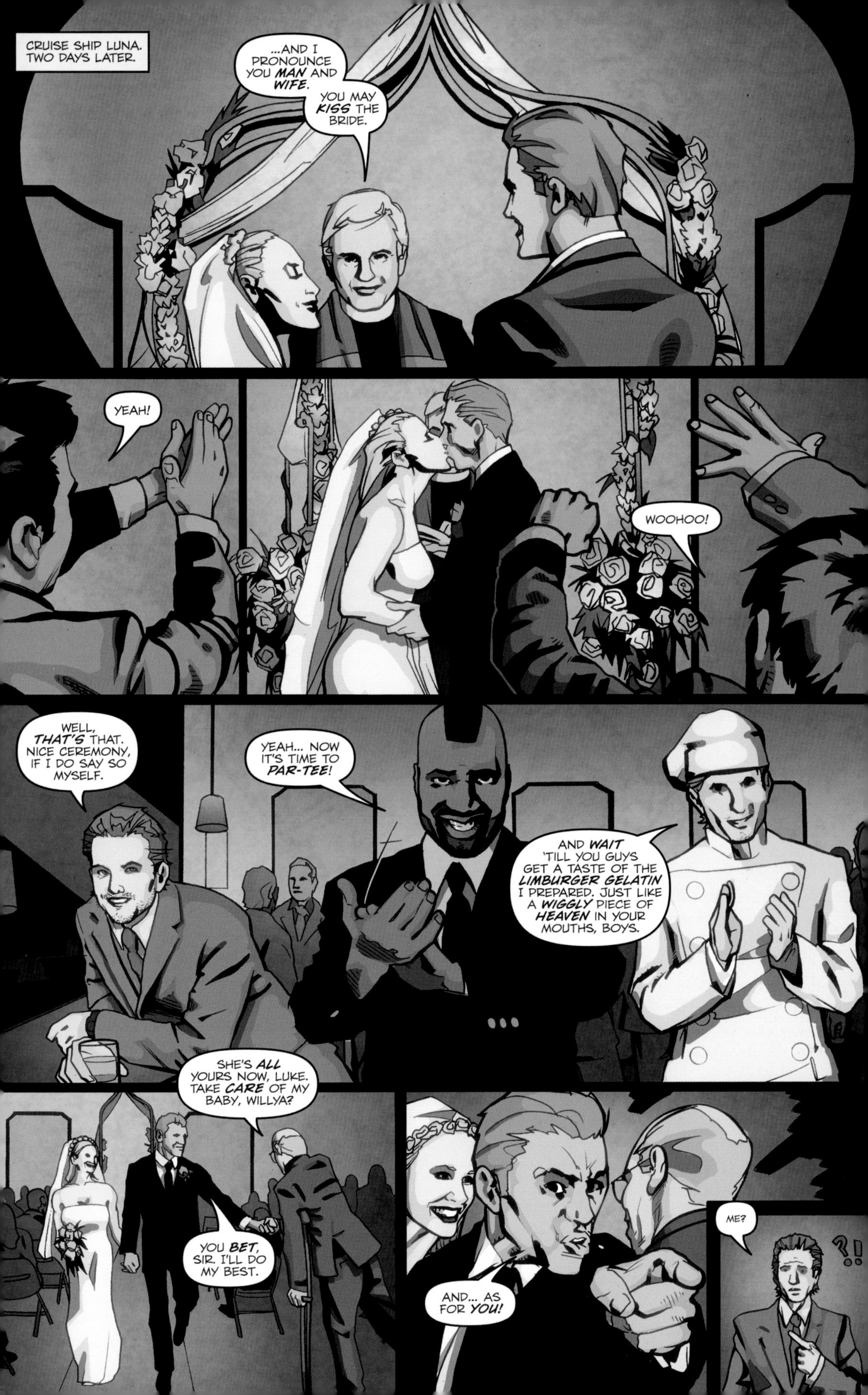
CRUISE SHIP LUNA. TWO DAYS LATER.
...AND I PRONOUNCE YOU MAN AND WIFE.
YOU MAY KISS THE BRIDE.
YEAH!
WOOHOO!
WELL, THAT'S THAT. NICE CEREMONY, IF I DO SAY SO MYSELF.
YEAH... NOW IT'S TIME TO PAR-TEE!
AND WAIT 'TILL YOU GUYS GET A TASTE OF THE LIMBURGER GELATIN I PREPARED. JUST LIKE A WIGGLY PIECE OF HEAVEN IN YOUR MOUTHS, BOYS.
SHE'S ALL YOURS NOW, LUKE. TAKE CARE OF MY BABY, WILLYA?
YOU BET, SIR. I'LL DO MY BEST.
AND... AS FOR YOU!
ME?
?!

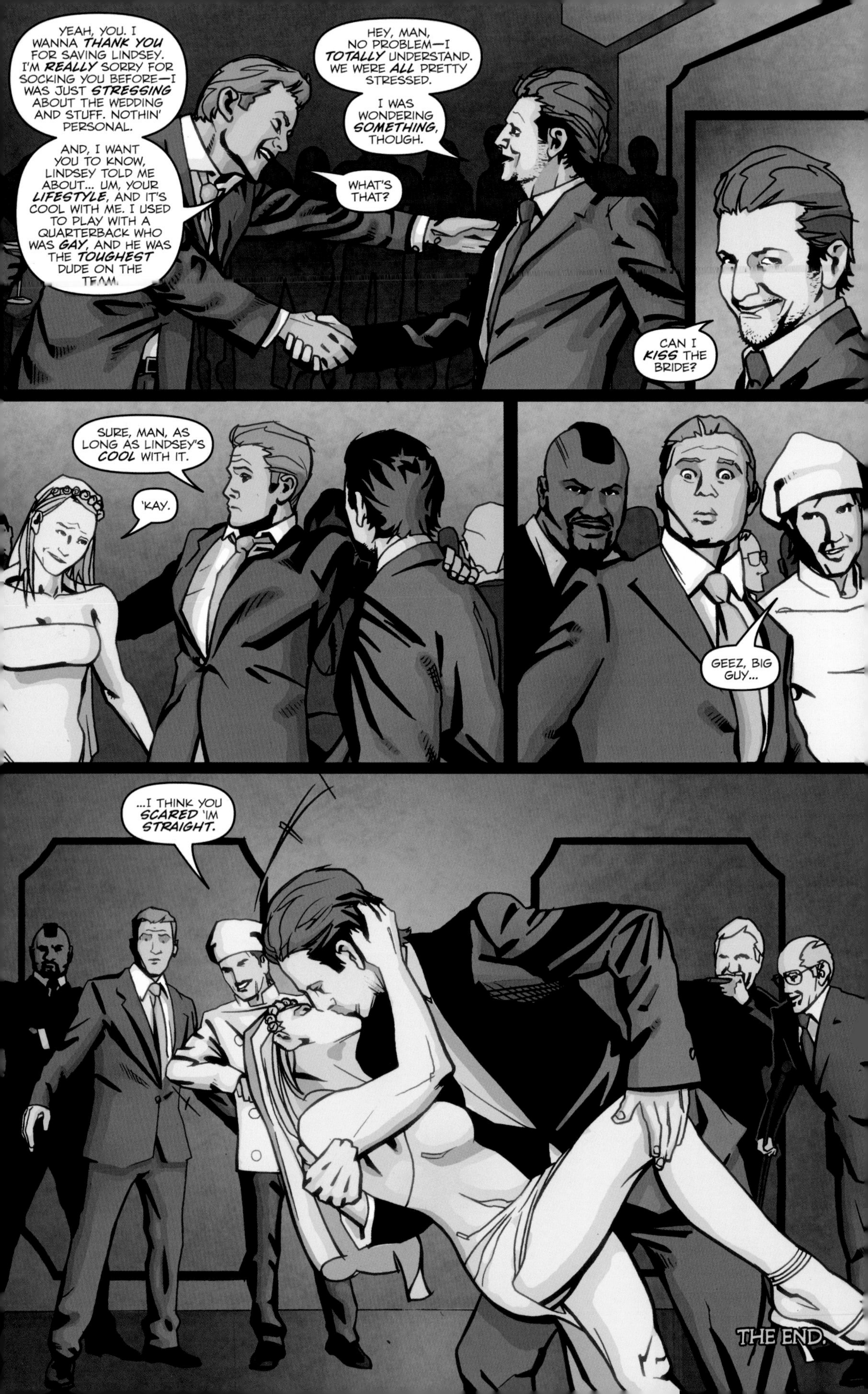
YEAH, YOU. I WANNA THANK YOU FOR SAVING LINDSEY. I'M REALLY SORRY FOR SOCKING YOU BEFORE—I WAS JUST STRESSING ABOUT THE WEDDING AND STUFF. NOTHIN' PERSONAL.
AND, I WANT YOU TO KNOW, LINDSEY TOLD ME ABOUT... UM, YOUR LIFESTYLE, AND IT'S COOL WITH ME. I USED TO PLAY WITH A QUARTERBACK WHO WAS GAY, AND HE WAS THE TOUGHEST DUDE ON THE TEAM.
HEY, MAN, NO PROBLEM—I TOTALLY UNDERSTAND. WE WERE ALL PRETTY STRESSED.
I WAS WONDERING SOMETHING, THOUGH.
WHAT'S THAT?
CAN I KISS THE BRIDE?
SURE, MAN, AS LONG AS LINDSEY'S COOL WITH IT.
'KAY.
GEEZ, BIG GUY...
...I THINK YOU SCARED 'IM STRAIGHT.
THE END.

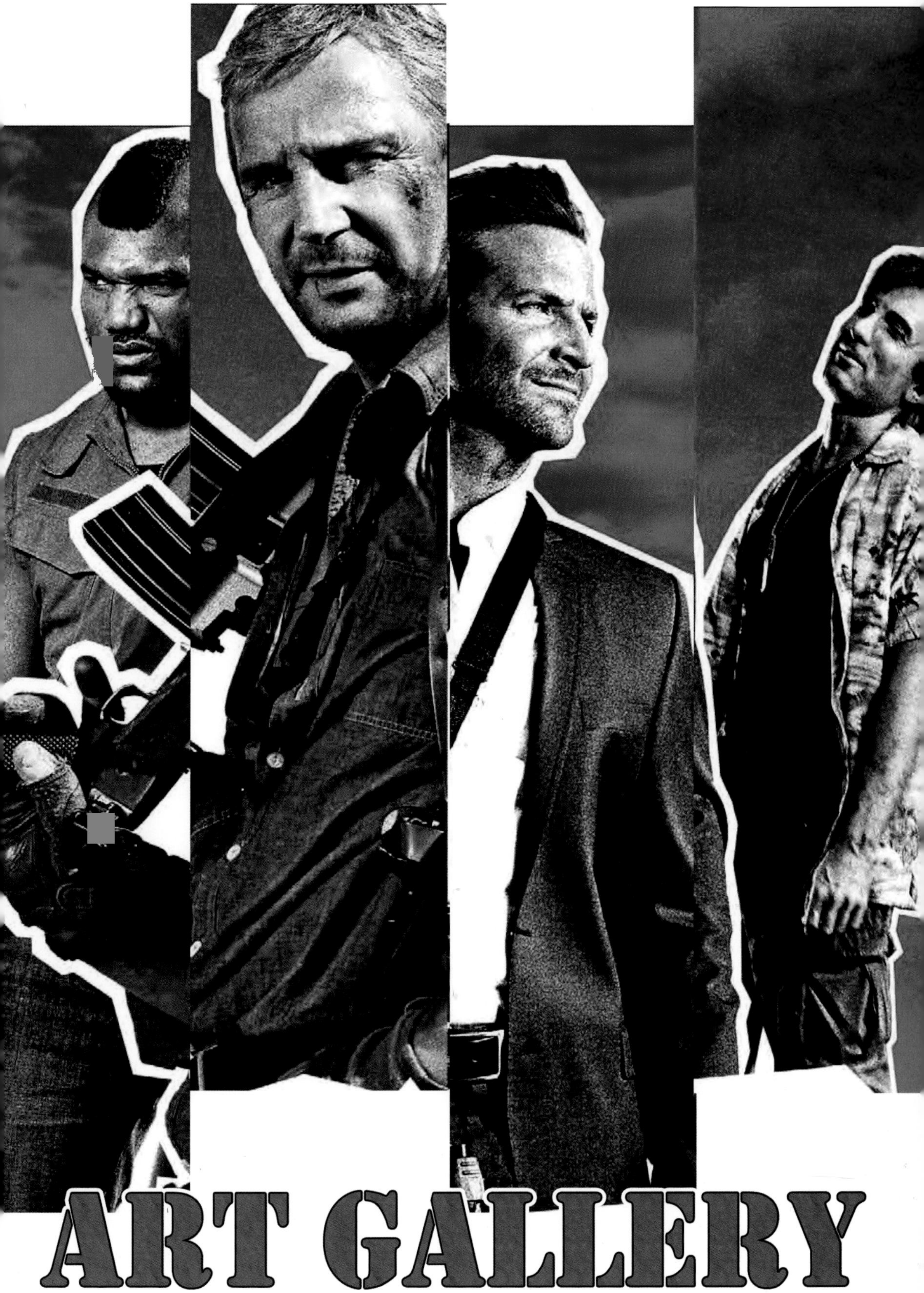

# ART GALLERY

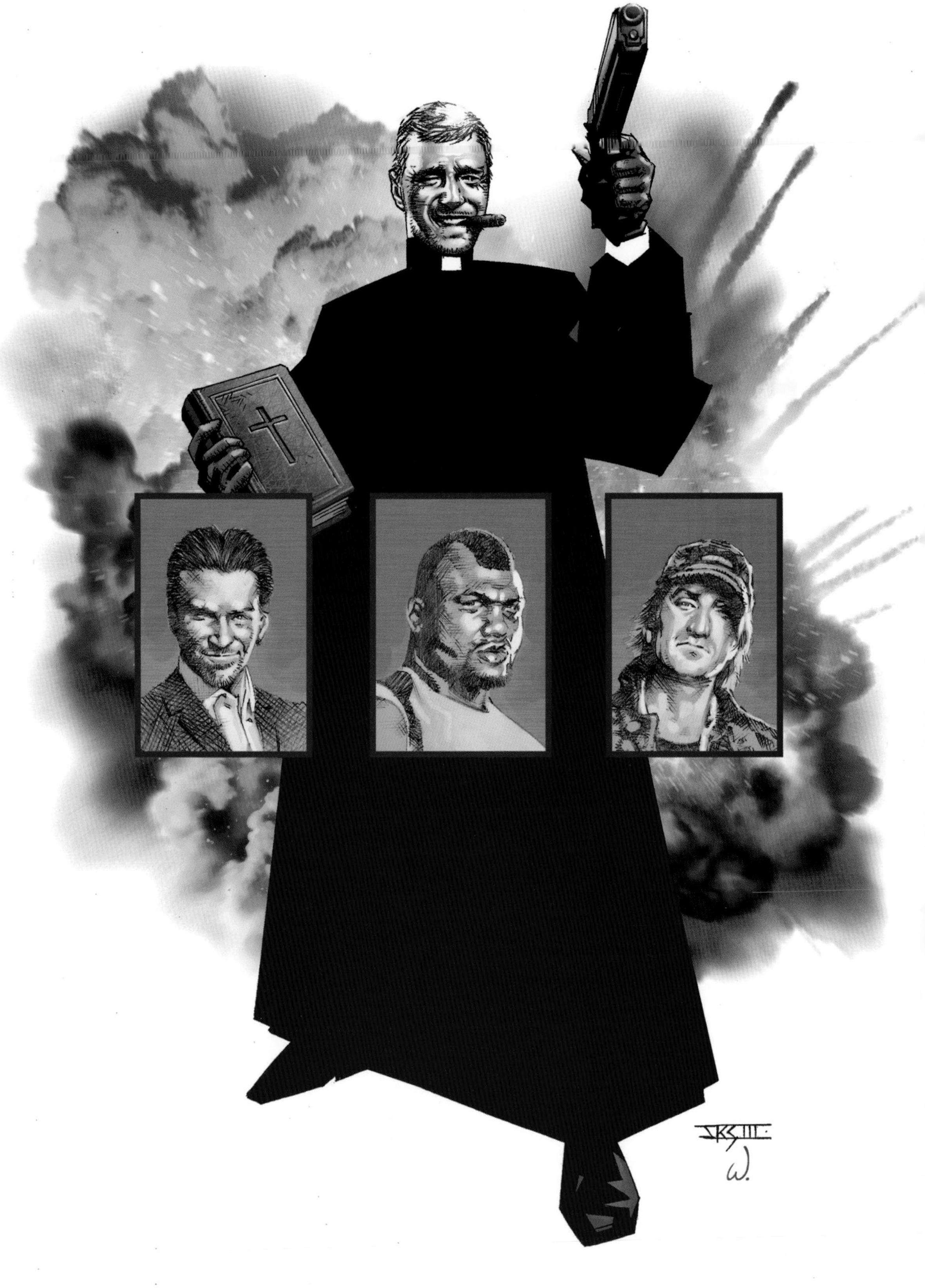

Art by John K. Snyder III ~ Colors by Jason Wright

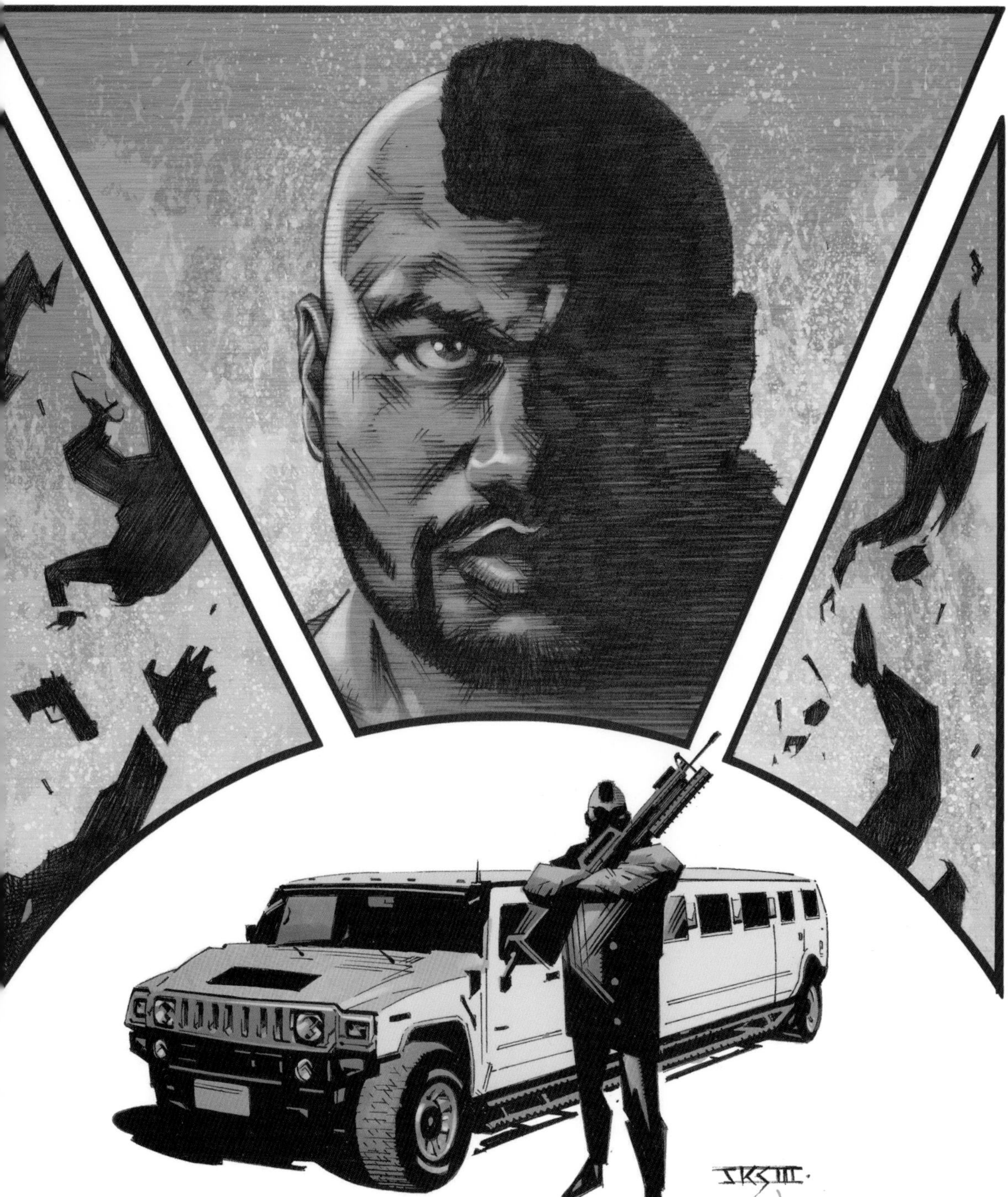

Art by John K. Snyder III ~ Colors by Jason Wright

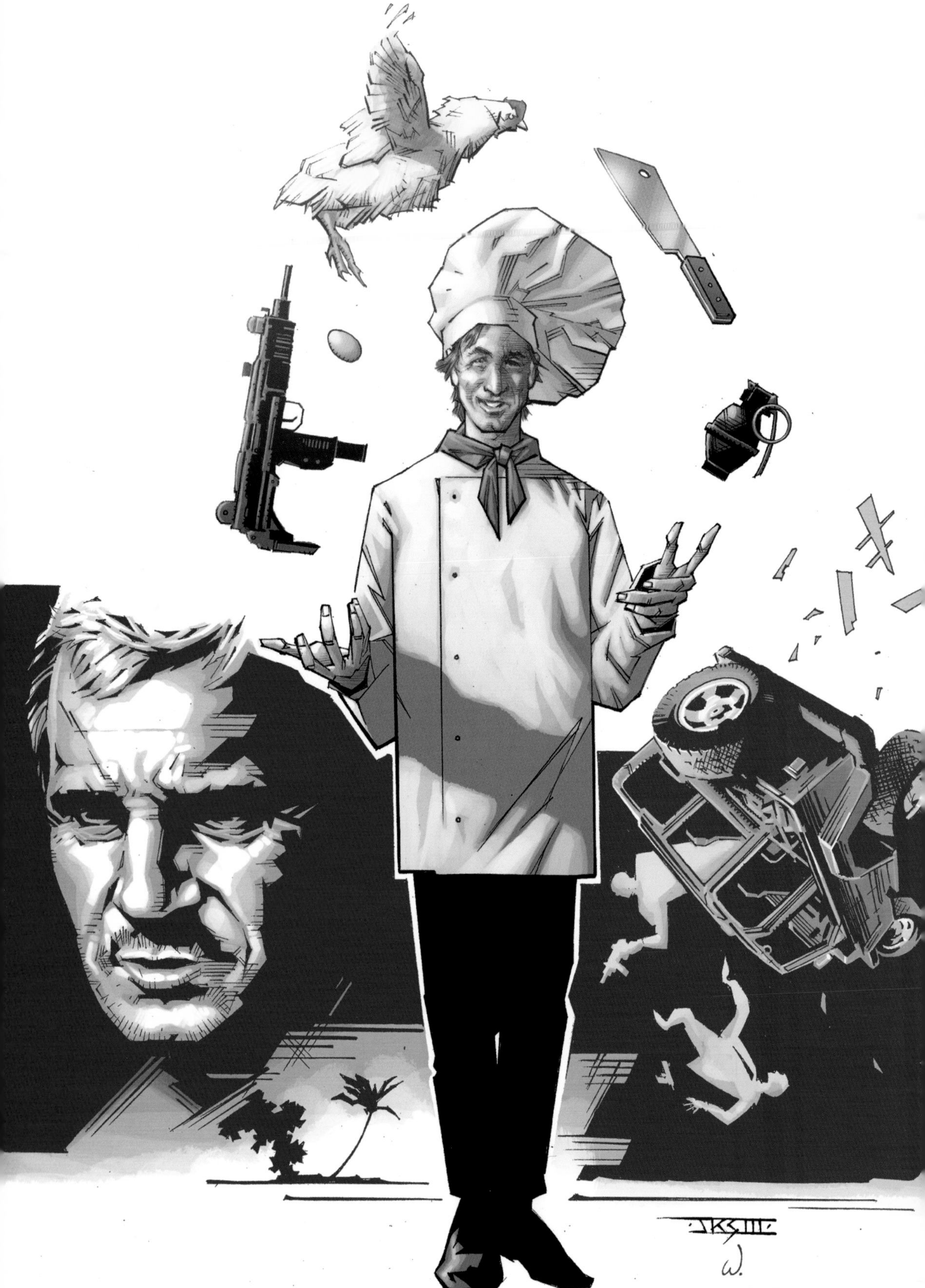
JKS III
W.

Art by John K. Snyder III ~ Colors by Jason Wright

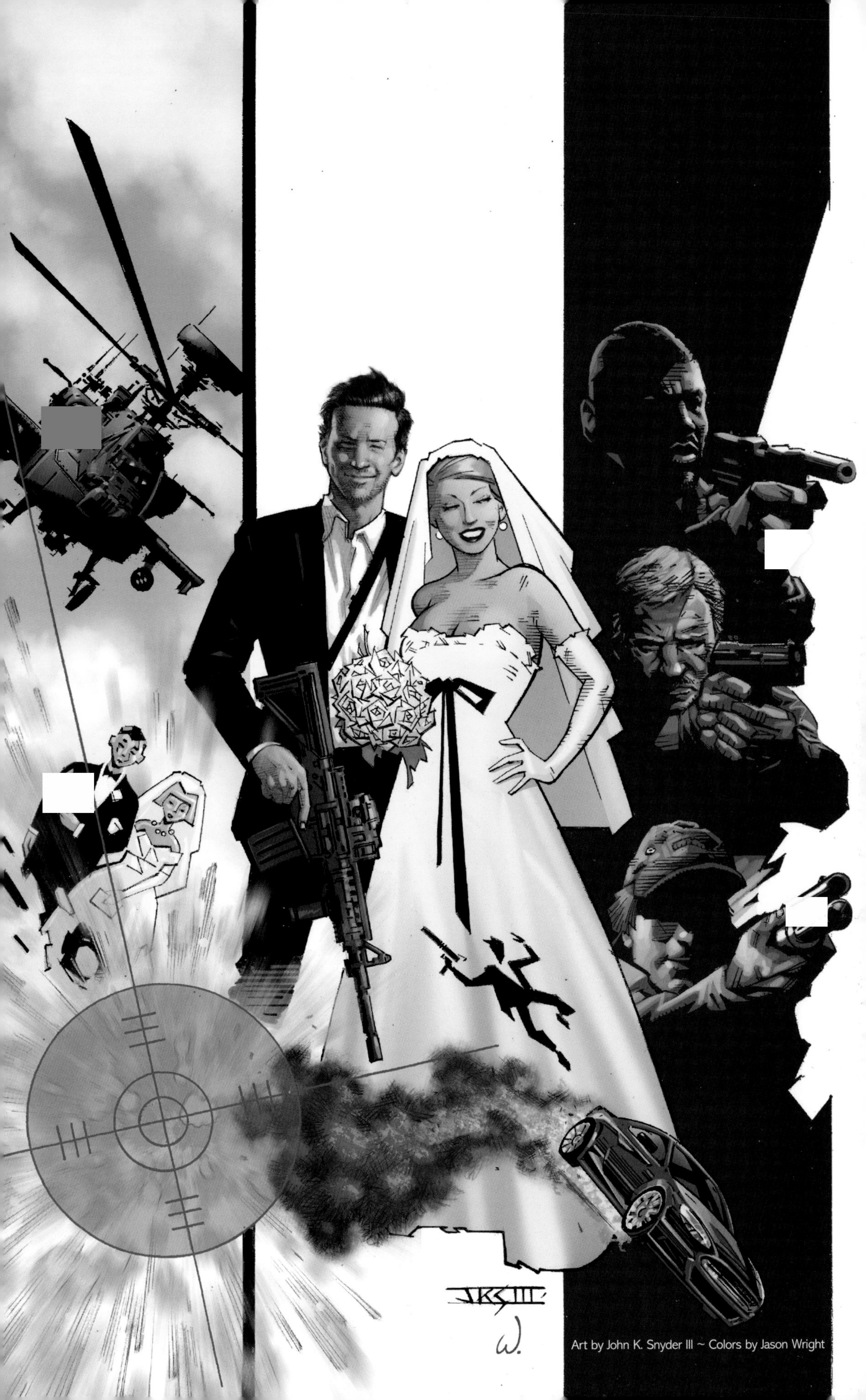

Art by John K. Snyder III ~ Colors by Jason Wright

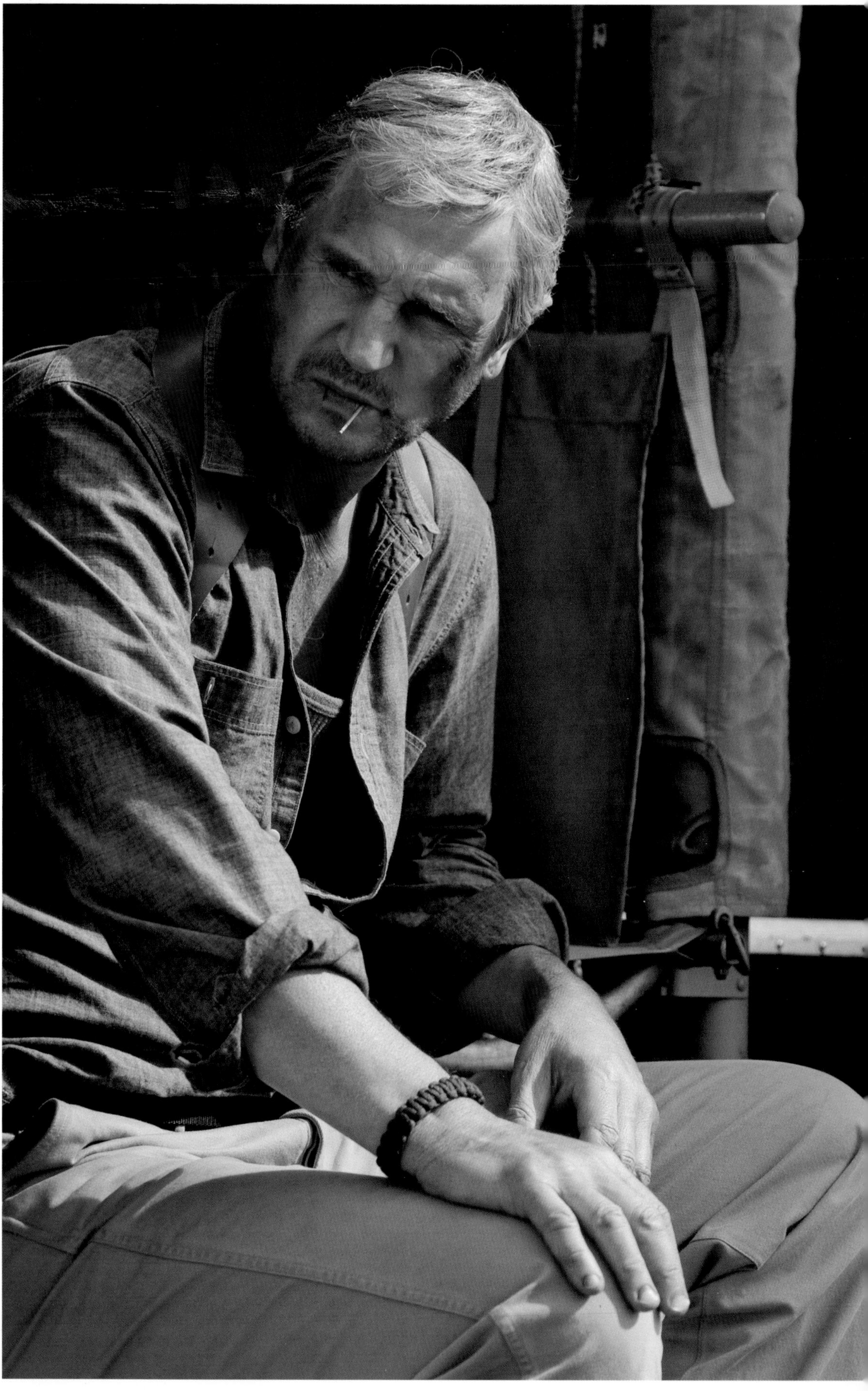

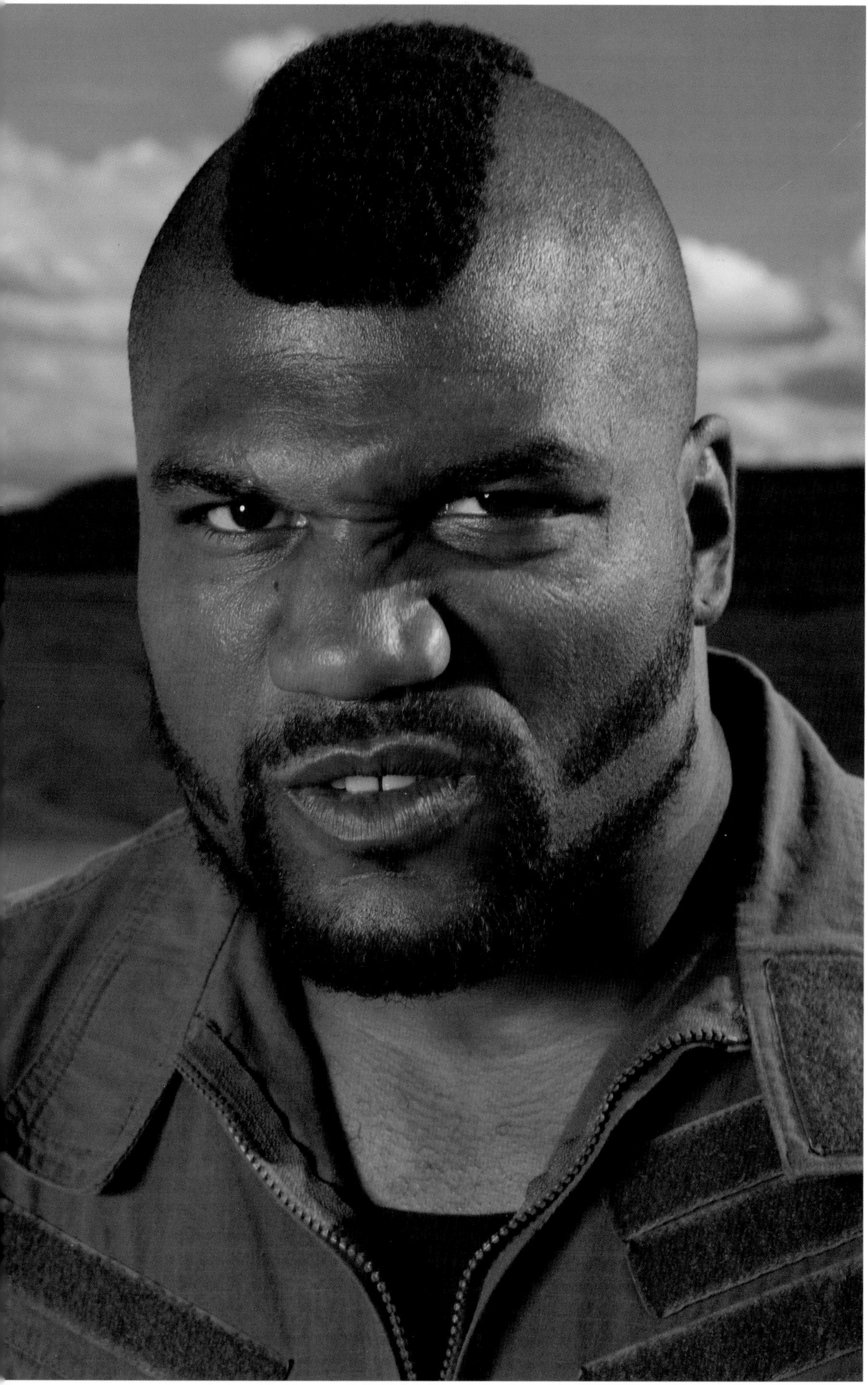

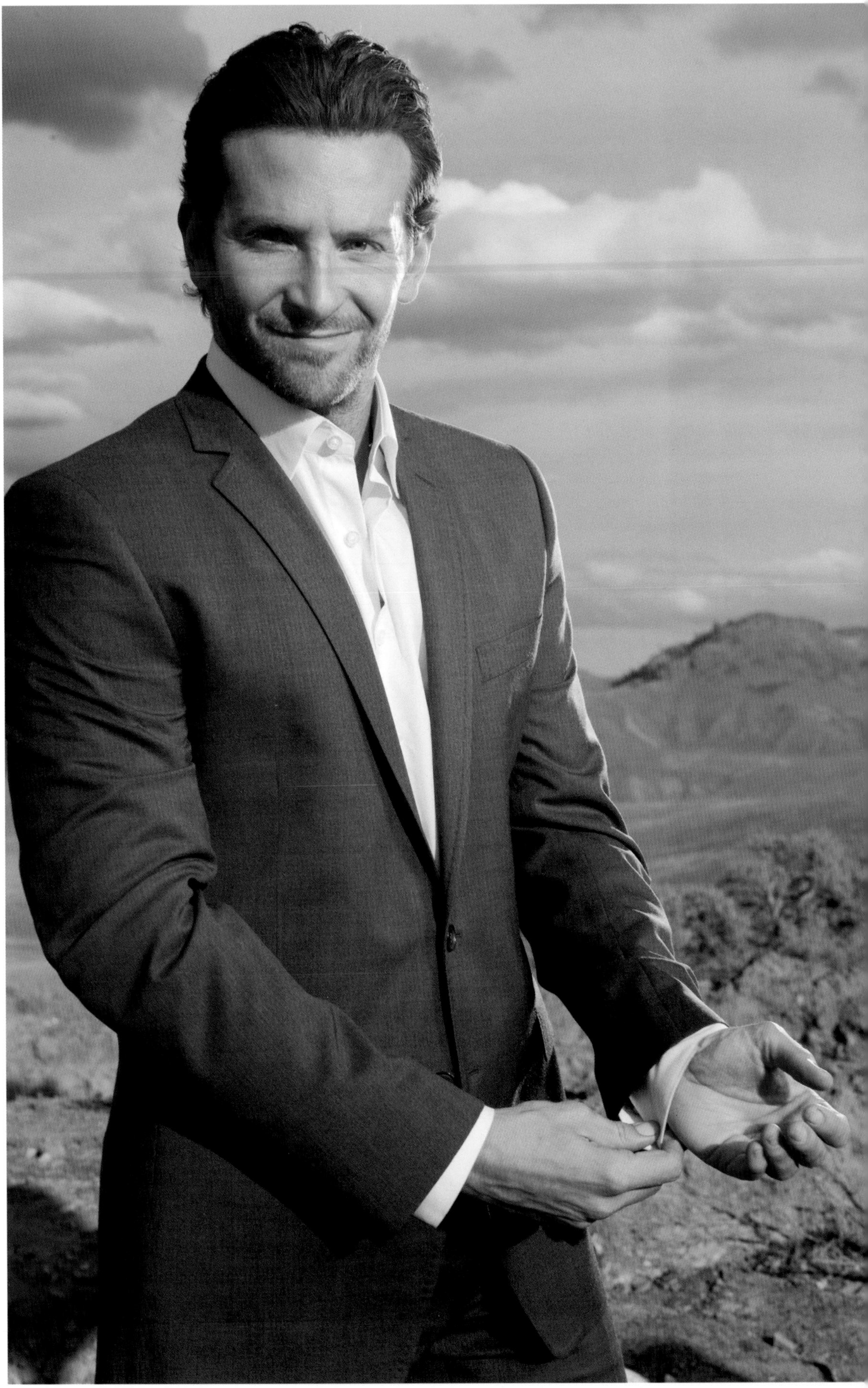

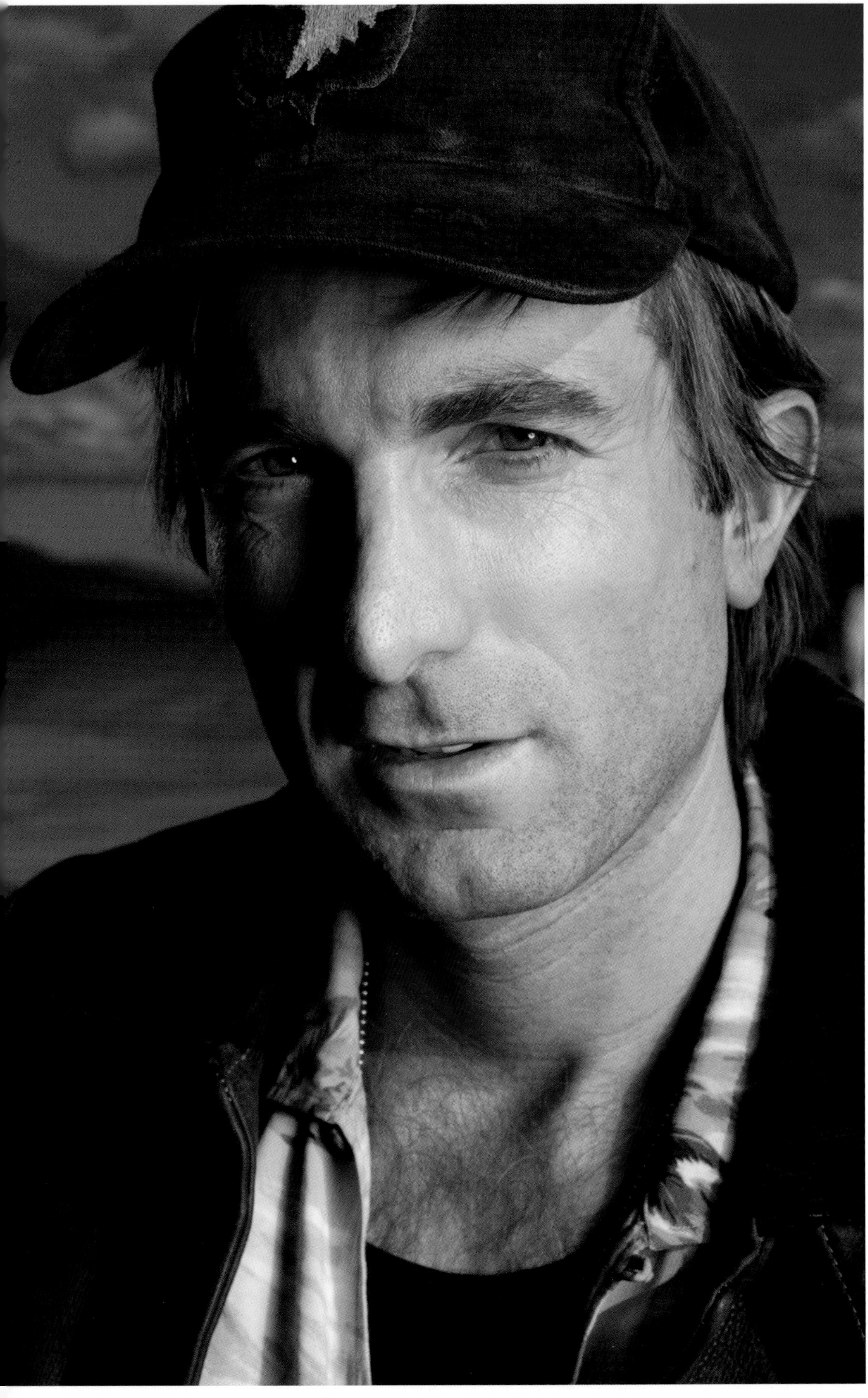

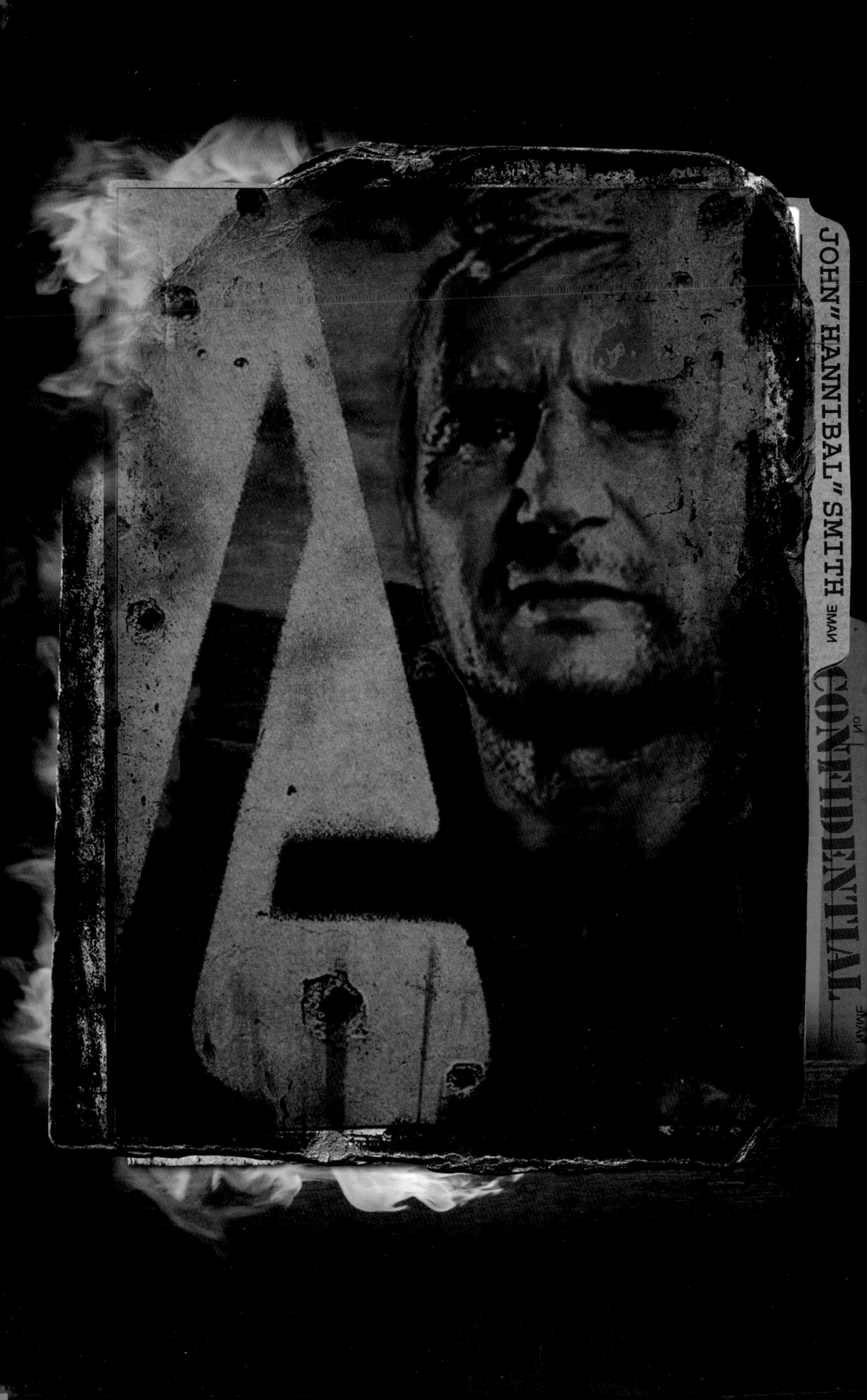
JOHN"HANNIBAL"SMITH
CONFIDENTIAL

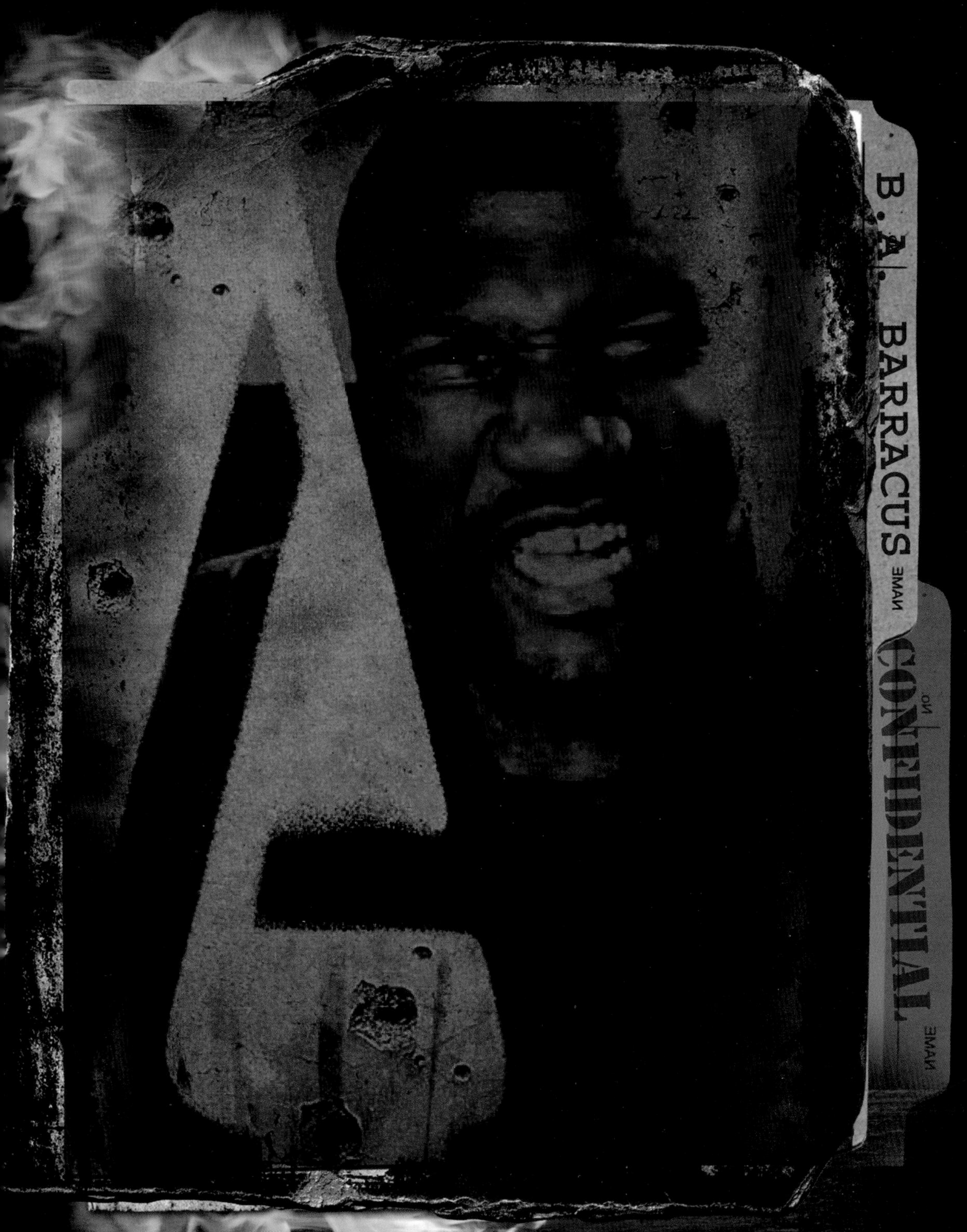
B.A. BARRACUS
NAME
CONFIDENTIAL
NO.
NAME

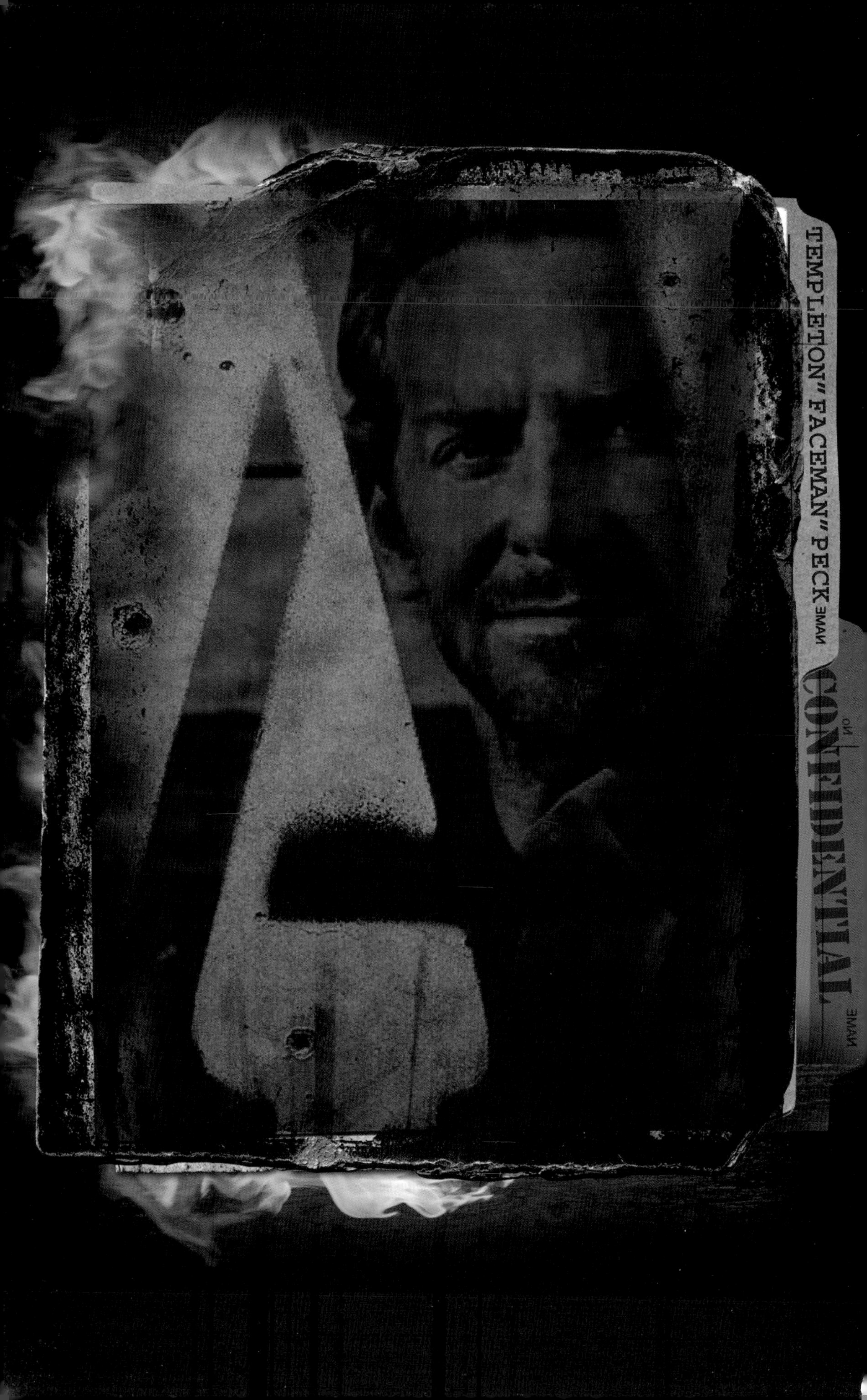

TEMPLETON "FACEMAN" PECK
CONFIDENTIAL

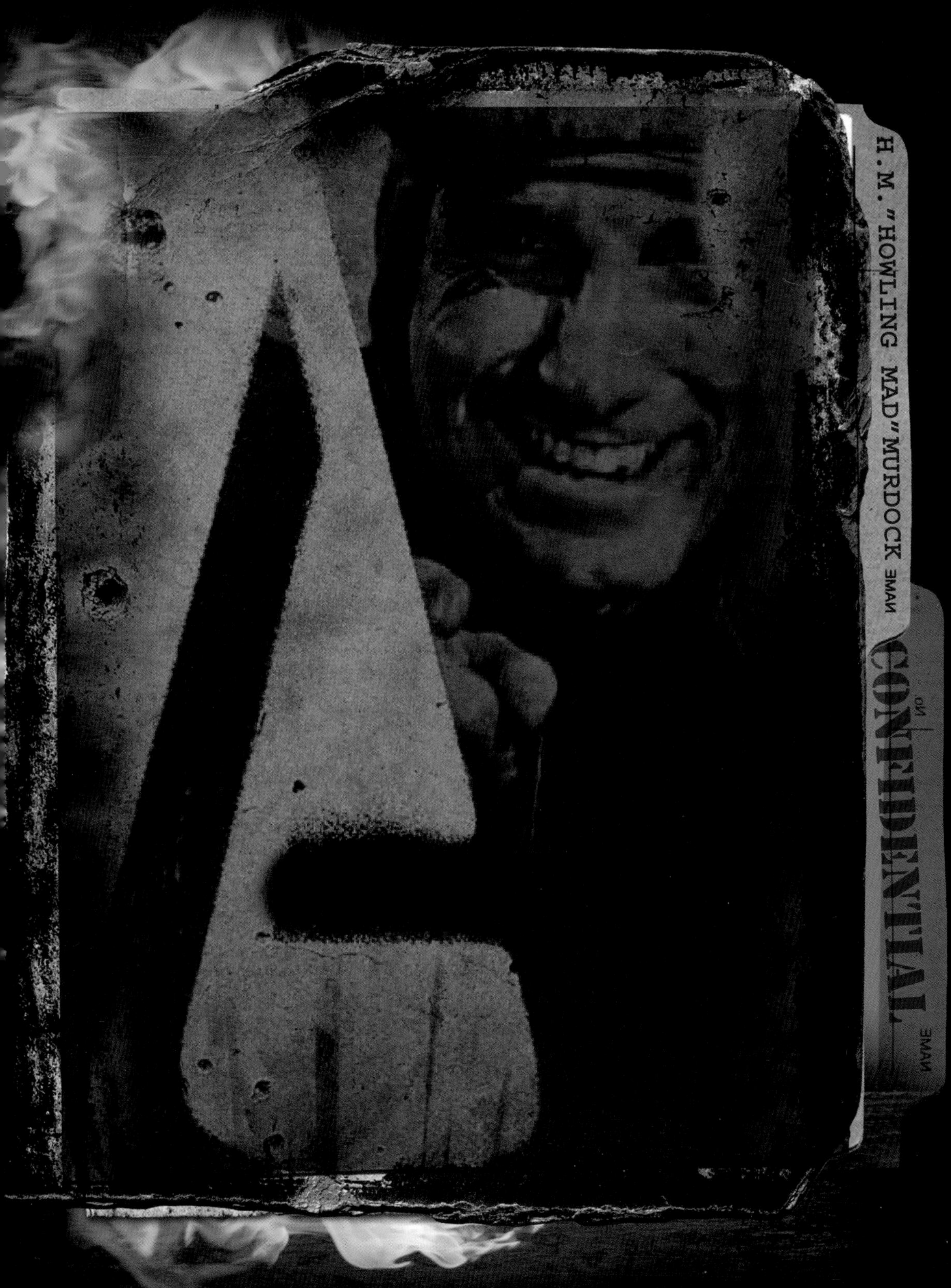
H.M. "HOWLING MAD"MURDOCK
NAME
NO
CONFIDENTIAL
NAME

# THE A-TEAM
## SHOTGUN WEDDING

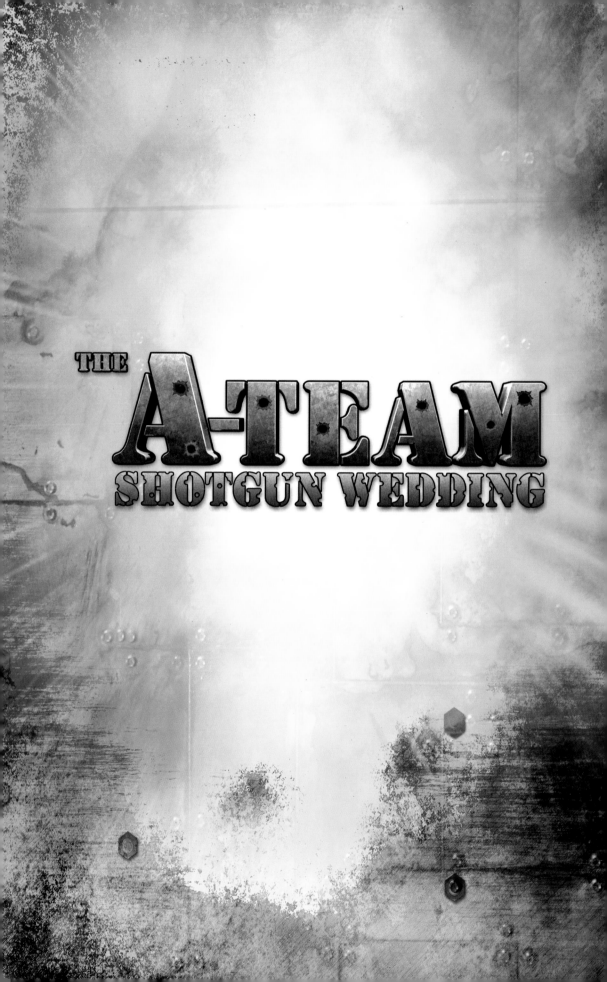